Yale Studies in English, 175

# THE CRAFT OF DYING
## A STUDY IN THE LITERARY
### TRADITION OF THE *ARS MORIENDI*
### IN ENGLAND

by Nancy Lee Beaty

New Haven and London: Yale University Press

1970

Published with assistance from the foundation
established in memory of Philip Hamilton McMillan
of the Class of 1894, Yale College.

Library of Congress catalog card number: 76–115365
International standard book number: 0–300–01336–1

Designed by John O. C. McCrillis
and set in Garamond type.
Printed in the United States of America by
The Carl Purington Rollins Printing-Office of the
Yale University Press, New Haven, Connecticut.

Distributed in Great Britain, Europe, and Africa by
Yale University Press, Ltd., London; in Canada by
McGill-Queen's University Press, Montreal; in Mexico
by Centro Interamericano de Libros Académicos,
Mexico City; in Central and South America
by Kaiman & Polon, Inc., New York City;
in Australasia by Australia and New
Zealand Book Co., Pty., Ltd., Artarmon, New South
Wales; in India by UBS Publishers' Distributors Pvt.,
Ltd., Delhi; in Japan by John Weatherhill, Inc.
Tokyo.

# Contents

# Preface

The aim with which the following study was undertaken, in partial
fulfillment of the requirements of Yale University for the doctoral
degree in English literature, still undergirds it: to make an intensive
study of Jeremy Taylor's *Holy Dying* that would take fully into
account the devotional tradition which nurtured it. Helen C.
White's valuable study of English devotional prose in the seventeenth century culminates in a single chapter on Taylor's *Holy
Living* and *Holy Dying,* as "the most representative and the finest"
of these works. Her brief commentary on the former, and briefer
note on the latter, suggested to me the line I wished my own study
to take. Taylor's masterpiece not only climaxes the devotional tradition in general: it represents at the same time the triumphant
artistic flowering of a single specialized subgenre of that tradition
—the ars moriendi. From its inception in the fifteenth century to
its culmination in the *Holy Dying,* the growth of this tradition in
England was consistent and intelligible. Since death impinges upon
all life, and a philosophy of death is therefore an integral part of
every philosophy of life, the emergent genre was naturally responsive to the richly varied influences of Renaissance, Reformation, and Counter-Reformation. Hence a consideration of Taylor's
Anglican synthesis should benefit from careful study of the various
stages in this tradition.

My method of approach was from the beginning highly selective.
Sister Mary Catharine O'Connor had already, in her exhaustive
study of the original *Ars moriendi,* provided us with a survey of
these works, and demonstrated their common indebtedness to the
medieval tract. I chose, rather, to analyze painstakingly one central
treatise from each of the major periods of religious thought and
orientation during which this tradition was developing, from the

germinal *Crafte of Dyinge* itself (the English translation of the
*Ars moriendi*) to the *Holy Dying*. For reasons explained fully
below, I selected Thomas Lupset's *Waye of Dyenge Well* to represent pre-Reformation English humanism; Thomas Becon's *Sicke
Mannes Salve,* the nascent Calvinism of Tudor England; and Edmund Bunny's adaptation of Robert Parsons's *First Booke of . . .
resolution,* the influence of Counter-Reformation devotion on
English Protestantism at the turn of the century. Each work lent
itself readily to fruitful criticism. Each revealed both a form and a
content firmly ordered by the theological premises and devotional
emphases of the religious position on which it was grounded. And
each, by epitomizing the contribution of its own period to the development of the ars moriendi as a literary tradition, furthered
significantly my understanding of Taylor's work as an artistic whole.

Obviously it is the *Holy Dying* alone that justifies such an intensive exploration of a devotional tradition which flourished for little
more than two hundred and fifty years. Yet this masterpiece, I am
now convinced, simply cannot be understood outside that tradition.
The inner logic of its structure, the true inspiration and significance
of its justly famous imagery and unique tone, the functional value
of even those elements which seem at first more inartistic—all
these, I believe, will be seen more clearly in the light shed by this
critical study of its predecessors. I have therefore assigned to each
representative work its full share of a chapter, and treated the *Holy
Dying* as climactic rather than central. At the same time, of course,
I have tried to control my material in such a way that the reader
will recognize without effort the relevance of all the earlier material
to a full appreciation of Taylor's splendid synthesis.

Necessarily, this study takes into account the major shifts in the
interpretation of man and his destiny which occurred in English
thought during the period covered. Even such relatively obscure
and practical books for laymen as those considered in chapters
1–4 do reflect these familiar shifts, and with a clarity that may well
fascinate students of intellectual and cultural history. All the same,
my focus throughout is on literary history and criticism—on the
progressive artistic enrichment of a small but significant literary
tradition. For this reason above all, I have tried to restrict the cita-

tions of historical and theological studies to those with immediate, commanding relevance to my own concerns. My interpretations of these different periods of intellectual and religious history are, then, simply those central ones available today to any interested student. (Where such a consensus is still lacking—notably in regard to the precise signification of the term "Renaissance"—I have tried to adjust the incidence of documentation accordingly.) Among those modern interpreters of Christianity whose influence, direct or indirect, pervades this study but is not acknowledged in footnotes, I owe particular thanks to the following: Roland Bainton, Henri Brémond, J. V. Casserly, Dom Gregory Dix, Dom Bede Frost, Etienne Gilson, Adolf von Harnack, A. G. Hebert, Geoffrey Nuttall, E. F. Scott, and William Temple. More explicitly secular historians whose names deserve special mention here, because not cited below, include P. S. Allen, E. K. Chambers, William Haller, F. M. Powicke, Preserved Smith, A. E. Taylor, and J. Tulloch.

Above all, I should like to acknowledge here, with a student's usual belated but heartfelt gratitude, my profound indebtedness to those scholars and professors whose lectures and guidance both in class and in conference—all true "clerkes" they!—have led me thus far toward an understanding of the history of Christian thought and spirituality: Franklin Baumer, Elizabeth Chase, Eric Dinkler, Grace Hawk, Walter Houghton, Paul Lehmann, Albert Mollegen, Davie Napier, Albert Outler, and Robert Rodenmayer. The last two will understand why my gratitude has had to be recorded not only in this "scroll of honor," but in a dedication as well. And, finally, Professor Louis L. Martz—as many another ex-advisee has testified before me—deserves not merely a separate sentence, but a separate and eloquent paragraph, for counsel, criticism, and encouragement far beyond the power of at least one of his apprentices even to suggest, much less repay.

Since more than a decade has passed since this study went through the first of many final typings, it gives me more than the customary pleasure to end these prefatory notes with a public expression of thanks too long delayed. I rejoice that my parents are still energetically pursuing the ars vivendi, for their loving support—in every sense—has been unflagging through the years.

Wellesley College honored me with an Alice Freeman Palmer Fellowship, and the Church Society for College Work, with a fellowship for its first Summer Seminar in Theological Studies; for both I was, and am, deeply grateful. The libraries of Amherst College, Columbia University, Princeton University, and the Yale Divinity School have been gracious in their hospitality and generous with their holdings. Professor Russell Alspach, of the University of Massachusetts, offered perceptive criticism when it was sorely needed. Above all, the practical and moral support extended to me by the families of John Camp and Harrison Young, Jr., has been unbounded and immeasurable, but must not go unrecorded. Without the aid of Mrs. Camp in particular, whose works of supererogation extended far beyond the patient and painstaking typing and proofreading of apparently endless drafts, I doubt sincerely that either the dissertation or the book would ever have reached completion.

N.L.B.

*Amherst, Massachusetts*
*January, 1970*

# The *Ars Moriendi:* Wellspring of the Tradition

It is a curious fact that the literary tradition of the "art of dying well" can be traced back no farther than the early fifteenth century, to the *Ars moriendi* itself. For once the obvious fountainhead of a literary stream is in fact its source. The Semitic authors of the Old Testament, perhaps because of their profound concept of "community," pay little attention to the passing of any one of its members. The classical authors of similar legends and biographies do often recount the last hours of a man's life in some detail, and in such a way as to suggest that his manner of dying may shed some light on the ultimate mysteries of human personality and its destiny after death—if only by testing to a degree the validity of the philosophy by which he has lived. Plato's description of "the end [of] the wisest and justest and best" of the men of his time[1] is merely the greatest of many accounts of deaths seen, and passed on to others, as suggestive commentaries of this sort. Without general agreement, however, on a frame of metaphysical reference for evaluating such death scenes, there can be no agreement as to what constitutes a good death—and hence no literature of specific advice on how to "make" one. The first fourteen centuries of Christian thought, on the other hand, are characterized by the common acceptance of metaphysical assumptions that seem, at first glance, preeminently congenial to the development of such a genre; yet the tomes of the Fathers and the medieval Churchmen yield little more than isolated and usually incidental references to this "art."[2] Some of the more compelling reasons for this silence will be sug-

1. *Phaedo,* trans. Jowett.
2. Sister Mary Catherine O'Connor, *The Art of Dying Well,* p. 24 n. 74, and pp. 17–21. Note also the meager selection of Patristic texts cited by later writers in the tradition.

1

gested later. For the moment, we need only recognize the fact that the *Ars moriendi* is, even though derivative in almost every detail, a truly original work—and hence of major significance despite its own want of literary value.

The generic title *Ars moriendi* actually refers to two distinct, though related, basic texts of the fifteenth century, each with its own variants and derivatives. The longer version is usually found under the heading of the *Tractatus,* or *Speculum, artis bene moriendi.* The shorter, generally associated with the famed block books of the same name, is, properly speaking, the true *Ars moriendi.* Both seek to instruct the Christian in the practical technique of dying "well and surely"—that is, to the glory of God and the salvation of his own soul. They are similar in their basic structure, their central themes, and their essential temper. And both were extraordinarily popular. As for the relationship between the two texts, Sister Mary Catharine O'Connor's tightly reasoned arguments[3] seem to me entirely convincing, and her conclusions will be accepted as valid for the purposes of this study.

The *Tractatus* was probably written in the first quarter of the fifteenth century, and quite possibly between 1414 and 1418 by order of the Council of Constance, which included among its reforming concerns an "emphasis on more devout Christian living" (p. 54). Such a genesis would help to explain not only some of the salient characteristics of the work, but also its rapid dissemination throughout Europe, since enthusiastic delegates would naturally take copies home with them. In any case, its anonymous author set out to provide for all Christians a handbook of practical, straightforward aid in the inescapable business of dying. His only predecessor of major importance was the great Chancellor of the University of Paris, Jean de Gerson (1363–1429), whose *Opusculum Tripartitum* contains a section entitled *"De arte moriendi."* Addressing himself primarily to priests, and secondarily to laymen needing further instruction in the faith—such as those caring for the poor and the sick (p. 22)—Gerson had chosen to limit himself

---

3. Ibid., pt. 1. "Literary History." Page references found in the text of the next two paragraphs allude to this exhaustive and indispensable study.

to a consideration of the art of helping *others* to die "well and surely." The result is a sort of "layman's ritual," a treatise whose "whole manner . . . is the cut and dried, unleisurely manner of the service books" (p. 23). In spite of its different orientation, this work became the major source of the *Ars moriendi*. Inevitably, since Gerson himself based the structure of his treatise on the liturgical office *De Visitate Infirmorum,* and since his adapter was very probably a Dominican and certainly a Churchman (pp. 50–60), the second most pervasive influence on the tract was the liturgy itself. Finally, for supplementary material, its author drew liberally on that apparently inexhaustible treasury of predictable works so helpful to all late-medieval writers: the Bible; Aristotle, Plato, Lucan, and Seneca; the Church Fathers *in extenso;* and the great medieval Churchmen from St. Gregory to Suso and Gerson himself.[4]

It is this *Tractatus* text, according to Sister Mary Catharine, which is the earlier of the two: the block book version is not a germinal form of the longer work, as hitherto was believed, but an abridged one.[5] Based on just one chapter of the *Tractatus,* the later *Ars moriendi*[6] consists essentially of a group of eleven woodcuts depicting, in expanded and animated form, the deathbed temptations of Moriens—to follow the same scholar's convenient appellation of the dying Everyman. Each woodcut, though sufficiently intelligible by itself, is accompanied by a single page of text. Thus, unlike the *Biblia pauperum,* the block book was designed for the literate as well as the semiliterate and completely unlettered among the people (p. 114). Ten vivid illustrations dramatize each temptation and its corresponding "inspiration"— that is, God's side of the argument, as revealed in Scripture and interpreted by the Church. In the temptation pictures, the sick man's bedroom is filled with grotesque little demons, no two of whom look exactly alike, swarming around and under the bed.

4. For the detailed sources of each point made in the treatise, see ibid., pp. 24–44.
5. Ibid., pp. 11–17. It is only one-third as long.
6. A facsimile of the *editio princeps,* ed. W. H. Rylands (1881), is in the Yale University Library.

Solid, vigorous little monsters, they embody effectively the reality of temptation, the power of hell. In the inspiration pictures, the room becomes almost cluttered as the demons are confronted by saints, angels, often the Virgin standing by in quiet benediction, and even, at times, Christ himself—on the Cross. The eleventh illustration represents the instant of death: the soul of Moriens is received by the heavenly attendants, and the demons, put to rout, scramble back to hell. Moriens, it is clear, has used his free will responsibly, "made a good death," and found eternal salvation. These woodcuts and their accompanying arguments, constituting the heart of the work, are framed verbally by a brief introduction and a still briefer conclusion which contain, in radically condensed form, much of the material from the other chapters of the *Tractatus.* Thus the text has, in a sense, its own integrity; and in several respects it is clearly superior, from an artistic viewpoint, to the original.

Consequently, a close analysis of the *Ars moriendi* might validly focus upon either version. This study will confine itself to the text of the *Tractatus* for three reasons: first, because it is the earlier and much the longer; secondly, because its values can be assessed without reference to those of the famous woodcuts; and finally because only this text is known to have been translated into English, and thus to have an indisputable niche in the history of English devotional literature. *The Boke of crafte of dyinge*—commonly referred to as the *Crafte of Dyinge*—is one of the many pieces ascribed to Richard Rolle until dismissed as spurious by Carl Horstmann in his 1896 edition of Rolle's works.[7] Horstmann identified it as a later translation of a Latin tract entitled *De arte moriendi*—a tract which he in turn ascribed tentatively to Rolle, but which is in fact a text of the *Tractatus.*[8] By focusing on this English exemplar of a work known all over Europe, we may conveniently trace the devel-

7. *Yorkshire Writers: Richard Rolle of Hampole and His Followers,* 2 vols., 2: xliii, 406. For his editorial criteria, see pp. xxxix–xl.

8. Rolle's authorship is ruled out by other than chronological considerations, too: Miss Hope Emily Allen "has found in the *Ars* not a trace of him" (O'Connor, p. 49).

opment of the literary tradition of the ars moriendi within the limited context of English history alone.[9]

In spite of its indebtedness to Gerson's *Opusculum*, the *Tractatus*, as represented by the *Crafte of Dyinge*, is reasonably well oriented to the problems and needs of the dying man himself. Generally speaking, it addresses the reader directly in his ultimate isolation when confronted by death; only occasionally does it assume that others may be present at the deathbed who are willing and able to offer help which is spiritually valid. Thus, Chapter I exhorts mortal man to recognize the significance of death and apply himself diligently to learning the art of dying "well and surely" while there is yet time. Chapter II—the heart of the treatise—describes the five paramount temptations with which the devil assaults all dying men, and arms the reader for the battle against them. For the most part, Moriens is presumed in this discussion to be a lone warrior, unsupported by family, friends, or Church; now and then, however, incidental services are suggested for which an ally might be enlisted. Chapter III consists of two alternative sets of interrogations—one specifically attributed to Gerson—designed to establish firmly the reader's saving faith. Although the presence of helpful bystanders would certainly facilitate the administration of this examination of conscience, Gerson's adapter maintains his own focus by asserting forcefully Moriens's freedom to interrogate himself in the absence of such aid. Chapter IV finds him still in possession of his reason and his senses, though drawing ever closer to the moment of death. Now, still on his own, he is urged to imitate Christ's actions on the Cross, and provided with short prayers to say "also longe . . . as he cann and may."

9. The text of *The Boke of crafte of dyinge* used for this study is that reconstructed by Horstmann from two of three groups of MSS, with MS Rawl. C894 as the basic text (*Yorkshire Writers*, pp. 406–20). While following his rendering in its editorial detail, I have expanded all abbreviations without italicization of the added letters; modernized *eth, thorn,* and *yogh;* adjusted the long *s, u* and *v, i* and *j* to conform to modern usage; and omitted his bracketing of occasional emendations that are clearly justified by alternative readings in the Harl. group of MSS.

It is at this point, as Moriens slips into irrationality or unconsciousness, that the author turns his attention to the Christians now
presumed to have gathered about the deathbed. Interrupting the
elementary chronological progression of the argument, he ad-
monishes all healthy Christians to remember their responsibility
for helping others to die in a state of justification. Then, retracing
his steps, he outlines the role that the concerned Christian should
play from the beginning of his friend's illness until the latter's
"last end." The sixth and final chapter, moreover, consists exclusively of prayers for use by such attendants. Moriens himself is
ignored, except as a subject for intercession, until the final prayers
of commendation. In short, Sister Mary Catharine's observation
that the "purpose of [Gerson's work] clings to parts of the *Ars*"
(p. 6, n. 35) is clearly correct. But is this transfer of focus from the
dying man to his friends basically illegitimate, after all? Technically
speaking, a student of the craft of dying might well consider the
course completed at the end of Chapter IV, with his own "departure" as a rational being. Emotionally speaking, however, any
Christian of liturgical temperament would consider such a work
disturbingly truncated. Do not these last two chapters deal with
topics about which he may legitimately be concerned? Surely a
fifteenth-century Moriens of formalistic bias would be reassured to
know that a well-defined—and effectual—pattern of behavior was
to dictate the actions of those responsible for his spiritual well-
being after he himself ceased to function as the chief actor in the
drama of death. The treatise closes on the note of quiet confidence
and triumphant hope struck by the great liturgical prayer "Go,
Christian soul, out of this world . . ."; and a pious reader of the
time might well feel that its author had remained faithful to his
central purpose of guiding one soul successfully through the difficult shoals of dying.

As this brief outline of its contents has indicated, the *Crafte of
Dyinge,* is, in effect, a "little conduct-book" comparable, as Sister
Mary Catharine expresses it, to contemporary works on "hunting
and hawking or on table manners for children" (pp. 2, 5). Furthermore, even as such, it is a remarkably meager work. Yet it was
precisely this thin, dry, skeletal handbook which subsequent genera-

tions found worthy of being fleshed out and clothed so that its presence is discernible in even the finest seventeenth-century works on death. Why? A detailed analysis of its argument and form is necessary if we are to understand its essential sturdiness, and also to follow the progress of its transmutation into such a durable work of art as Taylor's *Holy Dying*.

*The Crafte of Dyinge* opens with prefatory comments too time-less in their nature to require detailed consideration. A brief statement of the widespread need which the present book is designed to fill is followed by a quick indication of how it should be used, and then by a final proclamation of its profitableness to the reader. We need only note here the matter-of-fact assumption of the author that dying is in itself an experience to be dreaded. Not only to laymen, but even to the religious—those in orders—the "passage of deth" is difficult, dangerous, and "ryght ferefull and horrible" because of their "unkunnyng of dyinge." Its fearfulness is not considered a popular superstition, but a reality accepted by the educated and the devout as well as the ignorant.

CHAPTER I

Chapter I, "commendacion of deth and of cunnynge for to dye well," has a twofold purpose: to explain more fully the reasons why the craft of dying is the "most prophetable of all cunnynge," and to offer a preliminary general definition of what it means to die "well." In its assumptions about the nature of death and the ideal of the Christian life, it reflects significantly not only the climate of opinion that fostered the treatise, but also the temper of the man who wrote it. As regards death, it simply assumes that the Christian is already sensitive to its fearful imminence, that he associates the experience of dying with "agony (or stryfe)," and that he envisages this dreadful crisis as only the first of the Last Things. Yet the main argument of the chapter seeks to alleviate just that fright which these considerations might be expected to induce in the believer. Referring only casually, in a subordinate clause, to Aristotle's grim dictum that physical death is the most fearful of all fearful things, the author hastens on to assure the believer that the death of good men is precious in the sight of God, whatever their manner of dying;[10] and that these "good men" include not only martyrs but also "good cristen men" and, "ferthermore doughtlesse," all sinners, however evil, who die in contrition and in the faith, unity, and charity of the Church, standing firm against the temptations which beset them in their last hours. The penitent who dies "gladlye and wilfully," asserting reason over passion, suffering his dying patiently, conforming his will to God's—in short, accepting the inevitable as God's good will, "without any gruchchynge or contradiccion"—will find that death is for him, as for the "parfit cristen man," only a "goynge owt of presone and endynge of exile, a dyschargynge of a hevy bordone that is the body, fynysshyng of all infirmytees, escapynge of all perellys, distroynge of all evell thingis, brekynge of all bondes, payinge of dette of naturall dutee, turnyng ayen into his contree, and entring into blisse and joye."

The general tenor of this discussion is, therefore, primarily one of assurance and comfort. That it is not exclusively so is due to the author's inability to solve one of the basic problems that have plagued the Church from its earliest days: how to proclaim to sinful man the gospel of God's acceptance of him despite his sinfulness without thereby releasing him from the sense of moral obligation which makes possible human society as we know it. Theologically—and psychologically, for that matter—the answer is clear enough as regards the committed Christian. As sinner, he accepts the redemptive love of God with a gratitude which can express itself only through deeper devotion and holier living; and his persistent voluntary struggle to abide by the implications of the "two great Commandments" on which "hang all the Law and the

---

10. Since the author is here supposedly just translating the familiar sentence from "David the prophet," which he has quoted immediately before, this appended clause exemplifies clearly one of his methods of weighting his message. Another instance of such "exegetical translation," as it might be called, is found in the discussion of the temptation to despair (see below): he reassures the sinner by quoting Ps. 51:17 and then translating it as "Lord god thou wilt *never* dispice a contrite and a meke hert" (italics mine).

prophets" will tend to issue in daily behavior of a far higher moral caliber than that induced merely by the fear of punishment, whether human or divine. Practically, though, the Church has always had to recognize that the overwhelming majority of human beings are only too far from that stage of sanctification where they can really be trusted to behave responsibly without any motivation other than love. Hence the Christian ethic of gratitude has never been preached to the exclusion of more legalistic forms of moral sanctions. Instead, we find throughout Christian literature —even in such sensitive devotional works as Jeremy Taylor's— precisely that alternation of threats and "comfortable words" which characterizes, and weakens, this chapter of the *Crafte*.[11] A sharp warning to the genuinely evil interrupts the consoling reminder of God's infinite mercy toward the contrite sinner; and a final exhortation to all laymen to live, like the "religiouse," with "herte and . . . soule ever redy up to godward" tends to vitiate all the preceding assurance to the belatedly penitent. Nevertheless, the dominant tendency of this chapter is to reaffirm the Church's traditional message of consolation and cheer. It is in this light that the *descriptio mortis* quoted above should be considered: not as a mere series of hackneyed metaphors, but as a "commendacion of deth" whose very traditionalism is, as we shall see, its greatest justification.[12]

One other, less important, respect in which Chapter I reflects the thought of the late-medieval Church deserves brief comment because it adumbrates, however faintly, the impending battles over the Protestant doctrine of justification by faith alone. In his teaching about sin, the author of the *Crafte* tends to distinguish "good Christians" from "sinful men," and to consider "the chosen

11. Hence, too, the recurrent problem of the supposed conflict between God's justice and his mercy, which derives from precisely this false verbal opposition. See below, pp. 21–22, 28, 29; and cf. Daniel P. Walker, *The Decline of Hell,* pp. 4–8, 23–26, 40–42, and passim, for a discussion of the Church's support of the doctrine of hell as a moral deterrent.

12. As Sister Mary Catherine points out (p. 25 n. 78), it is suggestive that the author does not use the *De contemptu mundi* of Innocent III in this connection, although he is familiar with it.

people of God" and the "penitent" as two separate groups.
Not always consistent, he implies at times that all men stand
under condemnation as sinners; but on the whole he seems to
accept a threefold categorizing of mankind into (1) the religious,
in the sense of members of religious orders, (2) the righteous laymen, and (3) the sinful laymen. Reformation and Counter-Reformation will concur in readjusting the spiritual perspective of
Christian thought on this subject so that men's common sinfulness, or alienation from God, once more takes precedence over
their particular sins as individuals. And this shift will have important consequences for the development of the literary tradition of Christian dying.

CHAPTER II

Chapter II, "of the temptacions of men that dyene," opens with
a brief introduction asserting confidently that all must endure in
their "last siknesse and ende" temptations far more grievous than
any experienced during their lifetime. The discussion which ensues
of the five "most principall" of these is clearly the high spot of
the treatise not only for the medieval reader, as Sister Mary
Catharine assumes (pp. 27, 31, and passim), but also for the
modern student. Since it occupies almost twice as much space as
any of the other chapters (pp. 408–12), it will be convenient to
comment upon it in five separate units, following the sequence
of the original.

The first and greatest temptation is, of course, the temptation
to unbelief. The general structure of the discussion is noteworthy,
since it is followed, with a sort of careless consistency, in the
treatment of all five temptations. Also, it is one which Taylor will
use effectively for appropriate arguments in *Holy Dying.* First,
the author states briefly the dogmatic teaching of the Church in
regard to the particular virtue under attack by the devil. Faith, the
"fundament of all mannys soule-hele," is the all-important prerequisite to salvation, as St. Paul, St. John, and St. Augustine
testify. No matter how tempted to doubt, to stray slightly, or to
adopt superstitions, errors, or heresies, every Christian is bound

to give full faith and credence to both the principal articles of the faith and "all holy wrytt in all maner of thingis," though he need not "actually and intellectually apprehende" them; he is also bound to obey the statutes of the Church of Rome. The author reminds the reader that his salvation depends upon his remaining firm in faith—or whatever virtue is under consideration—but follows this warning immediately with general words of comfort. The devil, he assures Moriens, cannot prevail against any man who "hath use of his free will and of reason well disposed," for to incur damnation man must consent willfully to temptation.

Next he summarizes in broad terms the response required of the Christian, and offers specific suggestions for making such a response easier to achieve. Moriens's aim, in this instance, is to persevere and die in the faith, unity, and obedience of "oure moder holy chirch." As specific aids, therefore, he might have the Creed recited loudly before him, not only that he may be fortified in faith, but also that fiends, who cannot bear to hear it, may be drawn off from him; or he might consider the examples of biblical personages particularly noted for their faith, and also those of apostles, martyrs, confessors, and "virgyns unnombirable." Finally, the author clinches his argument by suggesting, more or less delicately, that practical as well as spiritual rewards await the righteous. The added inducement in the case of faith is a "double profytt" based on two biblical texts, the distinction between which is not made clear: that faith may "do all thingis," and that faith "gettith a man all thingis"—"as the hilles of Capsie be preier and peticion of kynge Alysaunder the gret conqueroure were closed to-gider."

The essence of the Church's teaching in the early fifteenth century in regard to faith is here distilled; one searches in vain for even a trace of contemporary distortions of emphasis or local doctrinal aberrations. The demonology of the times alluded to might appear to be an exception to this generalization. But the specific form in which man casts his understanding of the power of evil and its role in human life has never been considered a basic doctrinal issue. Satan, that is, has never been described in a creed. Thus the fifteenth-century vision of grotesque demons swarming about a deathbed may well be considered a vivid example of the naiveté and decadent concreteness of late-medieval thought,[13] but not necessarily an example of doctrinal heterodoxy. It all depends upon the interpretation of evil that such a vision embodies. In truth, the rhythmical intonation of familiar creedal phrases might well soothe a certain type of Christian suffering from momentary twinges of doubt, fear, rebelliousness, and so on. And the fifteenth-century observer might well visualize in concrete form such a dramatic liberation from the demons attendant upon illness. The demonology of the *Crafte* is more archaic in expression than in substance.

The second grievous temptation, directed against the "hope and confidence that every good man schuld have unto god," is the temptation to despair. Once again the argument—that salvation is always open to the penitent—is thoroughly traditional, and fully documented. When the devil reminds him of all the sins of which he has not been shriven, Moriens is to remember that the mercy of God exceeds even man's utmost ability to provoke his wrath and indignation, and that the only result of despair is to augment the everlasting pains which await the faithless. It is only when we note the selectivity of that documentation, the exegetical translation of Psalm 51:17 to strengthen its assurance,[14] and the absence of the usual warning reminder against considering this doctrine an excuse for evildoing[15] that we realize how heavily the author has weighted his discussion on the side to comfort. Indeed, the only reference here to the dangers of belated repentance is the mention of the evil man's shame and confusion when he sees Christ nailed to the Cross (as all men do, we are told, when dying) and knows that he is lost; and it strikes a jarring note quite at odds with the rest of the section. The other side of the argument has been given before in the *Crafte,* and will be heard again;[16] this is no sample of the

13. See Johan Huizinga, *The Waning of the Middle Ages,* trans. F. Hopman, chaps. 18, 12, and pp. 179–81, 240–43; see also below, pp. 47–48.

14. See above, note 10.

15. On the contrary, he reserves his strongest threat of hellfire for those who do *not* trust in God's love and forgiveness.

16. In Chap. V particularly; cf. below, p. 27–29.

fractious bickering over the validity of deathbed repentance which will mar post-Reformation works on Christian dying. For the moment, the author is simply marshaling, with more than ordinary care and effectiveness, arguments and practical suggestions to help Moriens in his battle against despair. The latter urge him to meditate on the crucified Christ, to remember that the virtue of hope is very commendable, and to take heart from the examples of numerous biblical personages saved in spite of great sinfulness.

It is the unusual eloquence of this section, however, even more than its argument, which reveals unmistakably the extent of the author's determination to preach the "gospel of reconciliation" (Rom. 5; 2 Cor. 5:17–20) to the frightened sinner of his time. He develops his answer to Satan's insinuations with a hyperbolic vehemence found nowhere else in the treatise:

> But therfor ther schuld no man dispaire in no wyse; for though eny o man or woman had do als many theftis or manslauters or as many other synnes as be droppis of water in the see and gravell-stones in the stronde, though he never had do pennaunce for hem afore ne never had bene shreven of hem afore, neither than myght have no tyme for syknesse or lacke of spech or schortnesse of tyme to be shreven or hem, yette schuld he never dispeire; ffor in such a cas verry contricion of herte with-in, with wyll to be schreven if tyme sufficed, is sufficient and acceptable to god for to save hym with everlastingly. [p. 409]

And his recommendation that Moriens think of Jesus on the Cross is itself a warmly reverent meditation on the crucified Christ:

> his heed enclyned to salve the, his mouth to kysse the, his armes I-spred to be-clyp the, his hondis I-thrilled to yeve the, his syde opened to love the, hys body alonge straught to yeve all hym-selfe to the. [p. 410]

Here, if anywhere, an emotional pastoral concern warms for an instant the impersonal authoritative tract.

The third temptation for which Moriens must be prepared is the temptation to impatience, "the which is ayenst charite bi the

which we be bounden to love gode above all thingis." The outstanding characteristic of this section is its meagerness of thought, in
comparison with that of the two preceding discussions. Here we
find no mention of Satan or his fiends, no helpful suggestions, no
inspirational examples of righteous patience from biblical or
Christian history. Moreover, the use of authoritarian citations is
noticeably different in kind. In his treatment of the temptations
against faith and hope, the author elaborates his arguments with
some independence, selecting authorities as his aides or allies; here
he is far more deferential. It is they who express *for* him the central
propositions of his discussion. Those who are mortally ill, he
observes, suffer great pain, particularly those who are dying—as is
most common—through illness or accident rather than from old
age. Nevertheless, those who are unwilling and unprepared to die,
who become "wood and witles" with rebellious complaining, sin
grievously; for their impatience shows their insufficient love for
the righteous God who permits suffering as punishment for sins.
Just as the contrite sinner offers himself to pain as satisfaction for
his sins, so should the sick man; for illness endured rightly (that
is, patiently, gladly and "willfully") is purgatory suffered before
death. Since the greater the sin, the greater or longer the illness,
let Moriens say, with St. Augustine, "Here cutt, here brenn, so that
thou spare me everlastynglye."[17] Without charity, the argument
concludes, no one can be saved; charity, "suffreth all thingis"—ex-
cluding nothing; Q.E.D., the Christian must endure patiently all
physical illness. "To hym that loveth ther is no thinge hard ne no
thinge impossible."

It would be difficult to overstate the contrast between this limited
and basically uncertain treatment of the virtue of patience—this
*miserere* in its minor mode—and Taylor's richly eloquent procla-

---

17. Interestingly enough, the problem of pain so disturbing to the
modern mind, so clearly inconsequential here, seems to have continued
"unrecognized," so to speak, well into the seventeenth century at least—
despite the intervening influences of Renaissance humanism. See, for example, Gordon S. Wakefield's observations on the approach taken by
Puritan devotional writers, in *Puritan Devotion: Its Place in the Development of Christian Piety*, pp. 133–34.

mation of the Way of the Cross as the very essence of the Christian life—an anthem as triumphant in spirit as it is traditional in substance. The enrichment of this one point over the two and one-half centuries with which we are concerned might well serve to epitomize the enrichment of the literary tradition of the ars moriendi as a whole.

With the fourth temptation, however, the temptation to spiritual pride, the discussion not only regains its earlier solidity, but even —considered as a whole—surpasses the literary effectiveness of the second section. Like the third, this section lacks specific aids and practical incentives to encourage the weak in developing the relevant virtue of humility; but its generalizations are handled firmly, with only a minimal and independent reference to authority, and its illustrative material is more lively than that of any other part of the treatise. This temptation, we are told, is the devil's weapon against "most relygiouse and devoute and parfite men." When he fails to undermine faith, hope, and charity, he then assails the Christian with "such maner of temptacions in his herte: 'O how stable arte thou in the feithe, how stronge in hope, how sad in pacience! O how many good dedis hast thou do!' " Because such an attitude clearly stands under condemnation by the "auctor of meknes," Moriens should humble himself, ponder his sins, and recognize that he never knows whether he is worthy of salvation or of damnation. Even here, though, the author weights his discussion on the side of comfort. Whereas his treatment of the temptation to despair carefully excludes warnings against overconfidence, here he just as carefully includes warnings against the opposite extreme of despair. Moriens must, he continues, remain strong in hope nonetheless, remembering that God's mercy is above all and that his desire is not the death, but the conversion, of sinners. Everyone, therefore, should follow St. Anthony, to whom the devil said, "Antony, thou hast overcom me, ffor when I wold have the up by pride, thou kepist thi-selfe a-downe by meknesse, and whan I wold draw the downe by disperacion thou kepist thi-selfe up by hope."

Familiar though its thought is, this section is striking in one respect—its vivid presentation of the devil. Scarcely more than mentioned before, he suddenly appears twice in person. In the latter instance (his encounter with St. Anthony), where he is completely externalized, the effectiveness of the passage rests solely in its unwonted use of a minor dramatic vignette as the vehicle for standard doctrine. Compared to Taylor's subtle presentation of the Christian's simultaneous awareness of both divine condemnation and divine acceptance, St. Anthony's simple oscillation between hope and humility is decidedly crude. Still, the anecdote is a lively example of the medieval mode of expressing the Church's paradoxical message. And Satan's first appearance, when he addresses Moriens directly, yet "in his herte," is even more effective. Here, his semicolloquial phrasing and exclamatory style communicate with real success the author's insight into the devious maneuvers of the human mind—and his wry smile at the pride which dictates them.

The fifth, and final, temptation, directed particularly against "most carnall men and seculer men," is the temptation to "avarice": the "over-much occupacion and besynesse a-bought outward temporall thingis . . . that thei hane loved inordinatly before," such as wives, children, friends, and "wordely [*sic*] riches and other thingis." The discussion of this promising topic is singularly disappointing, being characterized, as Sister Mary Catharine puts it, by "meager material and pallid phrasing" (p. 16). The author fails to elaborate in any way on the lures of the world and the flesh. Moreover, he is inconsistent in his definition of the corresponding virtue which Moriens is to display. Later on, as we shall see, he interprets total commitment to God's will in such a way that it includes a sensible concern for the state of affairs one is leaving behind as citizen, father, and so on. Here he demands, rather feebly and with no supporting citations of authorities, that the dying man put out of his mind all temporal and worldly concerns whatsoever. And most of the remainder of the section consists of repetitious groans over men's "perlous . . . and most inconvenient" refusal to prepare for death as they ought.

For these reasons, and because the arrangement of the temptations as a whole may be considered anticlimactic, it has been sug-

gested that the last two temptations are the work of a later hand.[18]
Yet there is really little reason to consider them afterthoughts. In
the first place, this final section follows the same general pattern
of development as the others, including the mention of practical
advantages that will accrue to him who "makes a good death." (He
will have satisfied God for his venial sins and even, perhaps, for
some of the debt incurred through deadly sins.) In the second place,
there is a wider discrepancy in tone between the fourth and fifth
sections than between, say, the third and fifth. And, most important of all, the entire work is, as Sister Mary Catharine says,
"truly medieval . . . in the anomaly of schematization somehow
combined with flagrant weakness in organization" (p. 10).

Even from the psychological viewpoint the sequence is by no
means as unjustifiable as Sister Mary Catharine would have us
consider it. "In the arrangement of the five temptations," she
writes, "there is no evidence of psychological plan, no working
from gentler to more violent, which according to St. Gregory is
the ordinary method of the devil. . . . The order is, upon the contrary, somewhat anticlimactic, with petty attachment to material
things following crimes as terrible as infidelity and despair" (p. 44,
n. 212). But the great temptations against faith, hope, and charity
beset all men at all times, and so simultaneously that any chronological order imposed upon a discussion of them is bound to be
false. Moreover, since victory over them is never more than relative
and partial, there are few Christians indeed who are not aware of
persistent spiritual conflict in all three areas of the inner life.
Hence it is perfectly logical to treat those temptations as a group,
following St. Paul's theologically meaningful arrangement in lieu
of some false chronological one. If, however, one then goes on,
motivated by a belief in the crucial significance of "making a good
death," to postulate a fourth as in fact *chronologically* climactic
—as the devil's final desperate maneuver to capture the citadel of
the soul—it must clearly be a temptation not only peculiarly forceful in the last hours of life, but also one less easily recognizable,

18. O'Connor, pp. 16, 43 n. 203, 44 n. 212.

more insidious, than the old, familiar, lifelong temptations. And
what more natural, more psychologically probable, than for the
devout religious to murmur proudly, "I have fought a good fight;
. . . I have kept the faith"? Or for the layman simply to be so preoccupied with setting his temporal affairs in order, so busy coping
with minutiae, that he "just never finds time" for spiritual concerns?

A brief recapitulatory coda reassures us once more, however.
The devil cannot, after all, prevail against a man unless the latter
"willfully consent." Since God will never burden one with more
temptations than can be borne with divine aid, Moriens need
only learn meekness to be safe. For, as St. Augustine says, "Thei
breken not in the forneyse that hane not the wynde of pride." Let
"everry man, ryghtfull and synfull, lowe hym-silfe fully unto the
myghty honde of god, and so with his helpe he shall surely opteyne
and have the victorye in all maner of temptacion, seknesse and
tribulacions, evyllys and sorrowes, and deth therto."

With this final affirmation of triumph for the humble, Chapter II
ends. The longest chapter of the treatise, it occupies almost one-
third of the work (about 3,250 of some 10,500 words); and its
introduction and conclusion are such that it is actually an isolable
essay in itself. Since it was probably the author's own distinctive
contribution to the contemporary discussion on the "craft of
dying,"[19] the central emphasis it is given is not really dispropor-
tionate. This chapter is in a sense, as it seemed to his readers, the
heart of his teaching.

CHAPTER III

With Chapter III, "the interrogacions that schulden be asked of
hem that were in her deth-bed while thei may speke and under-
stond," the author turns once more to Church tradition for aid.
Two series, one for religious and a second, much more detailed, for
laymen, are included. The brief preface does not announce this
fact, but merely explains that the interrogations which follow
should be administered to those that "drawen to the deth-ward"

19. O'Connor, pp. 27–29.

while they still possess reason and speech, so that "if ony man be not fully disposed to dye, he may better be enformed and confortid thereto." Based as it is on ancient Church custom, this chapter's usefulness is even more apparent than that of the second, the only one to exceed it in importance. Moreover, its content is even more thoroughly traditional, its tone even more obviously consoling. We are not surprised to find that it, too, became the foundation for later books on Christian dying.[20]

Both sequences of interrogations consist of seven general questions, but with meaningful variations. The first, ascribed by the author to "Ancellyne the bisshop," is a modified version of one of St. Anselm's—for the dying religious—but actually still older in origin.[21] It is brief and to the point. Semidramatic, it quotes the interrogator directly, but casts Moriens's answers, and other directions and comments, in rubrical form. The seven questions are as follows: (1) ". . . art thou glad that thou schalt dey in the ferth [*sic*] of Crist?"; (2) "Knowest thou well that thou hast not do so well as thou schuldist have do?"; (3) "Repentis thou the therof?"; (4) "Hast thou will to amend and thou haddist space and lyfe?"; (5) "Belevist thou fully that oure lord Jhesu Crist goddis son dyed for the?"; (6) "Thankyst thou hym thereof with all thy herte?"; (7) "Belevist thou verily that thow maist not be savyd but be Cristis deth and his passion?" After the first the author writes, "The seke man seithe, ye," and after each of the other six, "He answeryth, ye." After this satisfactory exchange, the hypothetical interrogator continues:

> Than thanke him ever thereof while the soule ys in the body, and put all thi truste in his passion and in his dethe onely, havyng truste in no other thingis; to this deth commyt the fully, with this deth cover the fully, in this deth wrap all thiself fully; and if it com unto thy mynde or by thin enmye be put into thy mynde that god will deme the, sey thus: Lord I put the deth of oure lord Jhesu Crist be-twene me and myn evell dedis, be-twene me and thy Jugement, other-wise I wyll

20. Otto Scheel, *Martin Luther,* I, 15, as cited in O'Connor, p. 31 n. 129.
21. See O'Connor, p. 34.

not stryve with the; Iff he sey that thou hast deserved damp-
nacion sey thou ayen: The deth of oure lord Jhesu Crist I put
be-twene me and all myn evell meritis, and the merite of his
worthi passione I offre for the merite that I shuld have had and
alas I have it not; Sey also: Lord put the deth of oure lord
Jhesu Crist be-twene me and thi ryghtwysnes. [p. 413]

This examination, we are told, is adequate for "religiouse and
devoute persones." Yet all men of both estates, according to
Gerson, should be "examyned . . . and informed more certeynly
and clerly" about the health of their souls. The second sequence,
therefore—based on one in Gerson's *De arte moriendi*—is much
expanded for instructive purposes; and it progresses with absolute
clarity, as the first does not, from the recognition of sinfulness to
the thankful acceptance of redemption. The first four questions
repeat those of St. Anselm, but each is defined and elaborated
upon with insistent churchliness. To die "in the faith of Christ,"
for example, is spelled out as to die believing in the articles of the
faith and in all Holy Scripture in all things "after the exposicion of
the holy and trew doctours of holy chirche"; forsaking all heresies,
errors, and opinions damned by the Church; and rejoicing that one
is to die "in the feyth of Criste and in the unite and obedience of
holy chirche." The fifth and sixth are new, designed to test more
fully the validity of a lay Moriens's contrition. Does he really
forgive, and seek forgiveness, for the love of Jesus Christ, from
whom he hopes for forgiveness himself? And is he eager to restore
fully all misgotten goods, even at the cost of bankrupting himself?
The seventh combines the last three of the earlier set, but reverses
the order of the last two, so that the examination ends more decisively on the note of thanksgiving. Furthermore, this set of
interrogations does not specify the response after each question,
but reserves a general promise for the conclusion: whoever can
answer each of these in good conscience and truth with "Yea" can
be certain that he is of the number that shall be saved. And Moriens
is reminded that he need not wait for another to put them to him
(since "ryght fewe" have the "kunnynge" of this "crafte of
dyinge"), but may interrogate himself in his own soul.

Without doubt the most notable characteristic of both sequences
is their common renunciation of the possibility of earning salvation through any merits other than those of Christ's Passion.
Whereas Chapters I and II contain occasional hints of inconsistent
thinking in this regard, Chapter III is uncompromising in its demand that all men, both religious and lay, recognize themselves as
sinners against the "hyghe mageste and the love and the goodnes
of god," dependent for their justification solely upon his mercy
through Christ. We have here, then, a fine example of one way in
which the extreme ritualism which characterized the "waning"
Middle Ages[22] could and did influence Christian thought and
literature for good as well as ill. The tendencies of the late-
medieval Church to degrade ritualism into sterile, even superstitious, formalism are suggested at the end of the Anselm questions. Moriens is to conclude the interrogations by saying *"In
manus . . . "* three times, and his community of fellow religious
are to join in. If he can no longer speak, the "convent," or the bystanders, are to say it by themselves three times, substituting *eius*
for *meum.* "And thus he dyeth surely, and he schal not dye everlastyngly." This rubric seems to reflect a superstitious faith in the
efficacy of the number three rather more than it serves any meaningful purpose. Yet liturgical tradition also ensured the perpetua-
tion and transmission of the Christian kerygma comparatively
unaffected by the thought or temper of any particular era. The
scholarly Gerson, anxious to deepen the spirituality of his time,
was active in his encouragement of new forms of popular devotion. Yet his interrogations for laymen are, even in the modified
version found in the *Crafte,* little less timeless than the ritual of
as much as seven or eight centuries before.

The emotional impression created by these stock lessons and
exhortations is one of singular gentleness, even sweetness, and of
joyful consolation. The questions are couched, it is true, in a
vocabulary so traditional that it borders on theological jargon. It is
rather the author's selection from the available terminology that
indicates the extent to which he has weighted his message on the

22. Huizinga, pp. 1–2, 6, and passim; and see my discussion below.

side of reconciliation as against prophetic denunciation. Thus, the second set emphasizes (citing St. Bernard) that the fear of the Lord is the beginning of wisdom; insists that Moriens acknowledge in detail the extent to which he has sinned against the God of righteousness; and examines and tests thoroughly the quality of his declared penitence. Yet the word *righteousness* occurs only once, the words *justice* and *judgment* and *damnation* not at all. Moriens has "displeased" and "grevously . . . offendid" the God who created him; has sinned against his "mageste," "love," "goodnes," and "kyndnes"; has rejected his freely proffered "graces." Therefore he should be—not "contrite" (a technical word)—but "sorry in [his] herte." Moreover, once penitent, he is to express that sorrow, not by breast-smiting or fearful groveling, but by praying for the grace of true repentance and a continued desire to amend his life, and by trying actively to carry out his new purpose as far as he may. The recurrent emphasis on the concept of grace is one of the most revealing characteristics of these interrogations.

Finally, and most tellingly, both sequences conclude with relatively eloquent pleas for a confident faith in the redemptive merits of Christ's Passion. Not "the Cross" alone, as Protestant teaching will so often phrase it; a warmer, more personal feeling informs both exhortations. This is particularly true of the first, quoted above, which also concludes St. Anselm's interrogations. Far more sternly than anywhere in the second sequence, its author reminds Moriens that he stands under condemnation. Yet the warning is treated primarily as a temptation of the devil; and it is counterbalanced by an unusually stylized and artistic expression of full trust in the redemptive efficacy of "the deth of oure lord Jhesu Crist." The second concluding exhortation, though more muted in style, urges Moriens just as earnestly to "commend and commytt" himself to the Passion of Christ, meditating on it as much as he can in sickness; "for thereby all the devellys temptacions and giles be most overcomm and voyded."

CHAPTER IV

The exhortation to meditate on the Passion which concludes Chapter III leads smoothly to the adaptation, in Chapter IV, of the devotional theme of the "imitation of Christ" to the needs of the dying. Indeed, the author scarcely pauses between the two, but introduces his "instruccion with certeyne obsecracions" by a "forthermore." Furthermore, he writes, since St. Gregory says that "every doynge of Crist ys oure instruccion and techynge," such things as he did while dying on the Cross should be emulated by every man at his "laste ende" to the best of his ability.

The extraordinary adaptability of the Gospel narratives to devout exegesis of this type is well illustrated by their use in this instance. The author manages, without undue strain, to find there a potent reinforcement of his doctrinal message. Christ, he tells us, "dyd fyve thingis in the crois": he prayed, cried out, wept, committed his soul to his father, and gave up the ghost willingly. The corresponding fivefold response demanded of the Christian "imitator" parallels neatly the theological structure implicit in the interrogations. For the ordinary mortal, to cry out is to "crye strongly" in his heart with the desire for forgiveness of sins and everlasting life; to weep is to weep in his heart with true repentance; and to commit his soul to God is to say in his heart (but preferably aloud also), "Lord god, into thin handis I commende my spirit; ffor truly thou thiselfc bought me dere." Here, too, therefore, faith leads to the acknowledgment of sin, which in turn leads to repentance, to the acceptance of forgiveness, and finally to glad commitment to the will of God. And this parallelism is, in its turn, underlined by an unusually deliberate parallelism of sentence structure as the author refers each point to Christ's example: "so a seke man . . . schuld prey" is followed by "soo shuld every man in his dying crye"; "so shulde every man in his dyinge wepe"; "so shuld every man in his ende"; and "so shuld every man in his deth." Such a precise balance must have been eminently satisfying to the medieval mind. And the reminder that the Great Exemplar of human holiness had also cried out and wept at the "laste ende" must have been comforting, too.

The remainder of Chapter IV consists of "obsecrations" to be recited by Moriens "also longe as . . . he cann and may." These are directed, in turn, to the Triune God, God the Father, Christ, "oure blessyd lady seynt Marye," the angels, and all the saints. In spite

of the practical brevity of these obsecrations, they mirror clearly—
as will most of those included in this study—not only the devotional idiosyncrasies of the time, but its basic religious temper as
well.

Above all, they reflect the distinctive fears and Christ-centered
hopes of the age. The first two are merely supplications for forgiveness, that "hell houndis devoure me not." The next three,
addressed to Christ, are clearly central.[23] The first, which calls on
him as "most swettest and most lovely lord my lord Jhesu Criste
goddis owen dere sonne," expresses most emphatically Moriens's
sense of unworthiness, coupled with trust in the "grace and mercy"
of that "lovely lord" whose passion will ensure his reception into
Paradise. The second consists of but one verse: "Lord thou hast
broke my bondis and therfor I shall thanke the with the sacrifice
of the oblacion of worship." Moriens is advised to repeat this frequently, since it is of so great virtue that, repeated three times in
true faith at a man's death, it will win him forgiveness of his sins.
The third narrows down the general thought of the first into a
specific plea for Christ's mercy on his soul "in hir streite passynge."
The fervor of this supplication epitomizes for the modern reader
the oddly fearful and intense concentration of the late-medieval
Church on the precise moment of death—and on the Christian's
behavior at that instant—as of peculiar spiritual significance.

The prayer which should logically follow at this point, one to
the Holy Spirit, is notably absent. Instead, Moriens pleads for
Mary's intercession on his behalf, "that for love of the, swete ladye,
he woll foryeve me my synnes." From the angels, as from Christ,
he begs assistance in the passing of his soul from the world, and
also general protection from his enemies and reception into their
"blissed company"; and he appeals particularly to that angel who
has been his "contynuall keper ordeyned of god." And, finally, he
is told to pray to "all the apostillys, martires, confessoures, and
virgines and specially to tho seyntis which he loved and wor-
schipped moste specially in his hele, that thei will helpe hym than
in his last and most neede."

23. Cf. the definition of *obsecrations* given in the *Oxford American
Prayer-Book Commentary,* ed. Massey Shepherd, p. 54: "entreaties addressed to our Lord recalling His redeeming acts on our behalf."

The undercurrent of fear at the prospect of Satan's last assault is clearly visible under the smooth surface of conventional phraseology. The conclusion of the chapter acknowledges its existence openly at last. Moriens is exhorted to say "thries or more" the following words (attributed to St. Augustine) or similar ones: "The pese of oure lord Jhesu Criste, and the vertu of his passione, and the signe of the holy cros, and the maydenhed of oure lady blyssed seynt Marye, and the blyssynge of all seyntis, and the kepinge of all angels, and the suffrage of all the chosen people of god be be-twene me and all myn enemyes visible and invisible, in this oure of my dethe. Amen." Then thrice this final verse: "Graunt me lord a clere ende, that my soule fall never downe-ward, but yeve me everlastyng blisse, that is the reward of holy dying." If Moriens is unable to do this, let another say them, changing the necessary words, and Moriens pray devoutly within his heart "and so yeld the gost up to god, and he shal be saved."

Considered as a whole, Chapter IV is more definitely a product of its time than any of the others. Its superstitious trust in the number three and in the inherent potency of certain prayers; its somewhat careless reference to the worship of the saints; its indifference to the Holy Spirit; and its delight in drawing precise directions for Christian behavior from the life of Christ—these are minor, though interesting details. What is of major significance is that it effectively counterbalances a real dread of the deathbed struggle with "enemyes visible and invisible" against a warm confidence in the saving mercies of man's "most swettest and most lovely lord."

## CHAPTER V

With the dying man now presumably beyond the point where he can help himself, we come to that lecture to the bystanders whose inclusion in the treatise has already been defended as valid (see above, p. 6). Chapter V presents us with a striking instance of medieval structure of the opposite type from that found in Chapter II: not overelaborate schematization, but apparent maundering diffuseness. Yet close analysis reveals an inner logic both rhetorical and pastoral, which is even more satisfying for being unexpected.

This "instruccion unto hem that shullen dye" is organized with
reference to two principles: first, that Moriens's friends are to help
him to follow instructions in the sequence already laid down; and
second, that they are to come to a fresh realization of the fact that
they, too, are among "hem that shullen dye." The first four of its
seven logical divisions—let us call them "paragraphs"—clearly
parallel, in a loosely knit way, the first four chapters of directions
for Moriens himself. The fifth, paralleling the final temptation (to
avarice) of Chapter II, is drastically misplaced in terms of rhetorical
symmetry; but its position is quite defensible in terms of pastoral
practicality. The sixth takes note briefly of the fact that these
hypothetical assistants are themselves Morientes, and exhorts them
to apply personally the principles of the "art of dying well." As
such, it is essentially parenthetical, yet psychologically valid. What
better time to admonish the healthy of their own need to learn
this art than at this moment, when they have been forced by circumstances to acknowledge the fact of human mortality and to consider its spiritual implications? The seventh and final paragraph
reasserts, as a sort of coda, the tremendous significance of "making
a good death" and, as a consequence, the incomparable value of
their enterprise.

Even the individual sections of this chapter are less disorganized
than they seem at first reading. The first is concerned primarily
with urging the friend or friends[24] to see to it that Moriens apply
in time the technique outlined in the rest of the treatise. (Too
many, writes the author sadly, delude themselves with expectations of indefinitely prolonged life, and die "or untestate or
unavised and undisposed.") In the light of its central purpose, its
general structure is climactic. Because all adversity is punishment
for sin, permitted by God, a priest should obviously be sum-
moned before the doctor, in any illness. More than this, however,
all spiritual ministrations to the sick should be ordered by the
assumption that the given illness is mortal; and these ministra-

24. The author confuses singular and plural throughout the treatise.
Merely for convenience in pronominal reference I shall assume from now
on the presence of more than one friend.

tions will include not only the appropriate priestly offices,[25] but also the friendly office of persuading Moriens to face up to the duties of dying well. Thus the friends' responsibilities grow heavier as the paragraph proceeds. That such burdens were no more eagerly shouldered in 1400 than they are today is indicated by the apparently repetitious discussion of spiritual factors in illness. The author introduces the topic as an argument on behalf of interference: he encourages hesitant friends with the eminently practical consideration that their intrusion upon the sick man's spiritual privacy may very well help him to physical recovery. For often, "as a certeyne decretall seyth, bodyly syknes commyth of the sicknes of the soule." The second mention of this interrelationship occurs when the friends, presumably having responded to the extent of summoning a priest, shrink from the far more distasteful chore of persuading the sick man to think of this illness as his last. Nowadays, he warns (citing Gerson), too many are given false hopes of recovery through "friendly" hypocrisy and blindness, and thus fall into everlasting damnation. True friends should urge the sick to contrition and confession; and, "if it be expedient for hym," this may improve his bodily health as well.

The second section is constructed on the assumption that Moriens, although now unquestionably doomed, is indifferent and unrepentant in spite of his friends' cogent arguments. Hence he must be prepared for, and assisted throughout, the devil's last attack. Because the state of Moriens's soul is such that he needs this aid, the author is much sterner here than in the earlier discussion, when the sick man was assumed to be following directions voluntarily, even eagerly. Now, for the first time, we hear the

25. Sister Mary Catherine, convinced that the "entirely orthodox" author "intended his little book to guide . . . those to whom the ministrations of the clergy were not available," dismisses this point as one "caught up in the thoughtless, gather-all way of the medieval writer" (p. 6). John McNeill challenges this view, however, arguing that the treatise is valid —as the author himself protests—for everyone under any circumstances. See *A History of the Cure of Souls*, p. 159. Accepting the latter hypothesis, I believe the reference to priestly ministrations to be not only relevant, but well-timed.

Church's solemn warnings in regard to the dangers of last-minute repentance. St. Gregory, St. Augustine, "and other doctours" agree that such deferred repentance is "unneth" saving contrition. The sick man must use his reason and will to make himself hate his sins and withstand his evil nature. Although the author's usual warnings against despair follow this passage with characteristic rapidity, the dominant tone of this paragraph is threatening, quite suitable to the hypothetical situation. Unless Moriens is brought somehow to a penitent recognition of his status before God as sinful creature dependent on Christ for his redemption, Satan will have won the battle before it is well begun. Hence the friends' concern should be focused primarily on helping him through the first encounter with the Enemy, and secondarily on assuring him of victory in those to follow if he will only fight "myghtily and manly." Once imbued with saving faith, he can overcome the other four temptations by himself. Indeed, he must; and the rest of his struggle with the devil is therefore not discussed here.

The third section, although tied in very closely with the interrogations of Chapter III, introduces the first real inconsistency in this parallelism. Besides examining Moriens to make certain that he dies a full believer, the friends may read, or have read, to him appropriate religious selections: either his favorites, or the Commandments, that he may meditate on the latter and consider his behavior for negligent trespasses. The reading period suggested here is the one originally placed in the struggle against the temptation to unbelief. Worse yet, the Moriens to whom one may read "devought histories and devoute praiers in the which he delyted moste in whan he was in hele" is a radical transmutation of the Moriens of only a moment ago. The discrepancy arises, of course, from the author's essential identification of Moriens with Everyman.[26] Since his aim is to deal with all possible contingencies, he turns here to the problem of awakening the pious as well as the callous to a sharp sense of sin. In later, more elaborate treatises, the split personality of Moriens will constitute a major artistic

26. The woodcuts in the *editio princeps* seem to underline this identification of Moriens by picturing him differently in each. Cf. O'Connor, p. 120 n. 41.

problem for their authors. In this skimpy work, though, it seems
a legitimate, and rather attractive, variation on the theme. Indeed,
in this context, the progression of thought even seems climactic:
friends may well find it more difficult to stir a devout Moriens to
contrition than a delinquent one. Hence the reading period, inserted here less for its inspirational value—its primary significance
in the earlier discussion—than for its potentialities as a conscience-
quickener. Once again we find the stern theme of judgment
stronger than the comforting one of mercy: "it is better and
ryghtfuller than he be compuncte and repentaunte with holsom
fere and dred and so be saved, than that he be dampned with
flaterynge and false dissimilacion." And now the warning extends
to the friends as well: it is even "devellike" to hide from a man his
soul's perilous state lest one *trouble* him a bit![27]

Because there is very little that spectators can do to help a
dying man apply Christ's example to his own last hours of life, the
fourth section is short. The miscellaneous helpful offices suggested are, however, loosely relevant to the topics of Chapter IV.
The friends are urged to give him an "Image" of the crucifix, or
of the Virgin, or of a saint which he "loved or worshipped" in
health. Also, they are to keep holy water nearby, and sprinkle it
often on or about him, so that "fendis mowe be voyded from
hem." The crucifix, we may infer, should remind him of the
spiritual duty of imitating Christ, while the other images and the
holy water should encourage him to start upon his final obsecrations and protect him from satanic distractions. Intercessory prayer,
as the most important, most effectual aid which friends can offer
at this stage, is mentioned last of all—with an urgent reminder to
pray "specially to oure savyoure lord Jhesu Crist."

It is at this point that the author suddenly inserts a reminder
that "no carnall frendis ne wife ne children ne riches ne no temporall goodis" should be allowed near the deathbed nor brought
to mind, save as Moriens's "spirituall helthe and profett" require.

---

27. This point is supported with a delightfully anticlimactic story about
the prophet Isaiah, whose unflattering warnings to the sick king illustrate
how one *should* behave; "and yet," the author adds honestly, as an afterthought, "he dyed not at that tyme."

Artistically, this constitutes a drastic departure from the rhetorical balance between this chapter and the preceding parts of the treatise. Its only conceivable justification lies in the realm of pastoral experience. One may hypothesize that the passage was dictated by vivid memories of priestly frustration as clamoring relatives interrupted the last solemn prayers at the deathbed with demands for Moriens's attention to their "carnall" problems, or with vehement protests against his penitent restitution of wealth sinfully acquired. Mere literary symmetry thus bows before the dictates of experience.

The pastoral effectiveness of the sixth paragraph, with its timely reminder that those who minister at others' deathbeds will soon lie there themselves, has already been affirmed. The argument is completely familiar except for one perceptive observation: "for in truth," the reader is warned, when "deth or gret seknesse fallith upon the, devocion passith owt from the." And the more serious the illness, the farther it flies away. In the light of its context, this seems like a discouragingly modern point. The author uses it, however, to underline his central precept: therefore, while thou hast "the use and fredam of thi wittis and reason well disposed, and while thou maist be maister of thi-selfe and of thi dedis," think on these things.[28]

This exhortation to the healthy leads smoothly into the concluding section of the chapter. Here the author's chief concern is to assure these healthy bystanders of the inestimable value of their aid (their "grette charge and diligence and wise disposicion and providence and besy exortacion") at the deathbed. By reiterating and reemphasizing the theme of the soul's perilous status at the hour of death, he impresses these potential assistants with a sense of their own importance. At the same time, though, he is of course impressing upon them by implication the danger in which their own souls stand. (Departing souls are in such need that if possible a whole city should gather around a dying man, as

28. This Augustinian precept, so vital to the literary development of the ars moriendi, became one of the bones of contention between Robert Parsons and his Calvinist "editor" Edmund Bunny; see below, chap. 4, pp. 187–88.

indeed some communities of religious do; "and therfor it is redde that religiouse people, and women, for the honeste of hir astate schall not ren, but to a man that is a-dyinge, and for fere [fire].") The tone of warning blends with that of assurance in this concluding passage. And the result is that Moriens's friends are enlisted in the struggle for his soul; instructed in the technique appropriate to the several stages of that struggle; praised for their invaluable assistance; and also made to see themselves, not as aides only, but as Morientes, intimately, personally concerned with the effectualness of these techniques—and all this in fewer than two thousand words. The author of the *Tractatus* does not deserve quite so much condescension as he receives from Sister Mary Catharine for his "want of method and . . . diffuseness" (p. 15);[29] nor should Chapter V be dismissed as "merely a loose series of directions," characterized by "flagrant weakness in organization" (pp. 44, 10). Like the other chapters, it does have a master plan, even though it is followed casually, with a confusing inattention to the niceties of tight logical organization.

Even more satisfying than the inner logic of its structure is its revelation of the author's fundamentally pastoral temperament. Every section of the chapter bears witness to his unusually clear-sighted observation of life as it is, coupled with a calm, practical acceptance of the situation confronting him. His vision of experience is limited, but it has not been distorted by being filtered through the lens of theological presuppositions. For example, he admits readily, with delightful candor, that sinners do exist who even when Judgment is imminent must be exhorted to withstand "the *delectable* thought of past sins" (italics mine). Again, he reveals his perceptiveness in using a sterner tone when addressing Moriens's friends than when speaking to Moriens himself. Everyman when on his deathbed is likely to need "comfortable words" more than denunciations; but Everyman when healthy will see in these same words chiefly an excuse for irresponsible failure to help his friend. It is the pastor, not the theologian, who recognizes

29. Cf. John A. Gee, *The Life and Works of Thomas Lupset,* pp. 143–44. As the less clearly constructed of the two texts, the *Tractatus* bears the brunt of Gee's criticism of the "formlessness" of the *Ars moriendi.*

such facts—whose understanding of human problems is neither determined nor delimited by abstract theory.

Moreover, it is the pastor—and the superior pastor—who accepts such facts with equanimity and seeks to act upon them both realistically and constructively. Because he is genuinely concerned to save souls, he is distressed by the dearth of interest in the art of dying "well and surely"; but he neither dismisses the gloomy statistics with the theologian's easy references to the doctrine of election nor overemphasizes them with the preacher's easy tirades. Instead, he states the facts resolutely, grieves at their implications —and promptly urges friends to rise to the challenge presented. Similarly, he accepts without rancor the need of weak man for some practical, even materialistic, motivation to goodness—and meets that need with the best arguments available to him. Finally, he even accepts the demands of this world upon the layman as to some degree legitimate—and acts upon this conviction without slavish reference to dogma. He includes among one's spiritual duties the making of a will and "laufully disposyinge for his household and other nedis if he have any to dispose for"; and he acknowledges, with some daring, that the presence of relatives may be necessary for the spiritual health of Moriens. In sum, the author of the *Crafte* reveals himself in Chapter V, even more clearly than elsewhere, as preeminently a pastor, concerned less with expounding Christian dogma than with relating it flexibly and creatively to existence.

### CHAPTER VI

The final chapter of the *Crafte* contains "praiers that shullen be seid upon hem that bene a-dyinge." Seven of the nine included are intercessions so similar in content and tone to the obsecrations of Chapter IV that virtually no further comment is needed. Four are addressed to Christ, one each to St. Michael and the Virgin, and only the seventh to "mercifull and benigne God" through Christ. Phrased in the traditional form of liturgical prayers, this one summarizes impressively in its petition the doctrinal teaching which has informed the entire work. Hence it serves as a fitting conclusion to the *oraciones* of intercession.

The last two selections, prayers of commendation addressed to the dying man, form a curious and revealing contrast to each other. In the first, the intercessors commit their "dere brother" to God, praying that he may be delivered by Christ from the torments of hell and received with gladness among the blessed in heaven, there to rejoice in the contemplation of God forever. Conventional enough, certainly, in its basic position; but unmistakably a product of the times just the same. With something approaching gusto, the prayer elaborates upon the horrors of hell, the anticipated triumph of Christ, and the glorious companies of heaven who are to welcome Moriens's soul. Above all, it assumes that "that foule sathanas with all his servauntis" will battle to the last possible instant to forestall that heavenly reception by winning the soul for hell. Moreover, its syntax is confusing, its phrasing and rhythm awkward to the point of being quite unsuitable for public recitation. Artistically and liturgically, in brief, it is the poorest prayer in the *Crafte*. Yet in that it "speaks to the condition" of the contemporary Christian, by quieting his distinctive fears and appealing to his most concretely visualized hopes of heaven, it does bear witness to the author's responsiveness to the pastoral needs of his audience.

In vivid contrast, however, he concludes this miscellany—and his treatise—with one of the great liturgical prayers of the Church, dating back to the eighth century at least, and still in use today: the *Proficiscere anima Christiana*. "Go, Cristen soule, out of this world . . ." This commendation dismisses Moriens very simply, in the name of the Father who created him, the Son who died for him, and the Holy Ghost who "was infounded" into him; and it prays that the traditional angelic host may receive him, and the saints and the prayers of the Church assist him, so that he may find everlasting peace in heaven, "by the mediacion of oure lord Jhesu criste." Here there is virtually nothing merely contemporary. In choosing for his final selection a prayer so traditional in its doctrinal content, and so confidently hopeful in its mood, the author displays once again a real feeling for climax. All the fearful dangers of death and Judgment in general and of dying in particular which have been implicit in so much of the work tend to be forgotten. It is as if, somehow, they had been disposed of once

and for all in the colorful and dramatic prayer immediately preceding this. Now the reader is free to close the book with the
emotional certitude that the dominant message of the Church is
still, as always, one of confidence, of hope, and of joy.

In the light of this detailed examination of the text, the *Crafte
of Dyinge* can be viewed as quasi-liturgical not only in substance
and spirit, but even in structure. Like the comparable occasional
rites of the Church, the *Crafte* attempts to deal with a crisis in
human experience by referring it, in a spirit of impersonal authoritarianism, to timeless Christian principles. Like almost all the
the liturgical offices, it also reflects in its dramatic inner movement those theological convictions which inform it—in this case,
the gospel of reconciliation in its entirety. Chapter IV, as we have
seen, clearly follows a fivefold division of this theological pattern.
Chapters II and III may also be fitted into it without strain. And
by ignoring Chapter V as irrelevant in this respect we may even
discern faintly the same five-part sequence in the organization of
the tract as a whole. Thus, Chapter I calls on the reader to acknowledge God's sovereignty in human life; Chapter II, to recognize his sinfulness, or the omnipresence of "Satan"; Chapter III,
to seek true repentance by thinking through his faith and its implications; Chapter IV, to accept the central redemptive significance of Christ in history and in human life; and Chapter VI, to
commit himself thankfully to God's will, now and for all eternity.
The drama of the Eucharist, though more complex, follows essentially the same pattern.

For all its valid structure, however, the *Crafte* is not truly a
literary creation; and the enormous popularity and influence of
the *Tractatus* in western Europe remain as yet incomprehensible.
The structure is *not,* in fact, apparent without close analysis. There
is no verbal clarity of organization; and even the inner logic ex-
pounded above is blurred by inconsistencies of thought and crudity
of expression. The argument is, moreover, extraordinarily thin.
About death itself it has almost nothing to say: dying is naturally
to be feared, for it is painful and will be followed by Judgment;
but death itself should be welcomed as release from the "wrecchid-

nesse of the exile of this world" (p. 406). Nor can the author envisage any attitude toward death except the two emotional extremes of fear and hope, or despair and confidence. On the whole, the tract has almost nothing to offer beyond a restatement of the clichés of the Christian gospel, and a rather superficial application of them to man's deathbed experience.

Worse yet, this meager proclamation of "good tidings of great joy" fails signally to communicate any sense of that joy. Its tone is static and flat, or monochromatic, almost devoid of dramatic and emotional overtones. The treatise is cluttered with traditional words and phrases so hackneyed that they have clearly lost whatever power they may have once possessed to evoke an emotional response. Such ecclesiastical clichés as "holy chirch," "holy martires," "synfull wrech," and "wrecchid sinfull man" are employed regularly and automatically instead of "Church," "martyrs," and "sinner" (or "man"). The connotations originally present in the expanded equivalents have long since disappeared. Other phrases just as trite compound the dreary effect: "laste ende," "carnall frendes," "gladlye and wilfully," "prophetable and good," "well and surely," "pacientlye and gladly," "reason and understondynge." The pairings of synonyms, in particular, is monotonously insistent. Often, it is true, they are merely the familiar couplets of native English and Latin derivatives: "hope and confidence," "ferefull and horrible," "grevouce and grete," "abyde and persevyr," and so on. Many of these couplets, however, seem to serve no useful purpose, and their inevitable recurrence becomes irritating: "open and certeyne," "ordeynynge and makinge," "loste and dampned." And a number of others seem to be dictated primarily by a yen for alliteration: in the "sorow and siknesse" of the body, one must withstand all temptations "myghtily and manly"; "provide and procure hym-selfe his soule-hele"—or "provid and purvey" *for* it; and, above all, abide "styfflye and stedfastly" in the faith. Even more pedestrian are those chunks of medieval argumentation which intrude upon this basically pastoral work. A tortuously clumsy sentence will set forth some aspect of Christian doctrine, support it by a quotation from the Bible or some "holy and trew" doctor, and include not only the chapter-and-verse source of the

cited authority but also an exegetical comment when necessary.
The affective potentialities of the author's few, sparse images are
stifled in such a context.

As a whole, therefore, the *Crafte* is, in its own right, scarcely
worth consideration as a literary work. It makes no attempt to
revitalize aesthetically that sense of joyful trust in God's mercy
which it declares is the fruit of Christian faith. Its impact on the
reader depends exclusively on the extent to which he responds to
the Christian kerygma itself, and to the Christian "Proclamation"
in its unadorned, skeletal form. Most forbidding of all, this minimal
doctrine is related to the reader's immediate concerns only in so
far as he is already disposed to acknowledge himself a Moriens
and seek voluntarily for help in playing that role. If he should,
perchance, insist on regarding himself as primarily a Vivens, very
little in the tract would "speak to his condition." Later writers in
the tradition will have to cope with precisely this problem; and
Taylor will solve it in the most magnificent passages of *Holy
Dying.*

Why, then, did such a mediocre work, thin in argument and
ineffective in expression, not sink predictably into the limbo
reserved for thousands of similar instructive and inspirational
treatises propagated by the Church? Instead, Emile Mâle tells us,
the *Ars moriendi,* in one version or another, was even more successful than the *danse macabre;*[30] and a large measure of this
popularity must be credited, not to the famous block book version,
but to the unillustrated, unimpressive *Tractatus artis bene moriendi.* Out of some three hundred extant manuscripts of the *Ars
moriendi,* "almost all," according to Sister Mary Catharine, contain, or derive from, this earlier version (p. 9). Latin manuscripts
are of course the most numerous, but the *Tractatus* has been preserved in German, Low German, Dutch, Italian, Spanish, and
French translations, too—as well as in the *Crafte of Dyinge.* It is
also the basic text of most of the printed editions which have come
down to us. Its immediate, widespread acceptance and prolonged
influence cannot be explained simply by reference to the so-called

30. *L'Art religieux de la fin du moyen âge en France,* p. 382.

death-consciousness of the Christian faith per se,[31] for the *Crafte* reflects an atmosphere radically at variance with that of primitive Christianity. Furthermore, as noted at the beginning of this study, the "art of dying well" was virtually nonexistent as a separate devotional tradition throughout the first fourteen centuries of the Church's history.

Only by considering the *Ars moriendi* in its historical context can we understand the secret of its power as the instigator of a unique literary tradition. Its appearance in the fifteenth century should be related, like other phenomena of the time, to the disintegration of the medieval synthesis as a whole and, in particular, to the distinctive exaggerations and distortions which characterized the religious temper of this period. The inextricable intermingling of religious and secular factors in the life of the "waning" Middle Ages is axiomatic, and it has been abundantly illustrated by Johan Huizinga in his brilliant study.[32] Nevertheless, it will be convenient to draw a distinction, however artificial, between the two, and to concern ourselves primarily with the interplay of forces constituting what may be called the "specifically religious" back-

31. See, e.g., Theodore Spencer, *Death and Elizabethan Tragedy*, pp. 4–8.
32. Esp. chaps. 12–15. As will be noted—especially by those who reject his portrait as excessively gloomy—I have relied heavily on Huizinga's general interpretation of this period in developing my own final critical evaluation of the *Tractatus* and its cultural significance. It can of course be argued—and has been, at length—that the fifteenth century may just as validly be seen, not as *Herfsttij*, but as the nascent springtide of a new age. Nonetheless, experience suggests that the true pastor tends to address himself to the obvious needs of the moment—its strains, its dislocations, its distresses, and his parishioners' resultant tensions and anxieties—rather than dwelling upon the bright future which may be latent in the present confusion. Furthermore, in those areas of thought and experience with which we are specifically concerned, recent studies seem only to buttress Huizinga's conclusions; see, e.g., John W. Blench, *Preaching in England in the Late Fifteenth and Sixteenth Centuries*, esp. chap. 5. For two somewhat differing contemporary evaluations of Huizinga's historiographic achievement, see R. L. Colie, "Johan Huizinga and the Task of Cultural History," *American Historical Review* 69 (1964): 607–30, and E. F. Jacob, "Johan Huizinga and the Autumn of the Middle Ages," in *Essays in Later Medieval History*, pp. 141–53.

ground of the *Ars moriendi.* Only a very few events included in every secular history of western Europe require passing mention, simply because their contribution to the late-medieval preoccupation with death can hardly be overemphasized.

Of these, by far the most important was the devastation of the bubonic plague in the middle years of the fourteenth century. Not only did this catastrophic blight focus man's attention on death to the point of obsession, but it is generally credited with having caused such widespread and irreparable dislocations in the social and economic spheres of life that the transition from the medieval to the modern era was radically speeded up. Second in importance to the plague—and intimately connected with it in many respects —is the fact that the other Horsemen[33] were also on the rampage during these years. In France alone, for instance, the Wars of Burgundy were exacting a toll of life matched only by that of her frightful droughts. Throughout western Europe, it is generally agreed, the widespread sense of insecurity was abnormally intense. Everything in his everyday life conspired to arouse in the "transitional man," regardless of his station, an abnormal sensitivity to the precariousness of life—not just his political, social, and economic well-being, but his sheer physical existence as well.[34] *"In media vitae . . ."*

Man's response to these disruptive conditions was one of emotional violence. We need not dwell here in detail on the crude extremisms that characterized every aspect of late-medieval life, since they are so ably discussed and illustrated by Huizinga. (See especially chap. 1 and pp. 163–64, 214–18.)[35] It is sufficient to

33. The Horsemen of the Apocalypse, as men were convinced: the expectation of the end of the world had become an obsession. Huizinga, p. 21.

34. "Perpetual danger prevails everywhere. . . . Bad government, exactions, the cupidity and violence of the great, wars and brigandage, scarcity, misery and pestilence—to this is contemporary history nearly reduced in the eyes of the people" (ibid., pp. 20–21).

35. Even Jacob supports Huizinga's emphasis upon the "coexistence" of antagonistic extremes, in the life of the period, as valid—including that between "extreme indecency" and "excessive formalism"—although he interprets the resultant tensions as creative rather than "decadent." See pp. 145–47.

note, in summary, that neither in a man's behavior nor in his thought, feeling, or spiritual insight was there any place for subtleties, shadings, refinements. Savage contrasts jostled each other elbow to elbow, or succeeded each other in mad oscillation within a single man. And each conflict between paired extremes was intensified and dramatized by the age's habit of ritualizing every facet of life.

On the other hand, as Huizinga demonstrates, it was precisely this same formalizing tendency of the late-medieval mind which during this difficult period was the chief deterrent to the relapse of civilized society—or semi-civilized, if one prefers—into anarchic barbarism.[36] The habit of seeing life as a fine art to be cultivated in minute detail does lead, in a decadent age, to indefensible excesses of various types.[37] In this "violent and high-strung" era, however, permeated with the "mixed smell of blood and roses,"[38] it was also an ameliorative influence of enormous significance for the preservation of civilized values. As we shall see, this general conclusion of Huizinga's is extremely illuminating when applied to the specifically religious area of late-medieval life.

Turning now to this (somewhat mythical) area, we find, as expected, the dislocations within the secular structure of life mirrored in little within the institutional Church. Despite the continuing popular acceptance of the sacerdotal sanctity of the priestly office, ecclesiastical authority was sharply challenged during this period, and declined with dramatic abruptness. The authority of the papacy was seriously undermined, first by the "Babylonian Captivity" of 1305–76, and secondly by the "Papal Schism" of 1378–1417. Simultaneously, the authority of the clergy in general was jeopardized by their increasing ignorance, indifference, and immorality.[39] What was scandalous to the deeply pious, whether

36. See pp. 34–35, 94–98, and passim; cf. Gerald R. Owst's observations on the primitivism of the preachers' threats in regard to death, purgatory, and hell, in *Preaching in Medieval England*, pp. 335–36, 345.

37. E.g., extravagance, pettiness, or sentimentality.

38. Huizinga, pp. 6, 18.

39. For a usefully compact yet well-documented survey of the Church's vices and failings at the opening of the sixteenth century, see Ernest W. Hunt, *Dean Colet and His Theology*, chap. 2.

priest or layman, was offensive even to the most casual nominal Christian; and this revulsion expressed itself in various ways throughout the fourteenth and fifteenth centuries.

Within the Church—but preferably well out of earshot of the people—reformers castigated themselves and their brethren,[40] and struggled for internal reform as well as for a solution to the external, objective problem of the papacy. Until they, too, degenerated, the mendicant orders were in the vanguard of the battle against clerical ignorance and indifference. And all orders produced extravagant ascetics in protest against the extravagant worldliness within their ranks, while genuine saints condemned by contrast the notorious sinners.

It is indicative of the temper of the times, however, that Denis the Carthusian, the "Doctor Ecstaticus"—a violent extremist in every respect—may be considered one of the truly outstanding representatives of the institutional Church of the period. The acknowledged saints, even those technically within the Church, were by and large pursuing the solitary, extra-ecclesiastical mystic's way. The individualism always latent in medieval devotion now burst into full flower. It was nourished not only by the poignant awareness of infinity induced by a revived Neoplatonism, but also, to some extent, by anticlericalism itself.[41] The mystical movement, minimizing as it did the liturgical worship and sacramental discipline of the Church, tended to draw the truly devout away from the mainstream of Church history. Hence, with a very few notable exceptions, such as the admirable Gerson,[42] the best

40. See, for example, Gerald R. Owst, *Literature and Pulpit in Medieval England* pp. 235, 242–86. In a recent University of California (Berkeley) dissertation, Caleb R. Woodhouse discusses such efforts at self-reform as those of Bishop Alnwick of Lincoln, arguing—in line with Owst's evidence —that they witness to the continuing faithful, creative vitality of fifteenth-century English Christianity despite all the better-known testimony on the other side. ("Religious Vitality in Fifteenth-Century England," *DA* 25(1964): 3528–29). See also E. F. Jacob, *Essays in the Conciliar Epoch,* esp. chap. 4, and idem, "The Fifteenth Century: Some Recent Interpretations," in *Bulletin of the John Rylands Library* 14(1930): 386–409.

41. See Pierre Pourrat, *Christian Spirituality,* trans. W. H. Mitchell and S. P. Jacques, 2:204–06, 336.

42. See Pourrat, 2:268–73, and Huizinga, pp. 174–75.

Christian intuition of the time reflected the Zeitgeist in its emotional intensity, but did not exert much constructive influence on contemporary official religious thought. The prodigiously versatile Denis—mystic and theologian, extravagant ascetic and adviser to princes, romantic individualist and uncompromising Churchman[43]—represents perhaps the most noteworthy experiment in trying to reconcile the two dominant strains in the religious temper of the period. Yet he was, for all his formidable brilliance and sincere piety, disappointingly uncreative, both as thinker and as Christian spirit.[44]

Meanwhile, outside the Church, the humanists were already contributing something to the revolt against ecclesiastical authority. The new literary criticism tended to undermine the documentary support for the claims of the papacy. The new moral sensitivity, appalled by the immorality of the priesthood, sought to bypass the Church almost completely through a new, practical interpretation of the Christian life. To seek God's will and then follow it as a rational, free, and morally responsible creature does not necessarily require submission to clerical authority and sacramental discipline, however freely it may permit such submission—or even lead to it, as theory is worked out in experience.

But the influence of the humanists' challenge was not yet widespread enough to warrant our dwelling upon it. Most important of all, for our purposes, was the revolt of the common man—the ignorant, the indifferent, or the normally sinful casual Christian of the late Middle Ages, whatever his social station.

In him, the various aspects of the mystical temperament take different forms, but are not transmuted beyond recognition. Ignorant of, or indifferent to, basic dogma and approved traditional forms of devotion, he embraced a mass of "facile beliefs"[45] and indulged in a bewildering variety of extraliturgical practices. In both beliefs and devotional techniques, the true mystic's legitimate

---

43. See Gerard Sitwell, *Spiritual Writers of the Middle Ages*, pp. 121–28. His sketch of Denis as man and devotional writer modifies judiciously Huizinga's well-known, almost melodramatic portrait (pp. 170–72). See also, for a full account, the *Dictionnaire de Spiritualité*, vol. 3, cols. 430–49.

44. Pourrat, 2:313–16; cf. Huizinga, p. 198, and O'Connor, p. 174.

45. Huizinga, p. 139.

individualism is seen in the ordinary man as sentimental cultism, ranging from the harmless or even helpful to the grossest, most primitive superstition. In the latter category must be included, for example, his obsession with the occult and his cultivation of black magic during this period.[46] And, finally, his emotionalism, unlike the concentrated intensity of true mystical devotion, manifested itself in similarly crude extremes of hope and fear—of exuberant joy, or delightful tenderness, set off against melancholy so black as to be at times genuinely hysteric.[47]

Again, our representative everyday Christian evinced, in modified form, some of the moral idealism of the humanists. The theme of most of his satirical laughter at the expense of the priest clearly seems to be, "He's no better than any average Joe." The implication of the satire, however, is not that the layman should therefore chuck the priest overboard, and the sanctity of his sacerdotal office as well, but rather that the priest should reform his ethical behavior to accord somewhat more closely to his (accepted) sacramental position. Underlying this type of anticlericalism, therefore, is not only a lingering moral sensibility, but also a strong basic loyalty to the sacerdotal principle.[48] Ignorant, indifferent, blatantly

46. Robert L. Calhoun discusses this phenomenon of the fourteenth century as a product of the recurrent tendency of frustrated human beings to turn in difficult times to supposedly outmoded superstitions: to propitiate the "powerful Earth Gods [with] old, half-forgotten . . . sacrifices [in] the sacred groves of our savage past." The wealthy and educated [or quasi-educated?] resorted, not to black rites, but to astrology and other forms of occultism. See *Lectures on the History of Christian Doctrine,* p. 332. The parallel to our own age—a full generation after Calhoun's comment—is startlingly close and, to me, suggestive.

47. Huizinga, esp. chap. 1 and pp. 22–28, 160–64, 176–78. Among the symptoms of hysteria familiar to modern medicine are, as Calhoun notes, the "dancing mania" and the appearance on the body of anaesthetic patches or stigmata (p. 332).

48. Huizinga considers this mixed attitude "perhaps the most insoluble" contradiction in late-medieval religious life (pp. 160–61). But William P. Ladd notes that the principle was so strongly embedded in medieval thought that it survived, in a modified form, in Lutheranism. See *Prayer Book Interleaves,* p. 13. See also Woodhouse, "Religious Vitality." On the other

sinful though the priest might be, as long as the errant layman
looked to him as sacramentally superior, and demanded that he be
morally superior as well, the position of the beleaguered hierarchy
was not too seriously endangered.

The most pernicious form of anticlericalism, then, was purely
and simply that of the new secularism. The ultimate revolt against
ecclesiastical authority is complete indifference—not only to the
claims of clericalism as such but, above all, to the claims of what
that clericalism professes to represent. The average, everyday
secularist of this period, just as absorbed in his worldly concerns
as his supposed betters, was just as deaf as they to the judgment
passed by the Christian ethic on his extravagant pride and his
boundless avarice.[49] *Here* was the true menace against the ecclesiastical status quo; and the Church sensed it.

"Hell was stoked," as Roland Bainton points out, "not because
men lived in perpetual dread, but precisely because they did not,
and in order to instill enough fear to drive them to the sacraments
of the Church."[50] The Church's response to these various challenges to its authority—particularly the challenge of indifference
—was in large measure responsible for that neurotic obsession
with death in its most gruesome and unspiritual aspects which
characterized the fifteenth century; and it is precisely this obsession in whose light—or darkness—the *Crafte* needs to be understood. In a passionate age, severely limited in its receptivity to any

---

hand, cf. the conspicuous insistence in *Everyman* upon the (sacramental)
dignity of Priesthood: one wonders if the anonymous dramatist doth not
protest too much. Popular skepticism may have been increasing somewhat
more rapidly than other evidence seems to indicate.

49. In the late Middle Ages "cupidity becomes the predominant sin,"
although "feudal and hierarchic pride [has] lost nothing, as yet, of its
vigor." Both "[manifest] themselves in the life of [these] centuries" with
"unabashed insolence." (Huizinga, pp. 19, 18.) Denys Hay argues pro-
vocatively that the chasm between the new capitalist's driving concerns—
legitimate as well as greedy—and the Church's traditional economic
theories led to his turning instead to the "ethical experience of Latin antiquity"—and thereby furthered not only the rise of secularism, but also
the cause of humanistic studies. See *The Medieval Centuries*, pp. 158–60.

50. *Here I Stand*, p. 28.

intellectual or emotional nuances whatsoever, Churchmen propagated the faith and defended the status quo with equally crude extremism, both intellectual and emotional. Largely because of the sheer facts of existence at the time, popular awareness of mortality was already keen. Hence the Last Things easily became emotional bludgeons with which to combat ignorance, individualism, immorality, and especially indifference—all alike. Closing ranks against these common foes, all the religious orders found that skulls, worms, fire, and brimstone were, in one way or another, singularly useful weapons in the battle for God and Church.

The Dominicans' special province was, of course, the combating of doctrinal ignorance, extra-ecclesiastical individualism, and secularistic indifference. For all these purposes, *Memento mori* was a most useful battlecry: death lent itself so well to courtyard preaching![51] As emotions became increasingly jaded, the Last Things might come eventually to amuse skeptic and renegade; but death itself must ever remain a sobering prospect to any human being. Lurid descriptions of physical death and its aftermath, as well as apocalyptic threats, became for the Dominican school of preaching attention-getters for the propagation of the Gospel; levers to force the errant back into the institutional fold; and violent stimuli to repentance and righteousness.[52] And the more one one was convinced of the need for immediate, as well as remote, preparation for death, the more apt he was to make his peace with the Church, thereby assuring himself of the aids of the Eucharist and Extreme Unction when the time came. It is not surprising that the tendency to narrow the interpretation of "making a good death" was furthered by the Dominican evangelists.

51. John Bromyard's monumental *Summa Praedicantium* includes over one thousand exempla, arranged under 189 topics, which represent the "gathered fruits" of fourteenth-century mendicant preaching. Indeed, much of the material dates back to the thirteenth, and the work itself perhaps to 1360 (Owst, *Preaching,* p. 279, and *Literature and Pulpit,* p. 224). Yet even so early a compendium contains a formidable mass of material relating to death: in the 1586 edition, seventy-five two-column quarto pages (Spencer, p. 24).

52. For the dominant themes of late-medieval preachers, see Blench, pp. 228–63; for their characteristic homiletic methods, see Owst, *Preaching,* pp. 334–43, and *Literature and Pulpit,* pp. 527–36.

Meanwhile, the Franciscan forces, advancing along tangential lines, were striving to combat indifference, whether moral or immoral, by propagating the ideal of Christian holiness motivated by love. For them, too, the reminder of death was a formidable weapon—but this time, the death of the Crucifixion. Aroused from spiritual lethargy by the full realization of Christ's sacrifice for them on the Cross, men were to be moved to gratitude, and repentance, and love, and thence to holiness of life.[53] Unhappily, the law of diminishing returns operated in this sphere as well as in others. The preachers found themselves elaborating on the Passion in more and more realistic (and imaginative) detail in order to evoke the same degree of response, until the agony of dying had itself become a popular theme embodied in the popular consciousness. Ultimately, the worshiper's attention shifted from the Cross to the dreaded anguish of his own imminent death.[54] Devotional emphasis on Christ's sufferings tended to deteriorate into decadent naturalism for sheer horror's sake—for a shiver and a thrill. The meditations themselves, formerly devotional or doctrinal reflections, were now "coloured descriptions"—mere "vehicles for emotional dissipation."[55] Franciscan preaching, too, had been corrupted by the popular proclivity for emotional orgies.[56]

Official Christianity cannot, then, be absolved of all responsi-

53. This ethical ideal was the corollary of Franciscan ecclesiastical theory, which looked to the life of the Apostolic Church as normative. Originally and inherently, therefore, Franciscan death-consciousness, like that of first-century Christianity, was characterized by a joyous assurance quite at variance with the lugubrious temper of fifteenth-century thought, particularly that of Dominican evangelism.

54. Spencer, p. 21. The mystics' contribution to this development is noted by Pourrat: as artists depicted their visions of the Crucifixion with steadily increasing skill, its physical agony became ever more vivid to the layman—and, by extension, the presumed pain of dying as such (2:320). The growing obsession with "realistic" detail reaches its climax in Grünewald's masterpiece of repellent naturalism.

55. Pourrat, 2:187. The progression from the twelfth to the fifteenth centuries is clearly marked by the meditations of St. Bernard, Pseudo-Bonaventure, Ludolph the Carthusian, and Henry Suso.

56. Mâle even thinks it probable that Franciscan preachers were the originators of the *danse macabre* in its earliest form (p. 362).

bility for the necromania of the late Middle Ages. The insecurities
of material existence account in large measure for the preoccupation of the age with the fragility of life, and with the most unpleasant physical aspects of death; yet the Church, for its own
purposes, joined only too loudly in the cry of "Death conquers all!"
The somber, but still essentially Christian, chant *In media vitae*
now has as its opposite extreme, not the joyous chorus "Death,
thou shalt die" of the New Testament, but the grim, primitive
cacophony of rattling bones, deathbed screams, and the rustling of
patient worms. No prophet arose in effective protest against this
sub-Christian focusing of death-consciousness on the physical;
indeed, the representative Denis *saw* devils swarming about a
deathbed, and described (with relish?) the horrors of dying as
reported to him by spirits of the departed faithful.[57]

Again, abnormal insecurity may be blamed for imbuing many
with either a disgusted contempt for the values of the present life
or a defiant worldliness in the face of extinction—both of which
reactions, incidentally, contribute equally well to the development
of such minor art forms as the *danse macabre.*[58] Churchmen,
however, supported and intensified this emotional extremism both
through the similar extravagance of their own behavior, and also
through the death-focused violence of their evangelical techniques.
Otherworldliness was now far from being—as in the Apostolic
Church—mere indifference to meaningless values, motivated by
the expectation of imminent glory, and strengthened by faith
in a triumphant Christ. It had come to mean instead, for most
men, the violent renunciation of values which were often keenly
felt, motivated largely by the terrified hope of minimizing inescapable tortures, and strengthened by faith in a Christ who had
suffered and endured. For the grounds of both these fears and
these hopes, we must look not only to the Zeitgeist as a whole, but

57. Huizinga, p. 172. Cf., by way of contrast, Luther's protest that
"divine majesty is at hand in the hour of death. We say, 'In the midst
of life we die.' God answers, 'Nay, in the midst of death we live.'" Quoted
in Bainton, p. 370.

58. See Huizinga, pp. 126–28; Mâle, p. 380; Douglas Bush, *English
Literature in the Earlier Seventeenth Century,* p. 4.

also, and specifically, to the Church's intensive exploitation of the homiletically effective themes of sin, death—whether man's or Christ's—and the other Last Things.

In summary, the institutional Church continued, as usual, to reflect the climate of opinion of its time with a sensitivity which its critics have often deplored. During this period, moreover, Christian intuition, momentarily absorbed in individualistic, extra-ecclesiastical—and incommunicable—devotional experiments and experiences, failed to counteract, as it had in earlier centuries, such tendencies in hierarchical thought and practice. Theological discussion and inquiry epitomized, with a very few exceptions, the general decadence of the late-medieval mentality.[59] On the popular front, the increasing religious literacy of the lay Christian consisted to a large extent of the acceptance without distinction of all doctrines, derivative principles, and mere suggestive legends as gospel truth, just so long as they could be imaged forth by preachers and apprehended visually.[60] With intellectual abstractions or gradations in significance, the ordinary layman was unable to cope at all. Educated minds coped—in a sense: for solid intellectual analysis they substituted precious niceties of quasi-logical distinctions, and for a sound philosophical realism, fantastically elaborated allegorical interpretations of anything and everything.[61] Small

59. For an analysis of the characteristic faults of this mentality, see Huizinga, pp. 214–18. Cf. Pourrat, 2:263, and below, notes 60–62.

60. Huizinga, pp. 148–59, 182, 261–62. Furthermore, the instructional tracts written for the literate laity exhibited the same weaknesses of oversimplification and underdiscrimination: "simple explications of the Creed, the Ten Commandments, the cardinal sins, the five joys of the Virgin, and the like . . . along with the liturgy of the church, formed the heart of parochial Christianity in the Middle Ages. It is not surprising, then, to find reflections of popular doctrine in the vernacular literature of all genres and of all levels of sophistication" (Robert W. Ackerman, "Middle English Literature to 1400," in *The Medieval Literature of Western Europe: A Review of Research, Mainly 1930–1960*, gen. ed. John H. Fisher, p. 81).

61. As early as the second half of the fourteenth century, "allegorical interpretations . . . reach the most tedious and absurd proportions imaginable" in Bromyard's *Summa Praedicantium* (Owst, *Preaching*, p. 304). For vivid illustrations of the age's "everlasting classification" of ideas and

wonder that the age as a whole seems lost in a welter of undifferentiated, but uniformly emotive, notions. At every social
level, Christian feeling, no longer controlled and channeled either
by the discipline of rigorous Church tradition and practice or by
that of sound contemporary thought, waxed frenetic, and dissipated itself in crude extremes of emotionalism. And these emotional contrasts, too, like all the others in the life of the time, were
dramatized and heightened by being concretized in appropriate
ritual.[62] The habit of expressing in visual terms his tender piety
or black remorse, his childlike rapture or inconsolable grief, made
it just as impossible for the late-medieval Christian to apprehend
the nuances of religious emotion as to appreciate subtleties in any
other realm of feeling.

   This, then, is the religious temper of the age which produced the
new genre of the ars moriendi: superficial in its intellectual approach to Christian doctrine and its implications; limited—or
solipsistic—in its spiritual insight and sensitivity; and extrava-
gantly emotional and dramatic in its expression of the crudest extremes of religious thought and feeling. Against this unusually dis-
ordered background the *Crafte* must be evaluated.

   Above all, it is to be understood as one more expression of the
ritualizing tendency of the late-medieval spirit—for good as well
as ill. In certain respects this approach sharpens our perception of
its weaknesses. As ritual, the *Crafte* mirrors only too clearly the
distinctive limitations of its period. Its platitudinous and thin presentation of the clichés of Christian dogma, marred by inconsis-

---

exaggerated absorption with symbolism, see Huizinga, chaps. 15–17; for a
splendid example of the sort of "perverse elaboration" that completely
destroyed the meaning of a parable, while pretending to "exegete" it, see
Blench, pp. 5–7.
   62. In the words of Lynn D. White, the entire sacramental system ultimately became so "concretized" that "sacrament yielded to spectacle." See
"The Significance of Medieval Christianity," in *The Vitality of the Christian Tradition,* ed. George F. Thomas, pp. 112–15. For examples, see
Huizinga, pp. 1–6, 40–45; Pourrat, 2:323; Ladd, pp. 45–46.

tencies of thought and deficiencies of insight, testifies to the intellectual superficiality and spiritual lethargy of official Christendom. More important, its very existence reflects that obsessive preoccupation with death and Judgment which led contemporary notables to evolve "solemn and sublime formalities" for dying comparable to those for, say, marrying or mourning.[63] And here, as elsewhere, the very act of formalizing an unusually intense response to one area of experience tended, per se, to perpetuate that cultural phenomenon.

On the other hand, the *Crafte* also epitomizes the constructive, positive functions of ritual suggested by Huizinga in general terms. Just as social rites and ceremonies operated, throughout these centuries of decadence and transition, to preserve civilized values in general from the ravages of unbridled passions, so, too, the Church's liturgical tradition operated to preserve the historic values of the Christian kerygma from the ravages of intellectual aberrations, devotional eccentricities, and excessive emotionalism. Amid a welter of extraliturgical practices, the historic offices continued to embody fundamental dogma—and newly devised "rituals" such as the *Tractatus* applied that dogma to the needs of the moment.[64] The *Crafte of Dyinge* deserves respectful attention as a worthy expression of that permanent tradition which transcends, and tests, the specific Christianity of any period.

Thus, its intellectual mediocrity is less significant, historically speaking, than its avoidance of the characteristic faults of contemporary thought. Its author presents basic Christian doctrine in a drastically simplified form; but he resists both the temptation to cast every statement into a simplistic image, and the temptation —at the other extreme—to indulge in fantastic preciosities of dissection and elaboration. Again, his devotional insights are limited, even superficial; but they are also admirably free from merely

63. Huizinga, p. 31. For examples, see ibid., pp. 163–65, and Virginia Moore, *Ho for Heaven!: Man's Changing Attitude Toward Dying,* pp. 119–20, 129.

64. By way of precedent, the author of the *Tractatus* could have cited St. Thomas Aquinas himself, who had devised a ritual in response to the demand for a special feast in honor of Corpus Christi. See Pourrat, 2:323.

transitory cultism, and quite devoid of any of the mystic's devotional individualism. In both respects the author evinces not only a pastoral common sense, but also a genuinely liturgical feel for the permanent. And, finally, this same liturgical spirit of moderation—tranquil because timeless—characterizes his unimaginative application of Christian clichés to a theme temporarily supercharged with emotion. His dry little conduct-book, channeling into an unpretentious formalized pattern of behavior the frenzied obsessions of the time, thereby reduced their disturbance-potential to a minimum. In all these respects, and especially the last, the *Crafte* exemplifies ritual at its best. Born in an age when religious thought and religious sensibility were alike distorted and corrupt, it reasserts the validity of the genuinely traditional in Christian doctrine and feeling—while doing it in such a way that the age was able to appropriate its message.

We have noted, for example, that the *Crafte* accepts the late-medieval view of man as above all Moriens, rightly fearful of the agony of dying which he must endure at any moment, as well as of the physical torments which await him beyond the grave. Yet whereas the Church in general tended to enhance this atmosphere of dread by elaborating with zest on the themes of deathbed horrors,[65] putrefaction, and punishments beyond the grave, the *Crafte* minimizes them. Instead, Everyman is seen primarily as Fidens, fortified against the tests ahead by the assurances of a loving God. Although the new spirit of the *danse macabre* had been in evidence for twenty-five years at least,[66] dancing skeletons and *réalisme funèbre* have no place here. Purgatory and hell receive minimal attention; the devilish tormentors are even made to seem rather ineffectual creatures. "Spirituall deth," we are assured, is far

65. Including, as early as 1340 (in the *Pricke of Conscience*), not only physical and spiritual agonies, but also horrible temptations by frightful devils. See Spencer, pp. 10–12.

66. Mâle postulates a fourteenth-century version of the *danse macabre* —"undoubtedly an illuminated manuscript"; but as a cultural phenomenon, he argues, this vision of death emerged only in the 1930s (pp. 47–48, 354, 361–63, 374–75).

more to be dreaded than physical death—but he who follows this simple ritual in faith "schal not dye everlastyngly." The assurance of the author is contagious.

Again, the *Crafte* follows its age in contemning this world and urging the reader to repent in time the multitude of specific sins to which his involvement in the world has led him. Yet whereas the Church as a whole thundered against worldliness, admired dramatic extremes of asceticism, and developed fantastic elaborations of its penitential system, the *Crafte* pursues its quiet purpose of restating fundamental doctrine and adapting it to the needs of its time. Extreme denunciation of the world and worldliness is avoided; indeed, room is made for legitimate concern about one's family and business affairs. True otherworldliness is not physical, but spiritual: "to have a herte and a soule ever redy up to godward." Men must of course repent their sins, but even more their essential sinfulness in not loving God above all else; and their repentance must spring from a new access of that love, rather than from fear of punishment. Most important of all, the whole tenor of the discussion on these points is one of comfort: the doctrines of grace and reconciliation are emphasized at the expense of apocalyptic threats.

And finally, we may note that the Passion-centered hopes of the period are accepted and modified in much the same way as its death-centered fears. The author follows his age in interpreting the *imitatio Christi* in a detailed and literal sense, and in displaying unusual warmth of feeling when describing the crucified Christ. At the same time, however, his meditation is devoid of the naturalistic and dramatic detail so familiar in other works of the time, both lay and ecclesiastical. Rather, it follows the traditional pattern of *doctrinal* reflections, designed less to evoke an emotional commitment than to expand and deepen one's understanding of a commitment already made. Here, for example, the frightened sinner is led to a fresh—and presumably heartening—awareness of two implications of his Christian faith: first, that his trust in the merits of Christ's Passion, simply as abstract doctrine, should reassure him in the face of the coming trial; and secondly,

that Christ in his mercy has actually left him, in that Passion, a
clearly defined path to follow to victory.[67] In short, "Fear not. . . ."

When the *Crafte* is read in the light of its own time, therefore, its very traditionalism is clearly recognizable as its essential virtue. Even its existence ceases to appear altogether mor-
bid, since, in Huizinga's terms, the *Tractatus* answered an "aesthetic need" of the age for a "style," or "form," into which to
channel its passions. Its contents reflect a "climate of opinion"
which its author could not transcend completely; but they also
argue forcefully, if indirectly, for a healthful moderation of that
climate. Even the pedestrianism of its tone is, in this context, laudable. Anonymous, impersonal, objective, utilitarian, it condemned
by implication the imaginative frenzies then corrupting Christian devotion. The stock quasi-liturgical structure, the labored
authoritarian argument, the clumsy sentence structure, the limited
vocabulary and meager imagery—all these support the author's
pastoral effort to speak to his contemporaries in the voice of authority and *traditio.* The true value of the *Crafte* for its own time
lay precisely in the extent to which its author was able to resist the
colorful potentialities of his theme and thus realize his pastoral
aim.

The *Crafte* is obviously an extremely limited work; indeed,
hardly a work of art at all. It was susceptible of vast enrichment
in every sense: philosophically, as a new intellectuality should
come to challenge its theistic and eschatological premises themselves; psychologically, as a new subtlety of perception should
suggest all sorts of new and complex reactions to the mystery of
death; and artistically, as a new aesthetic sensitivity should express with increasing skill every attitude toward dying and death
conceivable to the Renaissance mind. Nonetheless, it deserves
recognition, and even respect, for genuine virtues which have
gone too long unacknowledged. In the years to come, anyone concerned with the problem of death would have to take its message
into account—precisely because it was *not,* like the *danse macabre,*

67. Pourrat, 2:187.

an exciting but eccentric by-product of an eccentric age. One needed very little more than a belief in the moral obligation to die well and a willingness to accept the validity of deathbed temptation (however interpreted) in order to read the *Crafte*—or the Latin original—as a mine of authentic historic doctrine on the subject. The medieval Church could have found no abler, more persuasive spokesman for its position than the anonymous author of the *Tractatus artis bene moriendi.*

## CHAPTER 2

# *The Waye of Dyenge Well:* A Humanistic "Crafte"

Of all the sources of enrichment which were to contribute to the flowering of the ars moriendi as a literary genre, none was of greater significance than that of classical culture. Under the aegis of pre-Reformation transalpine humanism, the devotional tract was transmuted into a new literary type. Its intellectual horizons widened, its insights deepened, and it began to seek consciously an artistic form which should be worthy of its matter. The old wine of ecclesiastical tradition, now stale, was combined with the rather heady vintage of ancient death-literature, and poured into the new bottle of the classical moral essay. The indigestibility of such a simple mixture of the two traditions was not immediately apparent; it was, at first, too intoxicating. Thomas Lupset's *The Waye of Dyenge Well* (1534),[1] the finest exemplar of the humanistic "Crafte," witnesses forcefully to both the strengths and the weaknesses—the solid accomplishments and the inner tensions—of the early Renaissance in England.

On the Continent, the new classicism had started to modify the ars moriendi many decades earlier, if only in minor ways.[2] In

1. *A compendious and a very fruteful treatyse, teachynge the waye of Dyenge well.* . . . The text used for this study is that of the 1534 edition, as edited by John Archer Gee in his *Life and Works of Thomas Lupset,* pp. [265]–90. Aside from transposing *i* and *j, u* and *v,* and expanding ampersands, I have followed his rendering in every detail but omitted his notation of the original pagination.

2. For a detailed survey of representative fifteenth-century contributions to the new genre, see O'Connor, *Art of Dying Well,* pt. 4, pp. 172–80. Minor variations traceable to the new enthusiasms may be illustrated from the "Crafte" of Denis the Carthusian himself: his list of those who had to "submit to death" includes Paris, Venus and Adonis, Hector, Hercules, Plato, Plotinus, Cicero, Macrobius, Demosthenes, and Xenophon (p. 174).

England, however, where humanistic scholarship was later in taking to the field, its influence was still further delayed by the religious conservatism of Colet's circle. After 1490, when Caxton included a meager version of the *Tractatus* in one of his compendia, treatises on dying well spilled from the presses; significantly enough, even the busy humanists found time to produce their share. Yet so uncompromisingly orthodox in their religious views were the older generation that traditional elements continued to dominate their contributions to the genre until well into the sixteenth century. Thomas More's, for instance—the first section (ca. 1522) of a projected but never completed *Quattuor novissima*—is unmistakably traditional and derivative in spite of its use of classical material and its notable advance in artistic quality. It exalts *memorare novissima* above even the greatest of pagan philosophers, dwells on Satan's deathbed temptations, and affirms the invulnerability of Christ's Passion as Everyman's defense against these assaults.[3] Even his better-known *Dialogue of Comfort* (1534) is, for all its classicism, thoroughly Christian in its fundamental assumptions and method of argumentation. Erasmus, also, produced two treatises exhibiting the same differences in literary inspiration and the same conservatism in essence: the *De morte declamatio* (1517?), primarily consolatory in nature,[4] and the *De praeparatione ad mortem* (1953), thoroughly medieval

---

More important, the many editions of the *Ars moriendi* itself (over one hundred are extant from the fifteenth century alone) were supplemented rapidly by adaptations of various types. The most noteworthy are those in which the art of dying is already groping toward its ultimate reunion with the art of living. It seems to have been the English and the French—pragmatic and rational even then!—who rejected most firmly the late-medieval pseudological notion of splitting the two apart.

3. It is this work which includes More's valuable description of the "dance of death" once found in St. Paul's Cathedral; and it is the influence of the *danse macabre,* rather than that of the *Crafte,* which is reflected in his emphasis on the physical loathsomeness of death.

4. The first draft, we learn from a letter of More's (Dec. 15, 1516), Lupset "kept by him for some time." See Gee, pp. 53–54.

in both structure and argument.[5] It remained for Lupset, as the outstanding young hopeful of the second generation, to produce the essay which embodies most clearly the distinctive characteristics of the new learning—of Christian humanism as it developed in pre-Reformation England.

His equipment for such an achievement included not only a fine mind and admirable character,[6] but also an intimate relationship with the major humanists of his time. A protégé of Colet's in boyhood, he became a member of the Dean's household, and so devoted a disciple that he resolved to model his life on Colet's in every way possible. He may have studied Greek at St. Paul's School under Lily; he certainly studied at Cambridge under Erasmus, and probably helped the latter collate his New Testament with the ancient Greek MSS and edit St. Jerome's *Epistles.* After Colet's death, he became the equally devoted protégé, disciple, and friend of Erasmus. In London he naturally made the acquaintance of all Colet's circle, including particularly Linacre and More; and on a mission to Paris for the former, he met the great scholar Budé, who gave him an entrée to other continental humanists. A few years later, sent to Padua as tutor and chaperon of Wolsey's son Thomas Winter, he developed a close relationship with Leonicus, and an intimate friendship with a young scholar and devout Christian who was to become the great and controversial Reginald Cardinal Pole. Accepted, admired, and supported by such men as these—not to mention Pace and Wolsey—Lupset certainly had every reason to look forward to a brilliant career in public life as well as in the world of humanistic scholarship.

5. English translations were published in 1538 and 1543, and again in 1706. For a description of this work, see O'Connor, pp. 180–81. Although Colet contributed no work specifically in this genre, cf. his brief but suggestive exhortation in *A ryght fruitfull monicion concerning the order of a good christen mannes lyfe* . . . : "And in especyall haue in mynde, that thou shalt dye shortly, and how Christ dyed for the; the subtyltie and falsnes of this temporall world, the ioyes of heven, and the paynes of hell." Reprinted in Joseph H. Lupton, *A Life of John Colet,* 2d ed., app. D, p. 307.

6. See Gee, esp. pp. 65, 110–13, 156, and 174–83. Unless otherwise noted, I am indebted solely to this admirable study for the biographical information that follows.

Unhappily, this promise was never fulfilled, since he died of tuberculosis in 1530, at the age of thirty-five, leaving only three completed works of his own.[7] All three, written within the last eighteen months of his life, are short moral essays, classical in structure. The *Treatise of Charitie,* purportedly addressed to an "entirely beloved syster," is a specifically Christian moral discourse, modeled on the sermons of the "golden-tongued" Chrysostom.[8] The *Exhortation to Yonge Men,* addressed to a former student soon to become a merchant, is a Senecan moral essay almost exclusively classical in content, organized around Plato's analysis of the relative importance of soul, body, and world. The third and last, written only a few months before his death, is the *Waye of Dyenge Well.* This, too, is Senecan in structure, its supposed recipient this time a servant of Pole's; but it lies somewhere between the other two essays in its orientation, which is neither completely Christian nor wholeheartedly classical. That "one of the more advanced northern humanists of his day"[9] should concern himself at all with "teachynge the waye of Dyenge well" is expressive of the continuing power of the medieval religious tradition in Renaissance thought. That Lupset should attempt in this instance alone a fusion of Christian and classical elements is suggestive of the inherent adaptability of the medieval conduct-book to artistic elaboration.

As John A. Gee suggests, in his authoritative study of Lupset,[10] the young humanist's contributions to this artistic development have as their locus "a strong reaction . . . against the point of view, and possibly the formlessness" (or what he conceived to be the formlessness?) of the medieval works (p. 143). Even the full title

7. Despite his ill health, he was, we are told, "a hard student, but one who preferred to keep the results of his learning for his own private use and enjoyment, rather than publish them for the benefit of others" (Lupton [citing George Lily, the son of Lupset's old master at St. Paul's], p. 235 and n.).

8. Gee, p. 131.

9. Ibid., p. 180.

10. See above, note 1.

of his treatise hints at his very different approach to the conventional problem. *His* treatise will be "compendious," far richer in its thought, drawing on the wisdom of the ages to supersede the limited, incomplete, narrow *Crafte*. It will, moreover, be "fruitful" —an adjective whose biblical connotations lead us, correctly, to anticipate an argument oriented toward the art of living. (His use of the word "waye," rather than "art" or "craft" or "cunning," supports this implication for the same reason.)[11] And finally, to readers familiar with Lupset's humanistic predilections the word "treatyse" itself promises something more than a translation of a *tractatus*. We are not surprised to find that his discussion is characterized throughout by a careful fidelity to the traditional structure of the classical moral essay—a logical structure more or less concealed by a studied informality of manner.

Thus his introductory paragraphs constitute an adroit, but unmistakable, imitation of Seneca's personal introductions to his moral essays and epistles. John Walker, Pole's servant, is the Lucilius (or, better perhaps, the Paulinus or Polybius)[12] of this "letter"; and the concrete "fact" which is to serve as the springboard for abstract reflections[13] is, ostensibly, his "importune desire" that Lupset should "write to [him] the way of dyenge well" (pp. 266, [265]). For fifty lines the author protests gracefully that he should be released from his promise to comply with this request. Wise men agree that exceptions are implicit in all promises, since unforeseen hindrances may arise; hence he might plead the pressure of other work, and particularly his unworthiness—being neither a Socrates nor a Chrysostom—to discuss such a topic. He agrees finally to "say somewhat," but only on condition that Walker understand that the advice to come applies equally to both author

---

11. "Fruitful" was also, of course, a favorite epithet of the early Renaissance humanists for almost any of their own works, simply in implied contradistinction to the "barren" or "sterile" productions of the Schoolmen.

12. "Better" because the moral epistles addressed to Lucilius are shorter and more *intime* in content and expression than the moral essays. Paulinus is the supposed recipient of the *De brevitate vitae;* Polybius, of one of the *consolationes*.

13. Seneca regularly introduces his topics by means of this device.

and recipient. Thus the persona of the Roman moral epistolographer has been established: that of the urbane, cultured gentleman-philosopher, graciously desiring to be helpful, but politely diffident about the adequacy of his talents.[14]

As his letter unfolds, Lupset discloses his plan of organization even more explicitly than his models demand—perhaps as one facet of his repudiation of the formlessness of the medieval *tractati*. True, an historical anecdote is inserted casually as an enticing bridge from the personal to the theoretical section of the introduction. This latter, too, is developed with disarming ease, although it is a vitally important presentation of the two concepts on which the rest of his arguments are based, and on which, indeed, the justification for the treatise itself depends: his personal understanding of the grace of reason and of the distinction between worldliness and spirituality. Without these two premises his daring use of classical materials would be at best confusing. As soon as he has launched the reader onto the mainstream of his discourse, however, he drops most of this pretense of informality and sets out verbal markers which guide one insistently—almost officiously[15]—through to the end of the treatise. "Dienge well" is defined without more ado as "dyenge gladlye"; "dyenge gladlye" is defined in a brief passage as dying in faith, hope, and charity; and the remainder of his argument consists of a reasoned analysis of the two basic "lettes" to dying gladly—the fear of death, and the love of this life. This discussion, the core of his treatise, occupies roughly six thousand of the work's ten thousand words;

14. This traditional diffidence is seasoned with just a dash of that hero-worshiping humility so characteristic of the Renaissance humanist when deferring to the wisdom of the ancients. As Douglas Bush reminds us, such "profound reverence" was "not a genteel tradition," but a "dynamic faith"; it was "bred in the bone, and no amount of drill in grammar and rhetoric could kill it." See *Prefaces to Renaissance Literature,* pp. 21–23, 92–93. It is important, therefore, not to dismiss Lupset's traditionalism here—or elsewhere in his treatise—as merely glib or imitative; and nothing I say is meant to do so.

15. Somewhat in the manner of the pedagogue determined that, this one time, even the fuzzy-minded students shall be able to follow his outline. For Lupset's success as a lecturer, see Gee, pp. 87–101.

and four-fifths of it is concerned with the problem of man's apparently innate fear of death, only one-fifth with his inordinate love of life. The conclusion focuses again on the individual recipient of the letter, as Lupset advises Walker to apply personally the general truths now elucidated; but its organization remains as strict as that of the preceding analysis, rather than slipping once more into an apparent casualness. Walker is to adopt a rule of life, remembering death daily, fleeing from idleness, and praying without ceasing. The treatise ends with a brief intercessory prayer for Walker's safe passage through death to everlasting life.

Something of the curious intermingling of the old and the new in the early Renaissance is suggested even by this outline of the structure of the *Waye of Dyenge Well*. Static, analytical, and explicit in its organization, rather than dynamic, devotional, and implicit, its classical pattern is virtually the antithesis of the liturgical movement of the *Crafte*. On the other hand, both the concrete fact which inspires the essay and most of the concrete advice which climaxes it (not to mention the benedictory coda) are essentially medieval in spirit. Somewhere between the two extremes, finally, we must place Lupset's confident definition of "dying well," and his weighting of the hindrances thereto four to one on the side of man's fear of death. Here the Stoic literary tradition and the medieval heritage have combined forces effortlessly.

No rapid survey, however, can suggest adequately the earnestness of Lupset's struggle to fuse the two traditions under the ultimate truth, as he saw it, of the Christian Revelation; nor can it reveal the extent of his failure—the abundance of inconsistencies and latent contradictions in his thinking about, and in his emotional response to, the challenge of death. Time and again, throughout the treatise, Stoic concepts and ideals incorporated into his argument conflict implicitly with the accepted Christian teaching which they are designed to support and enrich. And time and again incongruities in style expose an underlying emotional tension as well: pagan intuition, dismissed by the mind as inferior to Christian truth, turns out to be unmistakably more vital, more stimulating to the emotions. For this critical understanding we must consider the text much more closely.

## Personal Introduction

Returning to Lupset's skillful introductory passage (pp. 265–66), we find that it reveals clearly not only the distinctive aims of the Christian humanist, but also his conspicuous superiority over his fifteenth-century predecessor in both intellectual equipment and ethical sensitivity. "How to die well" is, from the humanist's point of view, a problem of truly universal concern, since the Stoics discussed the topic endlessly. Hence the literary form of the moral essay is perfectly suitable for a reply to Walker's essentially Christian request for instruction. Within this framework, Lupset orders his argument so as to achieve a genuine fusion of the classical and the Christian understanding about death—but a fusion on certain specific terms.

On the one hand, the classics are to correct the medieval tradition wherever it has gone astray; and they are to enrich its valid insights. Thus, the treatise simply ignores from the start the whole issue of the deathbed, its dangers and opportunities, repudiating this emphasis in favor of a more enlightened, or humane, one on ethical living. The dictum that one must know how to live well before he can know, and teach, the way to die well, is a Stoic cliché; but it is one which harmonizes smoothly with the pronouncements of Christian thinkers from St. Paul to the compilers of the thirteenth- and fourteenth-century compendia.[16] In insisting from his very first paragraph on the inseparability of the two arts, and in reemphasizing the point (in terms of faith and works) before he has even approached his main argument, Lupset proves himself a loyal disciple of Colet and a worthy spokesman for English humanism. He also illustrates his axiom by recounting with the gusto of a conventional Stoic the noble suicide of Cato—thus reintroducing to Christian thought about dying the classical concepts of courage and honor. On the other hand, even the wisest of pagan insights must be subsumed in one way or another under the inherently superior teaching of the Christian Revelation.

16. St. Augustine states the Christian paraphrase succinctly in Sermon 249: *"Si bene vixeris, mali mori non poteris."* Quoted in O'Connor, p. 24 n. 74.

Cato and other exemplary pagans are subordinated emphatically
to Paul, Peter, and Jerome—indeed, to any man "exercised in
Cristes philosophye"—who "shulde here in speke more lyvely,
than al the subtyl clerkes of the olde grekes."[17]

The startling improvement in intellectual power and control
found in this passage is accompanied by a similar advance in its
artistic concreteness of expression. The epistolary form itself en-
hances noticeably the dramatic effectiveness of the essay, even
though the author remains the universal gentleman-scholar
throughout, while the recipient is given no individualizing traits
beyond a name and (later on) a vocation.[18] More important is the
vitalizing of cited authority: we are told, not merely what an authority said, but also enough about what he was, as revealed in his
life or death, to command our respectful attention to his words.
An individual *magister,* enunciating or exemplifying truths based
on wisdom and experience, supersedes impersonal *traditio,* speaking through disembodied names—hallowed, perhaps, but non-
human. Authority humanized is certainly more to our modern
taste, artistically speaking, than the "auctoritees" of the Schoolmen.[19]

17. Cf. St. Augustine, once again: despite his personal indebtedness to
the Neoplatonists, he insists that even the greatest of pagan philosophers
cannot be preferred to "the truth-speaking prophets, nor to any of the
apostles or martyrs of Christ, nay, not to *any faithful Christian man"*
*(City of God,* 2:14, as quoted by Leland Miles, *John Colet and the Platonic
Tradition,* p. 4; italics mine). Lupset's concept of the proper relationship
between the classics and the Christian gospel is, in short, the Clementine
or Augustinian position as distinct from that of Ficino and the Florentine
humanists. Roger K. Warlick demonstrates, however, that even Colet, the
"most conservative, the most English, of all the English humanists" was
"often not entirely successful" in his efforts to subordinate the pagan classics
to the Christian ("John Colet and Renaissance Humanism," *DA* 26 [1966]:
3893). In this instance at least, as we shall see, the disciple is assuredly
not above his master.

18. This statement, though accurate, is somewhat misleading, since
Walker does acquire an aura of reality through Lupset's complimentary
reference to his master, and also to Pole's affection for his servant.

19. For the Renaissance humanist, of course, this preference was more
than a matter of taste: whether scholar, philosopher, artist, or pedagogue, it
was a major article of his faith. Not only did he attack insistently—on

Equally conspicuous, on the other hand, are theological implications of real import for the subsequent history of Christian thought and literature. These may be called the "negative corollaries" of Lupset's positive achievements—negative, that is, in terms of their latent challenge, or even threat, to accepted Catholic orthodoxy.

The first corollary, and one of profound significance for the development of the literary tradition of the ars moriendi, is the radical modification that has occurred already in the historic Christian understanding of death. By a few deceptively simple steps, Lupset has gone far toward transmuting death from an ultimate existential challenge that must be met by Everyman to an abstract intellectual topic to be analyzed and discussed by the qualified few. For example, the focus of the *Crafte* is clearly on death as the inescapable final defeat of Everyman's efforts at autonomy. Whenever or however it may come, death is itself the uniquely universal problem confronting all men alike. Lupset's introduction of distinctions among kinds of death—natural death, death before one's time, and even suicide—blurs his focus to some extent, and tends to divert our gaze from death itself to living men and their differences.

Again, the *Crafte* assumes that man, confronted by the reality of death, is driven thereby to face the conditions of his own existence: his relationship to God as dependent creature. (The only alternative—that of death as the triumph of nothingness, death as ultimate negation—is of course unthinkable.) Face to face with

---

religious as well as rhetorical grounds—the Schoolmen's "painful and over-scrupulous alleging of authorities" (Colet, cited in Hunt, p. 100), but he exalted the giants of antiquity, and their potency as moral exemplars, with a fervor that sometimes bemuses us. So deeply embedded in the humanist psyche did this antagonism to the Scholastics and veneration for the ancients become, that more than a century later Jeremy Taylor still found occasion to exalt "those old wise spirits" (sixteen of whom he names in that very sentence) at the expense of "many of the latter schoolmen" (none of whom he names)—whose "triflings . . . added nothing to Christianity but trouble, scruple, and vexation" *(The Great Exemplar* in *The Whole Works of the Right Rev. Jeremy Taylor,* ed. Reginald Heber, revised and corrected by Charles P. Eden, vol. 2, Preface, sec. 44).

death, whether literally or contemplatively, one must perforce recognize the I-thou relationship between himself and God.[20] On his deathbed, then, if at no other time in his life, Everyman's attitude cannot but be devotional. Lupset's introduction of the classical virtues of courage and honor does indeed enrich the connotations of "well" in the phrase "dying well"; but it also reveals how far his classical enthusiasms have led him already from a God-centered, devotional orientation to death. These human virtues were relevant for the Stoic Moriens precisely because, in the last analysis, he could not be sure that any others mattered. The Christian humanist professes to be sure that the Christian virtues are of primary importance; but his endorsement, even temporarily, of the ideal of "dying with honour rather than living with shame"[21] suggests the power of the new thought over the minds even of those who considered themselves most orthodox.[22]

Finally, and above all, the *Crafte* sees death as a challenge which must be met—one which demands, not withdrawal and analysis, but commitment and action. Lupset, however, implies that "this lesson to lerne the way" is really a topic proper only for philosophical analysis: he protests that "the thynge" has "more difficulte in it" than is suitable for his "poore witte," and defers to the "mayster" who "knowethe both what our life is, and what the losse of the same is." This shifting of the problem from the religious to the philosophical sphere of life leads directly to the essential emasculation of death as a "doleful," "dreadful," omnipotent reality[23] before which one must come to terms with himself and with his God. In a very real sense, man escapes from the challenge of his mortality just so far as he can transmute the *fact* into an *idea* with which his finite brain is presumably able to deal.

20. See Martin Buber, *I and Thou*, trans. Ronald G. Smith, esp. pt. 3.

21. Cf., e.g., Seneca, *Ad Lucilium epistulae morales,* ed. and trans. R. M. Gummere, Loeb Classical Library, 3 vols., *Ep.* 70. All subsequent references to Seneca's epistles are to this edition.

22. Gee makes clear that Lupset considered all those who questioned the traditional faith "presumptuous" and "folishe medlars," and that he "dreaded any change in the *status quo*" (pp. 180–81).

23. See below, note 69.

Death has to that extent become subordinate to man, rather than man to death. And Lupset's imposition of a static pattern of organization upon his material contributes markedly to this escape, since the reader's first response must necessarily be one of passive understanding rather than of active obedience. Understanding may or may not lead to commitment, to appropriate action; but in any case, the challenge of death has been abstracted to a surprising degree.

Closely tied to these modifications in the traditional view of death is the second negative corollary: the emergence of the individual thinker and philosopher as the proper religious authority, rather than Christian *traditio*. Since dying is, for the *Crafte*, a universal and essentially religious experience, the Church is obviously the proper authority on how it should be done by the faithful. Lupset, absorbed in enriching his treatise with the insights of his classical masters, and with vivid accounts of their exemplification of their own teaching, fails—as did his fellow humanists—to recognize the long-range implications of his hero worship.

Of these, two are of notable significance for devotional literature. In the first place, his adoption of a philosophical orientation to his subject not only modifies the old understanding of death, but also challenges the traditional understanding of the power of sin and man's need for redemption. The moral insights of the classical masters—freshly realized through newly discovered works, widely disseminated in new translations, vividly dramatized in their own lives (and deaths)—did enrich beyond measure the thought and art of the Christian humanists of Lupset's age.[24] Inevitably, then, they cherished, and promulgated wholeheartedly, the familiar di-

24. For a most useful itemization of the humanists' *specific* contributions to classical scholarship, see Paul O. Kristeller, "Humanist Learning in the Italian Renaissance," in his *Renaissance Thought II,* pp. 6–7. Also among his numerous impressive studies is perhaps the single most comprehensive brief survey of the intellectual influences of these pursuits: "The Moral Thought of Renaissance Humanism," written for the Columbia University *Chapters in Western Civilization* (1961) and republished in *Renaissance Thought II,* pp. 20–68. The literature of twentieth-century scholarship in this area, both extensive and intensive, is of course inexhaustible.

dactic theory that literature and history were philosophy teaching by examples. Scorning the caveats of contemporary Tertullians, they insisted that classical exempla, as well as Christian, would not only teach men to understand the good, but also stir them to admire and emulate it. Lurking in these optimistic credos, however —as in the source materials to which they deferred so readily— is the ancient assumption that knowledge equals virtue, that understanding will in fact lead inevitably to right behavior.[25] This basic clash between classical and Christian interpretations of man, as yet only latent, will become increasingly severe in Renaissance thought.

In the second place, such a deference opens the gate logically to a floor of individualistic discourses, each based on "first principles," and each claiming the support of masters—at least in the beginning. And of the masters, the agnostic Stoics are the most compelling figures, not merely because their teaching and their deaths were written up with more artistry than those of the early Christians, but primarily because of their very agnosticism.[26]

---

25. Although the medieval lives of the saints were predicated on very similar assumptions, "it makes a difference," as Kristeller observes, "whether the persons whose lives are described as models of human conduct are Christian saints or ancient statesmen and generals, philosophers and poets" ("Moral Thought," p. 27; see also pp. 28, 43–44). For a sampling of representative statements of the didactic theory of history, ranging from Petrarch to Machiavelli, see Myron Gilmore, "The Renaissance Conception of the Lessons of History," in *Facets of the Renaissance,* ed. William H. Werkmeister, pp. 81–91. Even Machiavelli does not argue that the principle is invalid, only that it simply has not worked; his explanation, however, is scarcely that of St. Paul and the Augustinian tradition. Cf. Bush, *Prefaces,* pp. 92–94; and Herschel Baker, *The Dignity of Man,* pp. 270–72.

26. Classical authorities, we feel, are individuals; Christian authorities, potent but nevertheless still interchangeable names. (Cf. Bush, *Prefaces,* pp. 10–11.) With the single exception of St. Peter, whose position is unique, the Christian masters to whom Lupset defers are simply those most admired by his fellow humanists: St. Paul, St. Chrysostom, and St. Jerome. In any given context, his selection may be notably apt, or it may not. The certitude of saints is not especially dramatic.

Ultimately, the first principles themselves will be called into doubt by this process.[27]

Thus, by a few modifications, initiated in a conservative spirit of utter fidelity to his Christian heritage, Lupset is in truth undermining that heritage markedly—however germinally and unconsciously—in several fundamental respects. To point this out is in no sense to disparage the significance of his achievement, still less of the humanists' contribution to the intellectual and artistic development of the ars moriendi. Death had to be abstracted, to some extent at least—had to be understood as itself a human experience, a part of life rather than a shocking confrontation—before the literature of death could grow in any qualitative sense of the word. A problem of no less concern than before, it was now objectified to the point of rational and artistic manageability. The mind of man, hitherto paralyzed, could probe and analyze and explore; and his creative powers could be released to image forth truth as he understood it, and to interpret it.

For the same reasons, the claims of the Church to final authority had to be challenged, and those of individual reason, intuition, and experience asserted. Paradoxically, the loss of calm certitude as to the ultimate and all-inclusive truth of the Christian world view must be accounted of major significance in the development of a vital Christian death-literature. The denial of ecclesiastical authoritarianism leads to a new concept of religious authority which is far richer in its artistic potential. On the one hand, it is broadened to include all the wealth of classical civilization. Since the medieval indifference to the reality of time has not yet been superceded by the modern concept of history, the wise men of every age—classical

27. The seriousness of the threat which Stoic courage offers to Christian dogma (cf. Paul Tillich, *The Courage To Be*, chap. 1, pp. 9–17) is reflected quite sharply even in *Holy Dying*. Certainly Taylor's Christian eloquence is superlative, and his Christian control of individual Stoic exempla masterly. Yet even he does not place dramatic representations of agnostic nobility of character side by side with specifically Christian instruction; and even he, in an unwary moment, deserts his Christian principles to the extent of citing with unqualified approval an honorable suicide.

no less than patristic or medieval—may now be consulted, and cited, as contemporaries whose thought is immediately relevant.[28] On the other hand, since individual authorities are obviously no longer reconcilable in even the most casuistical sense of the word, ultimate authority must now devolve, in the last analysis, upon the individual. The voice of *traditio*—dispassionate, anonymous, professedly universal—becomes only one of many voices speaking to the Renaissance Christian about life and death and destiny. It is more than likely that he will find it a commanding voice, and in most respects authoritative; but in any case the final decision rests with him, and his personal integrity is directly involved. Clearly, therefore, the new intensity of thought and feeling which characterizes the Renaissance treatment of death is traceable in large measure to this dual modification of the medieval concepts of authority.

## THE DEATH OF CANIUS

The anecdote which supplies a smooth transition from personal remarks to theoretical premises is the tale of the good death of the philosopher Canius under the tyrant Caligula (pp. 267–68). This Lupset recounts in some detail,[29] with effective use of dramatic dialogue, and with unmistakable admiration for the protagonist of his story. Its essentials are as follows: (1) when Caligula, at the close of one of several quarrels with Canius, informed him that he was to be executed, the philosopher thanked him; (2) in the course of his ten days' respite, men marveled at his cheerfulness and untroubled spirit; (3) when the jailer and hangman finally came for him, he was playing chess, and insisted jokingly that the

---

28. Although "the development of an historical consciousness . . . was of course one of the great marks of the Renaissance mind" (Bush, *Prefaces,* p. 10; and see his *Classical Influences in Renaissance Literature,* pp. 13–15), the humanists' "sense of the life and style of the past" is clearly "incomplete"—"still far from the historicism of the nineteenth and twentieth centuries" (Gilmore, p. 80; and see pp. 76–80). Cf. E. H. Harbison, *The Christian Scholar in the Age of the Reformation,* pp. 34–38 and passim.

29. About seven hundred words long, it is only slightly shorter than each of the two introductory sections which it links.

jailer bear witness that he was ahead, so that his friend could not boast of victory after his death; (4) he reproved his mourning friends in Socrates's spirit, and almost in his exact words; and (5) finally, while those ahead of him were being beheaded, he pondered the problem of whether or not the soul perceives or feels its separation from the body, and promised his friends to bring word to them if possible of the truth in regard to this problem, and also in regard to the state of men's souls after death.

After the first, third, and fifth of these points, Lupset inserts exegeses so that his reader will be sure to understand just exactly why Canius's behavior was laudable in each instance. By thanking the tyrant for his unjust sentence, the philosopher indicated that Caligula's mad rages were so intolerable that death under his regime should be accounted a "benefit and a good tourne." By joking over the chess game, he "playde with deathe," and thus by his "quiete harte gave a foule checke mate to the tyrantes crueltie," since the brute power of "mightye princes" is always rendered impotent by the lofty spirit which scorns their threats. As for Canius's final farewell, Lupset cries that "this mans mynde was worthye of an ever lastynge lyfe, that was not onely to the deathe studious of knowlege, but also in the selfe death founde occasion of lernynge. It was not possyble for any mannes mynde to contynue his studye longer, or to a ferther poynte than this noble philosopher dyd."

The intellectual contributions of the ancients become increasingly evident in this passage, as a few more clichés of classical death-literature make their appearance. Most important, for our purposes, are those which assert the relevance and validity of specifically human values even in the face of death. These Lupset adopts enthusiastically. They include the familiar exaltation of the virtue of courage;[30] the argument that one should learn indifference to death for the specific purpose of freeing oneself thereby from the power of temporal tyranny;[31] and the belief that a man's

30. Cf. esp. Seneca, Ep. 24, for one of the clearest presentations of this very common theme.
31. Cf., e.g., Seneca, Ep. 26, 70, and 77.

death should be regarded primarily as the final touchstone for evaluating the quality of his life.[32] All these notions tend implicitly to shift the focus of our attention from Moriens, in his helpless finitude, to Vivens, seen both as ethical individual immersed in complex social relationships,[33] and as isolated personality whose integrity is itself an ultimate value. This Stoic doctrine of man is most fully revealed, however, in the account of the death scene itself. Here Lupset approves explicitly of Canius's clutching to the last possible instant his selfhood—and his selfhood understood in its sociological context, as well. The dawn of a new age is upon us.

It is worth observing, in this connection, that Lupset nowhere reflects the enthusiasms of his own circle so clearly as in this commentary on Canius's death. This "noble philosopher" merited immortality, according to Lupset, not primarily because he accepted death gladly, with Stoic resignation and fortitude, but—in the last analysis—because he evinced until the last possible moment the most laudable intellectual curiosity! The exaltation of questing intelligence as man's noblest attribute in the face of death was of course a hoary tradition of classical death-literature dating back at least to the *Phaedo.* Nonetheless, the fervent tone of the dedicated scholar-adventurer of the early Renaissance seems as unmistakable as the Platonic echoes of Canius's rebuke to his companions for their grief.

The literary quality of this exemplum is almost worthy of Lupset's classical models. Again one must applaud his careful construction. In a casual, informal sentence quite in the mood of the preceding passage he introduces the story of just such a master of living and dying as he has professed not to be himself. Then, after a succinct topic-sentence stating that Canius's way of accepting death revealed his "great spirite," he plunges into his tale. It moves

32. Cf., e.g., Seneca, *Ep.* 26.
33. Unfortunately, according to Seneca, who argues fervently for what may be called "enlightened selfishness." See *De brevitate vitae,* in *Moral Essays,* ed. and trans. John W. Basore, Loeb Classical Library, 3 vols, vol. 2, esp. viii, 3–5. All subsequent references to the moral essays are to this edition.

along with admirable rapidity. Irrelevant information is rigorously
excluded—for example, the precise reason for his quarrel with
Caligula, or just exactly how he spent his ten days of grace. Lupset
focuses on the three crucial scenes: Canius's response to the news
of his doom; his reception of the hangman; and his last moments
of life. Moreover, each is made into a small dramatic sketch, developed with a colloquial liveliness which verges on the ludicrous
in its sober Stoic context. Canius's response to Caligula's death
sentence is to turn "with lowe courtesy" and say, "My most gentill
prince I hartely thanke you"; he adjures his chess companion to
"make no false crakes" that he has won the game; and at the place
of execution he stands in "a musynge dumpte" until aroused by
his friends.[34] The commentary following each of these vivid
scenes is too brief to impede the progress of the story. Rather, the
impression left with the reader is one of well-paced movement
characterized by a skillful alternation of narrative, dialogue, and
commentary.[35] Obviously such concreteness and variety impart a

34. Prof. Bush's observations on North's translation of Plutarch seem
to me strikingly applicable to Lupset's achievement in this respect: its
"power . . . is not merely a matter of word and rhythm; it arises from a
feeling that he shared with other men of the age, a reverence for the
special greatness of ancient heroes combined with an instinctive sense of
contemporaneous intimacy. Hence he ranges freely from the colloquial and
slangy to the poetic, and on all levels he is dramatic" (*Prefaces,* p. 14).
Interestingly enough, North also studied at St. Paul's under William Lily
(Lupton, p. 171).
35. Cf. Gee, p. 184. In view of Gee's thorough analysis of Lupset's
prose style, it seems unnecessary to elaborate further here upon its admirable qualities. See ibid., pp. 183–97, and the cross-references there
noted. Gee argues convincingly that

> no one before [Lupset] wrote English expository prose which is at
> the same time both as dignified and graceful without being so
> rhetorical and labored that it lacks ease, and as clear and idiomatic
> without carrying the natural simplicity of colloquial speech to an ex-
> treme. . . . More was the first to write modern English prose before
> 1530. The best English prose written before that date was by Lupset.
> [pp. 183, 197]

In sum, Lupset is an outstanding representative of the "School of More,"

vitality to Lupset's work which is in striking contrast to the monotony of the *Crafte of Dyinge.*

The tale of Canius is, then, a well-constructed and truly entertaining sample of the Stoic biographical exemplum, recounted with the enthusiasm of a thoroughgoing humanist. At the same time, Lupset's treatment of it reveals something of the unrecognized inner tensions of the Christian humanists in their approach to death. The metaphysical assumptions which make such behavior meaningful are obviously those of the highest agnostic humanism; yet Lupset so obviously reveres Canius that the reader is drawn quite naturally—if not in strictest logic—to assume that he is similarly sympathetic to his hero's presuppositions about life and death and destiny. The rationalization of the Christian humanists, made in all good faith, was that such integrity of character, such nobility of behavior, represented the highest possibilities open to man *before* the Incarnation. Nonetheless, the emotional appeal of these agnostics is, for all their presumptive insufficiency of understanding and faith, unmistakably greater than that of the all too familiar Christian martyrs, with their cheerful certitude.[36] The two traditions have been reconciled intellectually, but not as yet fused emotionally—nor, as a consequence, artistically.

THEORETICAL PREMISES

Since Canius's "mynde" was worthy of everlasting life, his story leads forward directly and easily into an interpretation of the grace of reason. Lupset's discussion of this channel of grace constitutes, together with that which follows—his understanding of the meanings of *worldliness* and *spirituality*—the most important

---

even though "too old"—in the phrase of R. W. Chambers—"to be a typical member." He, too, blended the best in the classical tradition with the best in the native devotional tradition to achieve a lucid and flexible prose style which was to become "part of the inheritance of every educated Englishman" (R. W. Chambers, "The Continuity of English Prose from Alfred to More and his School," in Nicholas Harpsfield, *The Life and Death of Sir Thomas More,* ed. E. V. Hitchcock, Early English Text Society, O.S. 186, pp. cxlvii, lvi, and passim.

36. Cf. below, pp. 94–99.

section of the treatise from the historical viewpoint (pp. 268–70).[37] Not only is it a crucial premise of the argument which is to come, but it is, in effect, the apologia for all future efforts to incorporate classical culture into the Christian world view. The Fathers had used similar arguments in their struggles to preserve the records and values of classical civilization; but the lingering hostility displayed by a man of Colet's stature to any classical literature that lacked the "salutary flavour of Christ" suggests how far the Christian Renaissance had to go to recapture that broad vision of the early Church.[38]

Lupset introduces his central thesis with the skill we have come to expect. Such stories as that of Canius, he remarks, often make him ponder "what a strength of knowlege is in mannes brayne, to serche and to fynde by hym selfe the truthe, if he enforce his wittes to lerne." For Canius and many others like him, not having the advantage of Christ's teaching, were not supported by the rules of faith, which teach us the way to the "perfyghte knowelege of all prevy misteries"; nor strengthened by His preaching to "sette lyttel by this life"; nor encouraged to love "vertue above nature" by Scripture's promise of "an other place, wher vertu receiveth her crowne." Lupset marvels that such "naturall men" could so "rise

37. Gee's outline (pp. 141–42) of the introductory portion of the *Waye of Dyenge Well* places the forthcoming "essay on reason" together with the tale of Canius, under the general heading *"Man has ever been blessed with the means of attaining a knowledge of God's will."* This unit and the "essay on spirituality" are seen as two major subdivisions of *"Prefatory remarks leading more definitely to the main theme."* Since the two theoretical premises seem to me both logically and structurally inseparable, I prefer to consider the exemplum a separate-and-equal unit linking personal and theoretical prefatory remarks. This disagreement, though inconsequential, perhaps indicates more clearly than pages of analysis how well integrated Lupset's introduction is.

38. See Gee, pp. 29–31; see also above, note 17. For a more comprehensive, and more philosophically oriented, historical survey than Miles provides of the changing attitudes of the western Church toward the classics, from apostolic times to the Renaissance, see Paul O. Kristeller, "Paganism and Christianity," in his *Renaissance Thought: The Classic, Scholastic, and Humanist Strains,* pp. 75–79.

above theyr nature" as to scorn death, and, without any certainty of
another life to come, set the power of the spirit against the power
of tyrants. For death is "the thynge that in this worlde by nature is
made mooste doubtfull, moste terrible, most heynous, and most
worthy to be fered, to be eschewed, and by al meanes, ways, gynnes,
or crafte to be escaped."

This transition section accomplishes several purposes very
adroitly. The detailed summary of the advantages of Christ's teaching—advantages which Canius did not enjoy—applies a checkrein
to the reader's (and the author's?) classical enthusiasms; reimposes
the Christian perspective on the discussion; and points forward to
the coming Christian modifications of the Stoic version of dying
gladly. Also, as phrased by Lupset, it contributes to the point he is
preparing to make. By passing quickly over the "prevy misteries"
of the faith, by emphasizing as the core of Christian ethics those
two specific principles held in common by the medieval and Stoic
traditions, and by dismissing heaven as "an other place" in which
these virtues will surely be rewarded, he underlines both the universality of ethical principles and also the acceptability to God of all
who abide by them. Similarly, his elaboration of Aristotle's dictum
that death is the "most terrible of all terrible things" is well-placed.
It, too, points forward to the body of the work as an assurance that
he has not forgotten his central purpose; more important, it serves
to underline his thesis by reminding us of the dread nature of the
challenge which Canius and his fellow philosophers had to meet
without the aid of Christ's teaching. Having in this dual fashion
aroused our sympathetic admiration for the unenlightened but
noble pagans, he is now in a position to expound convincingly a
doctrine still revolutionary in 1530. This he spills out, with an
emphatic repetitiousness which is quite startling.

Reason, the universal grace, is bestowed on all men alike, he
asserts. Holy Scripture teaches him that ever since Creation God
has given man

> sufficiente grace to knowe the ryghte, to se the hye majestie of
> vertue, to fynd out the trewe dignite of the soule, to perceyve
> the vanyte of this presente lyfe, and fynally, to understonde

wherin stondethe the pleasure of god, and wherin standeth
his displeasure. Ever by goddes mere goodnes man knewe what
was well to be done, and what was contrarye yvelle to be
done. It is a lawe written in the harte of man with the fynger of
god in our creation, to be enduced by reason to praise alway
vertue, and to thynke synne worthye of disprayse. [p. 269]

Through grace man's mind sees farther than his physical sight,
feels more sensitively than his five senses, and considers the loss
"of bloudde or of breth . . . a smalle trifell" whenever it is not
blinded by the darkness of the body, which "stomblethe atte everye
strawe in this worlde."

In short, "the truthe" discoverable by reason is equated with the
will of God, which is, in its turn, to be understood as essentially
*ethical.* Any man who will, therefore, may come to know the good,
to praise and revere it—and also to understand, in the light of this
reverent knowledge, the dignity of his own soul and the relative
vanity of worldly values. The thoroughgoing ethical orientation of
this analysis of reason—not to mention the definition of the truth
which reason seeks—is in the best tradition of English humanism.[39]
Once again, however, we find in this early treatise a failure to
recognize at least some of the significant theological implications
of the new enthusiasms, and hence a recurrent disturbing discrepancy between old and new which will be utterly lacking in
Taylor's *Holy Dying.*

39. Eugene F. Rice, working with continental treatises, associates a
growing tendency to consider wisdom a moral, rather than intellectual,
virtue with the increasing secularization of the period (see *The Renaissance Idea of Wisdom,* esp. chaps. 3 and 5); and Kristeller observes that
*"most* of the philosophical treatises and dialogues of the humanists are
really nothing but moral tracts" ("Humanism and Scholasticism," in his
*Renaissance Thought,* p. 106; italics mine). Yet no one seems disposed to
doubt that the Christian humanists of Colet's circle were both entirely
orthodox and distinctively pragmatic in their outlook. Robert P. Adams
goes even further: the English humanists' attempt to apply the "New
Learning . . . boldly to the construction of a vastly improved, peaceful society," he says, resulted in "profound and imaginatively penetrating social
criticism" that bespeaks true "intellectual and moral daring" *(The Better
Part of Valor,* p. 20).

Despite his exaltation of the grace of reason, Lupset himself clearly views natural man as in some sense "fallen" man, although he does not use the term: man instinctively worldly, rarely inclined to "enforce his wittes to lerne" the truth, and all too often prevented by the "darkenesse of the bodye" from following the truth which he does perceive. Yet hidden in the humanist's determined efforts to reassert the dignity of the soul, and his admiration for those who triumphed by reason and will over their natural selves, is the tendency (still no more than embryonic) to rest content with his own bootstraps as moral uplifters. Here, for example, we find the affirmation that man's mind *"hath* a grace" (italics mine) to "see" farther than his eyes, and so on. Does Lupset really mean us to understand that man *possesses* this particular grace—i.e. as a discrete, completed gift, so to speak—or merely that he is the recipient of this continually renewed manifestation of God's all-encompassing gracious concern for him? In all probability the latter. Nonetheless, the phrase is suggestive. Carried to its logical extreme, the line of thought at which it hints has for its terminus the conviction that man can save himself: reason ceases to be one channel for God's grace, and becomes itself redeeming grace—and a natural possession of man.[40]

In any case, the God presented in this passage differs far more radically from the late-medieval God than Lupset's Rational-Ethical Man does from Everyman. His essential attribute is goodness—a goodness exhibited toward man ever since his creation of the world. If this God is no longer the terrifying Judge of absolute

---

40. The relative weakness of Lupset's assertions of man's fallenness is more clearly evident when they are juxtaposed to those of an earlier generation, such as the following excerpt from Colet's commentary on the Epistle to the Romans (translated by Hunt): man's

> will is distorted, his understanding darkened, his memory weakened, his carnal appetites inflamed, and the causes of disease and death, both of the body and the soul, are endless. There is nothing here but iniquity, ignorance, powerlessness, downfall, destruction; nothing but the cold of wickedness, the absurdity of folly, the winter of death; nothing but dissolution, going astray, deformity, disorderly living, baseness, shame. [p. 11]

righteousness before whom the medieval sinner trembled, neither is he the God of love, of mercy, or of compassion. Rather, he is, quite simply and impersonally, the creator and upholder of moral law, and, as such, a remote Being whose interrelationship with the individual soul must be mediated *through* the moral law. The divine-human encounter which lies at the heart of Christian devotion has, by implication, disappeared. And so, too, as an inescapable corollary, has the God-focused sense of sin which distinguishes Christian contrition from the mere acknowledgment of man's ethical shortcomings.

The meager Christology of the *Waye of Dyenge Well* follows logically from the foregoing considerations. In spite of the uncompromising, even impatient, orthodoxy of Lupset's professed faith,[41] the creedal propositions about the nature and work of Christ are of minimal significance in his argument. The essential function of the Incarnation is to set the seal of supernatural certainty on the revelations of reason. The "prevy misteries" revealed to those who accept the "rules of faythe" embedded in "Christes philosophye" interest him very little; the theology of reconciliation, scarcely at all.[42] Nowhere, for example, does he consider explicitly the problem of how to cope with the "darkenesse of the bodye" as one endeavors erratically to live well in order that he may die gladly. Christ's role as ultimate authority—as Teacher, Master, and Son of God—is emphasized repeatedly; his role as Redeemer is barely mentioned.[43]

41. See above, note 22.

42. This relative indifference is particularly striking to the reader who searches for some reflection of the English humanists' devoted labors on St. Paul's Epistles. Cf., per contra, Colet's strongly Christocentric philosophy, his lifelong concern with Pauline soteriology, and his interpretation of the mystics' "purgative way" as ending in the sacrament of Penance and reconciliation. See Hunt, chap. 5; Miles, p. 29; and Helen C. White, *The Tudor Books of Private Devotion,* chap. 13, esp. pp. 226–27 and chap. 14, pp. 236, 240, 245–47.

43. An interesting passage in one of Erasmus's letters informs us that "over the High Master's chair [at St. Paul's School] is a beautifully wrought figure of the Child Jesus, seated, in the attitude of one teaching; and all the flock, as they go into and leave the school, salute it with a

Finally, we may note that Lupset's discussion of the grace of reason does, however indirectly, signalize the approaching revitalization of the doctrine of the Holy Spirit in the thought of western Christianity. Explicitly, his treatise takes no more account than does the *Crafte* of this concept. Nonetheless, his optimistic picture of man does serve to remind us of notions long dormant in Christian thought: that man was created "in the image of God"; that the creative capacities, rational powers, and moral nature connoted by this phrase have been distorted—not destroyed—by his Fall, and are recoverable in Christ; and that the work of the Holy Spirit is precisely that of leading man to Christian commitment, guiding his growth in faith within the community of the Church, and thereby restoring in him the *imaginem dei*—understood *primarily in terms of his interrelationships with his fellowmen.*[44] The slighting of these more positive views of man and of his social and ethical responsibilities left a vacuum in man's total world view; and it is this vacuum which is being refilled from the wellspring of classical culture. The *imago dei* must be rediscovered in man's nature before his persistent repudiation of it can be felt poignantly once more.

The second of Lupset's premises is equally indispensable for the effective fusion of the two traditions. In order to justify the ancients' claim to moral authority even in the Christian era of history, and even in so specifically religious a field as that of "dying well," he must assert the validity of their own type of spirituality. This he does by defining the distinction between worldliness and spirituality in terms of one's response, not to the grace of revela-

---

hymn. Above it is the face of God the Father, saying, 'Hear ye him' [*Ipsum audite*]; these words were added at my suggestion." (*Opus Epistolarum Des. Erasmi Roterodami,* ed. P. S. and H. E. Allen, vol. 4, pp. 517–18, trans. Hunt, p. 14).

44. The New Testament in general lays special emphasis on the work of the Holy Spirit in inspiring and directing the Christian *koinonia;* and almost all of the fruits of the Spirit, as listed by St. Paul (Gal. 5:22–23), imply interpersonal relationships: "love, joy, peace, longsuffering, gentleness, goodness, faith, meekness, temperance . . . "

tion, but to the grace of reason, which he has already established as universal. The intimate connection between the two premises is suggested by the lack of a paragraph-break between the two discussions, or even a clear line of demarcation between sentences. The final sentence of the "essay on reason," with its somewhat anticlimactic reminder that the body "stomblethe atte every strawe in this worlde," serves also to introduce the new topic.

The worldly man, as Lupset sees him, is one who pursues with his senses and his wits the values of this life alone, who "clymeth not in no consideration above the myste of this valeye." Men of "this weake sorte" have always constituted the majority of mankind. The spiritual man, uncommon but present in every age, is one who strives to discover wherein the essential dignity and value of anything lie, and to determine how much we should esteem it—that is, one "in whome the mynde and spirite chefelye ruleth." The distinction between the two has nothing to do with either learning or orders. A tailor, shoemaker, carpenter, or boatman may be spiritual, a master of arts, doctor of divinity, dean, or bishop worldly, in spite of both "cunninge and dignities." It is clear, then, that the "temporalle mynde" sees nothing sweeter nor more pleasant than life, and thinks it "a bytter thynge" to die, while the spiritual mind thinks it "a bytter time to indure the space of this life," and finds "swetenes" and joy in death, whereby the soul will be rid of the "heavye burden" of the body. "For lyke as the prince of this worlde never agreethe with god, nor yet the bodye with the soule, nor the earthe with hevyn: so he that studieth for this tyme, hath clene contrary opinions to hym that foloweth the spiryte."

For all the persuasiveness, and even charm, of this argument, a close examination of its thought and expression reveals once again the ambivalence lurking in Lupset's attitude toward the two heritages he is working to reconcile. As the "new man," he approaches the theme of otherworldliness in a spirit of enlightened moderation. His definition of "worldly" avoids ascetic implications, and would serve well enough even today. His emphatic assertion of the universality of *mind*, as he uses the term, precludes any

imputations of intellectual or religious snobbery; it also suggests
delicately the anticlericalism of the ethical reformers of his time.[45]
His use of the word *sweet* in regard to death is a characteristically
thoughtful choice, since it is common to both traditions.[46] Further,
we may note that his familiar confusion of *mind* and *spirit*—ordi-
narily suggestive of unthinking acquiescence in classical usage—
is justified here by his central purpose of broadening the meaning
of *spirituality* to include more than exclusively devotional connotations.

His medieval heritage was not, however, to be dismissed or
transcended quite so easily. The simplistic dualism which informs
his very mode of thinking is perhaps the evidence of this fact which
strikes us most forcibly. Mind vs. body, Satan vs. God, earth vs.
heaven, sweet vs. bitter—such pairings of extremes are still instinctive, even to a highly educated mind. Moreover, the content
of his thought is similarly medieval in its extremism, which goes
far beyond that of either the Stoics or even the Platonists in its
hostility to the values of this life. The insights of the classics into
the complexities of reality have not yet been assimilated. The attempt to combine a medieval otherworldliness with undigested
Stoicism is going to involve Lupset in awkward inconsistencies
before he is through: since life is obviously not, for him, bitter
"durance vile," and since death will be treated as something to be
"endured" rather than welcomed, he will, in effect, end up by
aligning himself with the damnable worldly! His ambivalence in
this regard is suggested by the very vehemence of his conservatism.
One feels that he doth protest too much.

Lupset now concludes his introductory section with dispatch,
tying together smoothly its various parts. Addressing himself di-

45. A similar humanist jibe at clerical worldliness is incorporated into
the exhortation to John which climaxes Lupset's argument (p. 283; quoted
below). Neither, of course, implies a thoroughgoing antisacerdotalism:
Lupset twice refers to those in orders as essentially different from laymen.
Cf. Hunt, chap. 2, esp. pp. 22, 44–50; Miles, p. 135; and Adams, pp.
281–85.

46. Seneca, however, scorns the adjective *(dulcis)* as an "effeminate
word" for an "act so honorable and austere" as dying *(Ep. 67).*

rectly again to "good John," he promises that "these contrarye
opinyons" will seem less remarkable after they have "considered
the thyng it selfe, what shoulde be death"—a Stoic cliché which
points forward into the central portion of the work. Soon Walker
will see whether Canius should be more praiseworthy for his
"lyttell regardyng" of death, or the English traitor Francis Phillip
—whose wretched cowardice is herewith described briefly as a
reminder-by-contrast of the splendid behavior of the Roman.
Happily, it provides us as well with another short dramatic interlude before the solid chunk of analysis which lies ahead.

   Quite properly, Lupset begins the central portion of his work
with a short paragraph reviewing the axioms—as he conceives
them—of his subject, and also their most immediate corollaries
(pp. 271–72). To die well is, he asserts with finality, "in effecte to
dye gladlye"—that is, "in a sure hope to lyve ageyne." One who
entertains such a hope is not only "wery of this worlde," but has
also "lived well here." For there can be no gladness in death without a "full truste of opteynynge the rewarde of vertue, partelye
by the truste and fayth of a good mynde, partely by the mercye of
god, that fulfilleth ever our insufficiency, yf we bring ought with
us worthi of his favour." That is, we must come before God with
souls clothed in "a perfecte faith, and an ernest wyl of doing wel";
but "a full truste" requires "the strength of charite," of "good
workes" which stir and quicken our faith that Christ's merits will
supply our deficiencies. Hence the heart fortified by faith, hope, and
charity is cheerful, ready to die gladly

> eyther to be ridde from the bondes of this prison, or to opteyne
> the lybertye of heven: bothe wayes commeth from a good
> lyfe passed: so that surely no man can dye well, that lyveth
> not well, for ever deth is a sorrowfull thynge to the yvell
> lyver, by cause he hathe nothynge to laye before the mercy
> of god whereuppon he maye take hope and truste to be made
> worthy of the sure lyfe, in the whiche deathe medleth
> not. [p. 272]

Therefore, we need only analyze the hindrances and aids to our dying gladly, and we shall have found the "waye to dye well. For in my mynde these .ii. be allwayes one, to dye well, and to dye gladly."

The equating of *well* and *gladly* is of course the basic cliché of both the Christian and the Stoic traditions.[47] Yet the way in which Lupset seeks to justify this truism provides us with an interesting sample of his technique for subsuming Stoic insights under the Christian whenever he deems it necessary. Running through Stoic death-literature are three major threads of advice on how to die gladly. Philosophical insight, acquired through the proper use of reason, will teach one the true significance and value of both life and death. The cultivation of the virtues proper to man—i.e. the learning how to live well—will deepen a man's insight, free him from slavery to necessity, and prepare him to die well. And dying *well* is defined more or less explicitly as accepting necessity in a spirit of indifferent resignation. To die *gladly* means, therefore, to meet the exigencies of one's mortal nature with freely chosen willingness—or even to seek death *before* it is strictly necessary, if by suicide one may assert more forcefully the dignity and values which make life meaningful. For Lupset, this Stoic pattern of thought is purified, as well as crystallized, in the Christian Revelation. Philosophical insight becomes faith; the pursuit of rationally established virtues becomes charity, which perfects faith and makes hope possible; and resignation to the inevitable becomes hope of heaven. To die gladly becomes, therefore, more than acquiescence, in *apatheia* and moral integrity: it connotes genuine cheerfulness because of one's hope of heaven based on faith made perfect in charity. The Christian virtues, far from contradicting the Stoic insights, confirm and transcend them.

In view of all the subtle shifts in Lupset's thought in the direction of (ethical) this-worldliness—not to mention the outpouring of Stoic sentiments which is soon to come—the firm otherworldly orientation of these axiomatic definitions is particularly interesting.

---

47. Cf. esp. Seneca, *Ep.* 30 and 61; and Cicero, *Cato maior de senectute,* ed. and trans. William A. Falconer, Loeb Classical Library, secs. 21–23.

His understanding of *gladly* does focus rather more on Moriens than on God, unlike that of the *Crafte's* author *("Thy* will be done"). Of greater significance, however, is its thoroughly medieval assumption that an eternal afterlife of either bliss or misery awaits each one of us. Thus, the evil-liver faces a "sorowfull" death, not because—as Seneca would say—he has become a wretched slave to necessity,[48] but simply because his destiny is apt to be extremely unpleasant. Actually, in the light of Lupset's moral idealism, his warning seems rather casual, voiced as it is in a clause which is rhetorically anticlimactic. One feels that is is automatic, that damnation means little to him, either conceptually or affectively.[49] On the other hand, his concern for ethical living leads him very close indeed to the extreme position regarding man's salvability which the Puritans are to decry as the heresy of salvation-through-works. That Lupset's traditional orientation is chiefly instinctive is implied by his admonition that a good man must not only hope for heaven, but also be "wery of this worlde" and eager to escape "the bondes of this prison." His reliance on the hoariest of clichés is suggestive.

Having now established all the requisite premises, the treatise moves on—via a self-consciously precise transitional paragraph— to the topic which, following both the *Ars moriendi* and the ancients, the Christian humanist considers most important: the hindrances to "the gladde desyre of dyinge" (pp. 272–87). These, as he sees them, are the fear of death, and the love of this life. "If these two blockes be taken out of our stomakes, we shall fynde an easye and a playne waye to the ende of our pourpose." For he who neither fears to die nor loves to live is prepared to die gladly.

Above all, he begins (pp. 272–74), we must learn not to fear death if we would learn to die well:

And yet howe I shulde prove, that death is not to be feared, I canne not well telle, seinge the hole power of nature sheweth,

48. See e.g., *Ep.* 26, 54, 70, and 77.
49. Occasionally he seems to refer, though vaguely, to meditation (or contemplation) as a desirable act of Christian devotion (pp. 268–69, 284, 287). In each case, the topic of meditation is to be heaven.

that of all thynges death is moost fearefull: and to reason
ageynste nature, it were paraventure not soo harde as vaine.
For what canne reason prevayle, if nature resiste? It is a
thynge to farre above mans power, to stryve or to wrastelle
with nature, her strengthe passeth the myghte of our wyll,
what helpe somever we take of reason or of auctoritie: nother
counsayle nor commandement hath place, where nature dothe
her uttermoste. [p. 272]

Although it may well be intensified by love of this life, fear of
purgatory and hell, and fear of the "sore painefull panges" of
dying, this natural fear precedes and goes deeper than these emotions. This is proven by the fact that little children are terrified
by threats made in sport. The existence of a few who, through
learning or courage, seem unmoved by death does not belie the
truth that nature implants fear in most. Other proofs are the
willingness of men to endure any wretchedness for the sake of
prolonging life a bit; the exhibition by so many of the most shame-
ful fear as death approaches; and the preservation by mankind of
stories of apparently fearless deaths as if they were miraculous.
Hence, although excessive fear is reprehensible, there is "a meane
measure of fere in dethe, that may be rekened honest and juste,
bycause nature maketh it necessary." Yet reason tells us that we
should not fear the unknown, but only evil. Since we do not know
death, we do not know whether it is in itself good or bad. Let us,
therefore, pause now to consider the nature of death and whether
in itself it be good or evil.

   The most striking aspect of this argument's classicism is neither
its use of clichés dating back to the Socratic dialogues, nor even its
adoption of the classical tendency to personify nature. It is, rather,
the emergence here, in unmistakable form, of a new mode of
thinking which itself drew on ancient models for inspiration and
example. Lupset is clearly striving to return to first principles and
then think through their implications with a logical thoroughness
which is to be sound rather than artful. He is renouncing, not only
the authoritarianism of the scholastics, but above all the finical and
fruitless hairsplitting which characterized late-medieval "disputa-

tions." He is trying to stretch his mental muscles in a new way; and his attempt is remarkably successful. Actual existence is brought to bear on abstract theory both in his vivid picture of the child's terror at the prospect of being thrown out of "some hye windowe," and in his perceptive interpretation of the sheer fact that men preserve and treasure stories of courageous deaths. These are welcome signs that a new strength, a new humane sensibleness, is being introduced into men's thinking.[50]

It is interesting to observe, moreover, that Lupset uses his mental powers to go far beyond his classical masters in arguing that nature virtually demands that men fear death. Both Cicero and Seneca minimize the intensity of man's fear, and overestimate the ease with which the philosopher can overcome it. Lupset goes out of his way to correct their perspective—with a wry humor as well as vehemence.

The "consideration" of the nature of death which Lupset now incorporates into the *Waye of Dying Well* (pp. 274–78) is a familiar element of classical death-literature;[51] but here, too, the humanist carefully subsumes ancient philosophy under Christian truth. He must pause to summarize for his reader the "advancement of learning" on the subject of death itself before he can move on to the universal clichés clustered around the teaching that death is per se neither good nor evil, but indifferent. The argument proceeds lucidly, yet contains at the same time suggestions of Lupset's intellectual and emotional ambivalence in relation to his topic. On

50. Cf. Huizinga, *Waning of the Middle Ages*, pp. 271, 307–08. Kristeller lists among the key "general features" of the Renaissance "an atmosphere of intellectual fermentation that begins with a restatement of ancient ideas . . . and ends with a bold proposal of consciously new and original alternatives." See "Changing Views of the Intellectual History of the Renaissance since Jacob Burckhardt," in *The Renaissance: A Reconsideration of the Theories and Interpretations of the Age,* ed. Tinsley Helton, p. 45.

51. Like others considered in this chapter, it is traceable at least as far back as Plato's *Apology* and *Phaedo;* but see, e.g. Seneca, *Ep.* 30 and 82, and *De consolatione ad Marciam,* xix, 5. Cf. also Cicero, *Epistulae ad familiares,* ed. and trans. W. Glynn Williams, Loeb Classical Library, 3 vols., *Ep.* 5, sec. 16; and *Ep.* 6, secs. 4 and 21.

the one hand, he develops with a sure touch his Christian modification of the Stoic truism that all who are born must die: death, he
says, is the necessary departure of soul from body after the latter
has forsaken life. He employs without hesitation authoritarian
arguments, theological as well as biblical. "It is the creatours wyl,"
he avers, "that nothynge in this worlde shall have a soule, but man
alone"; and not only reason but, even better, "our mayster the son
of god" teaches us that "the ymage of god in us is perpetuall." And
at just that point where Seneca would be likely to introduce the
thought that evil enslaves man in a living death, Lupset refers
instead to the concept of sin, "the lyvynge dethe of the soule" which
springs from our "frowarde wyll" and corrupts the *imaginem dei*
within us.[52]

On the other hand, his rather detailed summary of the agnostic
doubts of "some olde clerkes," from which "the unfallible doctrine
of Christe hath now delyvered us al," hints at a degree of sympathy
for their position. The passage as a whole implies that the fear of
total extinction is one which must be dealt with at some length,
not dismissed as no longer relevant in the light of the Christian
dispensation.

Lupset now plunges spiritedly into the traditional consideration
of whether death be good or evil. He extends and adapts the
classical arguments for death's being "indifferent" in such a way
that they become genuinely Christian, yet still permit the pagan to
enter the other world on a virtually equal footing with the enlightened man of faith. Deductive reasoning establishes the principle that "death considered alone by hit selfe, is nother good nor
yvell," but only "the circumstances, the maner, the fashyon, the
cause of deathe, or that goeth before death, or that foloweth dethe."
Hence the Christian need not fear death unless he has done nothing
to justify him in hoping for God's favor or mercy, or, worse, has
done so much evil that he can have "no trust of escaping damnable
punyshement." Nor does the non-Christian need to fear death
unless, by "false imagination," he has "none hygher thought of

52. Note, also, the argument from analogy that death precedes the departure of the soul *as life precedes its entrance at birth.*

lyfe" than the beasts, for whom death is the final "conclusion of their being." And surely "unworthy he is to have in hym the power of understandynge, of thynkyng, of provydynge, of lernynge, of teachyng, of divisyng, of remembringe, of lovyng, of hatyng, of resonyng, of counsaylynge, of infinite moo gyftes, who somever jugeth hym self to have no more than a swyne or an ape hath." As the body learns through the senses, so the soul "walkith to his understandynge" through these mental powers, and is made worthy either of everlasting life or of everlasting death, "for the damned soule lyveth in deth without ende." In conclusion, the fear of death is the "working of nature"; yet the "strength of mannes minde fully fastened in fayth" may certainly overcome it "victoriousely," since the pagan's "mighty and valiant minde" was able without the support of revelation to "subdewe . . . the power of all affectes."

The uneasy reconciliation between the neo-Stoic and the Christian traditionalist in Lupset becomes increasingly apparent in this passage. The new moderate exalts the "powers of mynd" so enthusiastically that his list of them not only spills over into redundancy, but even includes the emotions of love and hatred. And he uses those mental powers to rationalize a broad-minded and warmhearted optimism about the destiny of his own and almost everyone else's soul. At the same time, the orthodox Christian, still close to his medieval heritage, considers the nature and will of God, or even martyrs' heavenly crowns, valid minor premises in his deductive reasoning. He turns instinctively to the story of the Passion for traditional examples of good and bad deaths, and uses them in a stock manner: the contrasting deaths of the thieves, though physically identical, and the evil death of Judas because of his "cursed desperation, his dampnable mystruste of goddes mercye, his dispitefull refusynge grace."[53] Above all, he insists—albeit as something of an afterthought—on the real possibility of everlasting damnation, or "deth without ende"; and he considers "the maner of hym that dyeth" a valid clue to the soul's chances of escaping it.

<hr/>

53. Both illustrations are found in the block book *Ars moriendi* specifically, as well as being commonplaces of Christian teaching and preaching.

Thus, in the very course of persuading men to renounce their narrow, obsessive concern with deathbed behavior per se, the early humanist enunciates with precision just that traditional theory which alone justifies such a concern.

Other, minor inconsistencies and contradictions come to light when we refer to preceding sections of his treatise. He begins this argument by saying that certain knowledge of the nature of death is impossible to living men—but he has just finished transmitting precisely that "certayne determination," which he then asserts to be final truth according to the "unfallible doctrine of Christe." Again, he affirms as self-evident the proposition that natural reason condemns suicide as "abhominable"—but he has cited Cato's noble suicide with an admiration worthy of Seneca. Finally, he recognizes and tries explicitly to resolve the conflict between these rather glib solutions to the problem of fear and his own eloquent demonstration earlier of the instinctive and ineradicable nature of that fear—but his resolution is unsuccessful on the emotional level. The relatively clear-eyed focus of the first parts of the treatise seems to be blurring.

This latent uncertainty manifests itself with explosive clarity in the section which follows (pp. 278–81). Lupset's powers of organization, both philosophical and literary, collapse completely. Seneca has carried the day. Ten of the Stoic's favorite arguments are now offered for our consideration. Of these, the first nine are neither subsumed under the Christian faith nor even organized coherently in themselves. Indeed, Lupset contents himself for the most part with either direct translation or close paraphrase of the Latin original. Since these arguments will reappear constantly from now on as indispensable ingredients in the consideration of "dying well," it will be convenient to summarize them now, when they are still found virtually in their original form.

    1. A learned pagan writes that we should care neither for life nor death in itself, but only to live well and die well.[54] (And Christ

---

54. For Seneca's statement of this Socratic precept, see *Ep.* 70. Cf. also *Ep.* 49, and Cicero, *De Senectute,* sec. 19. For precept (2), cf. *Ep.* 30, 49, and 77. For (3), cf. *Ep.* 4 and 36 (alluding to Epicurus). For the first sen-

forbade Christians vehemently to care for death; so they should be even more ashamed to be afraid.)

2. We should set little store by death, because it is not rare and therefore frightening, but a common, familiar, daily occurrence in our sight.

3. It is ridiculous to fear death, which is never present, but always either still in the future or in the past, so that fear can never encounter the thing feared.

4. Man persists in musing on the length of his life, over which he has no control, rather than on its quality, which he can indeed determine. Similarly, he struggles (in vain) to analyze or intuit the nature of death, instead of seeking (with success) the way of dying well. ("This madness John I truste, you wyll put of. . . .")

5. It is good to accept death gladly as an escape from evil living.

6. Not to fear death frees one from that wretched thralldom to Fortune which we see in those who value life too much.

7. It is as foolish to fear death as to fear old age, for both are inevitable, whereas only the uncertain merits fear.

8. If it is the pain of dying which is feared, one should remember that after death there shall be no pain, and that if it be intense, it will be short, since no extreme pain can last long.

9. It is as foolish to grieve that one cannot live for a thousand years to come as it would be to bewail not having been born a thousand years ago. You were not; you shall not be. "So that one mynde shulde be in us, as well to remember we shall not be, as to remember we ones were not. It is no newe thyng to dye, our fathers, our grantfathers, our great foresiers be gone the way that both we shal go, and al that folow us must come the same."

As assembled by Lupset, this potpourri of Senecan precepts is even more indiscriminate than the above paraphrase reveals. The degree to which he has lost control of his material may be suggested by his handling of the theme of *memento mori* in this con-

---

tence of precept (4), cf. *Ep.* 22 and 70. For (5), cf. *Ep.* 70. For (6), cf. *Ep.* 6, 36, 70, 77, and *De brevitate vitae,* V, 3. For (7), cf. *Ep.* 24, 30, and esp. 77. For (8), cf. *Ep.* 30 (quoting the elderly Bassus as quoting Epicurus). For (9), cf. *Ep.* 77 (Lupset substitutes "grantfathers" for "mothers").

text. At the end of the eighth argument—that the pain of death, if intense, must be brief—we find this curiously misplaced observation: "Every way deth is a thing never to be feared of a wyse man, and never to be out of mynd both with good men and wyse men." Then he moves on immediately to the ninth argument, belying the obvious implication of this sentence that "every way" has now been explored. As for the adjuration to remember death continually, its position in the context makes it seem a wildly irrelevant non sequitur. An explanation is suggested, however, by Lupset's assumption, in discussing the intensity of pains to be felt at death, that there will, in fact and without question, be pains, however minimal.[55] In other words, his emotional orientation to the death scene itself is still strongly medieval; and therefore the thought of death-pains reminds him promptly of the duty of meditating constantly on death, including the agony of dying. This duty he mentions automatically, even employing the traditional distinction between *good* and *wise* men, although in terms of his own analysis it is tautological. The devotional exhortation is tacked onto his argument as a mere afterthought.

The tenth and climactic argument witnesses in quite another way than the first nine to Lupset's responsiveness to Stoic thought. Here, disregarding his earlier conventional assertions that the Christian should consider life bitter and death sweet, he presents the key appeal to necessity with an eloquence both startling and suggestive. "More over," he writes (as if he had never before mentioned the fact that death is inescapable!)

> in as moche no labour, wyt, craft, nor diligence prevayleth to escape dethe, no power, no ryches, no auctoritie helpeth, but all indifferentely be called of dethe, all without choyse must folowe the trayne of deathe, no corner can hyde us, no walles

55. Seneca doubts strongly that dying is painful, and refers to it in *Ep.* 26 as a "melting away"; at worst, he agrees with Epicurus that if there *should* be any pain, it must necessarily be short *(Ep.* 30). Lupset, per contra, has Canius refer to death with flat assurance as "this short pange of death"—thereby assuming a position just halfway between the *Crafte* and Seneca at his most confident.

can defende us, no waye nor meane, no intreatie, no prayer, no suite, nothynge under heven can kepe us from deathes hande. Let us than take a lusty courage of this desperation, seinge there is no remedy: lette us manfully go to it. . . . In this necessitie of dethe we nowe be all, it is vayne for us to flye or to ron awaye, our feare can fynd no place of flyght. Lette us imagine the trouthe as in dede it is, that we be al betrayed to dye. . . . Lifte up therfore your hart onely bycause there is no remedy, desyre not to flie when there is no place to runne to, lette necessite gyve you a courage, if al other strength decayith. [pp. 280–81]

Nowhere else in the *Waye of Dyenge Well* can one find a passage in which old and new are so truly reconciled in expression as well as in thought. In general, the treatise reveals its pioneer status quite as much by its compartmentalized diction as by its inconsistent and sometimes contradictory argument. The preponderance of traditional Christian vocabulary in "Christian" passages, and of classical vocabulary in distinctively "classical" passages, is striking. Here, though, we find that skillful amalgamation which indicates that the author has so fully absorbed his material that it has become somehow new, possessing its own integrity rather than merely deriving from one or the other literary tradition. As in the tale of Canius, Stoic expressions, enlivened as usual by colloquialisms, predominate. This time, they are also bound up inextricably with a variety of Christian references. Man, instead of being mortal simply by definition, is "betrayed to die"; death, instead of being merely his terminus, is personified into the invincible lord of the *danse macabre;* and his victims, instead of merely resigning themselves courageously to the inevitable, are to "lift up their hearts" —a liturgical command fraught with positive connotations. In this instance, clearly, Lupset is not shackled within one literary—or philosophical—frame of reference.

Despite its effective peroration, however, this sequence of classical arguments against the fear of death remains unsatisfactory as a whole. Lupset has indeed assimilated thoroughly the concepts of the dignity of manhood and the virtue of courage; and he has adopted to a notable degree the Stoic exaltation of the life of reasoned virtue. (Walker is to flee this "madness," not this "sin.") Still, several of his arguments are simply inapplicable to the problem of death as one considers it within the context of Christian thought. The Stoic concept of the dignity of manhood as such is still only a partial realization of the concept of the dignity of the unique personality created by God and potentially capable of sonship to him. Thus, Seneca's rational appeals to universal experience in order to prove the madness of fearing death may seem naïve, or cold, or both, to the modern reader; but within the context of his own thought they are not unreasonable. For the individual Stoic realizes the fullness of his selfhood precisely by accepting with dignified and courageous *apatheia* the dictates of necessity, including his oneness with mankind in mortality and all that this may imply. This is to place a higher valuation than medieval thought does on the living personality which is thus confronted and challenged by necessity. Nonetheless, its emotional orientation is essentially negative, since the individual is, in the last analysis, still Everyman in the face of his ultimate defeat by death. Stern reminders such as Seneca's were intended to stiffen the Stoic's backbone, to encourage him to play the philosopher, to act the man—in short, to assert human values *in spite of* their apparent irrelevance to, and lack of justification *by,* any external reality.[56]

56. Eloquent modern presentations of this position, ranging from Bertrand Russell's *A Free Man's Worship* to, say, Tom Stoppard's *Rosencrantz and Guildenstern Are Dead,* are of course so numerous as to defy even selective listing in a footnote. Dr. Ignace Lepp's brief observations on the "radical individualism" of Stoic courage, in the face of meaningless death, and on the various forms of revolt advocated by French absurdists since Heidegger, are provocative: the more explicitly these existentialists reject the Stoic serenity of a Seneca, the closer they seem implicitly— to me, that is—to the heart of the Stoic position, the essence of Stoic nobility. See *Death and Its Mysteries,* trans. Bernard Murchland, pp. 90–91, 131–33, 147. Seneca's *Ep.* 102, with its fervent "intimations of immortality," may safely be disregarded in this context as atypical. The characteristic Stoic view anticipated on occasion a mildly pleasant afterlife, but more commonly either nothingness or absorption into the divine Essence. Cf. Seneca, *Ep.* 63, and Cicero, *De Senectute,* secs. 21–23; Seneca, *Ep.* 54, and Cicero, *Ep.* 6, secs. 3–4, 21; Seneca, *Ep.* 36 and *Ad Marciam,* xxvi, 6–7.

These same arguments were to become increasingly beside the point, however, as the Stoic tradition became genuinely fused with the Christian in a new realization of the uniqueness of the individual personality and of its value *as sustained by God.* Lupset, adopting wholesale the new and exciting appreciation of man, does not recognize that such arguments as these will need radical modification if they are to be relevant to Christian thought once that thought has really appropriated classical insights. Hamlet, for one, will give Seneca's more superficial arguments. short shrift. Death is common to all men? "Ay, madam, it is common." It is ridiculous to fear that which is always non-present? "What dreams may come when we have shuffled off this mortal coil must give us pause." And so on. Christian certitude will be undermined by many factors, among them classical agnosticism; yet the Christian tradition will at the same time carry the classical concept of individual significance to its logical extreme, religiously speaking. And the new doubt will be all the more poignant for the new awareness of personal values. Of such implications latent in his enthusiastic classicism, Lupset is quite unaware.[57]

His handling of the remainder of this portion of the treatise (pp. 281–84) does suggest, however, an awareness that Seneca's arguments have led him rather far afield, both as artist and as Christian. A sudden reference to Canius reminds us of his original scheme of organization, and introduces a new series of historical

57. Cf. Bush, *Prefaces,* pp. 73–74. The view of death as "the complete extinction of a vital personality . . . negation or annihilation" Bush characterizes as pagan, whether or not the context of such an utterance is explicitly Christian. As for *Hamlet,* "whatever degree of Christian atmosphere we allow or do not allow to [it], the hero's reflections in the graveyard are almost purely pagan." This approach seems to imply that the pagan and Christian views are wholly disjunct, so that pagan utterances are identifiable as such no matter what the period of the Christian death-literature in which they are embedded—i.e., that there simply can be no resolution of the conflict between the Stoic warning "You were not; you shall not be" and Christian faith in personal resurrection. As this study will make clear, I cannot agree entirely with this position. Yet it is clear, at least, that any reconciliation of the two views is impossible until Renaissance Christians become sensitive to the threatening power of this particular Senecan argument. Hamlet, in short, makes a clear distinction between trivial *consolationes* and crucial Challenge; Lupset does not.

exempla, which provide dramatic illustration of the abstract argumentation which has preceded them. Moreover, this series includes only one more Stoic anecdote—the defiant response of Theodore the philosopher to tyrannical threats—plus the addendum that "of suche coragious aunsweres the storyes of paynymes be fulle." Then Lupset shifts abruptly to the exempla of Christian tradition, reimposing his Christian perspective on the discussion with the following flat pronouncement: "But moche more the bookes of Christened men be fulle of suche ensamples." Neither reason nor learning, he asserts, could strengthen men's hearts as much as "Christes faythe" did the "holye martyrs," who not only were fearless in the face of death, and of all the tortures devised to "make deathe more paynefulle than deathe," but even seemed to "stryve to have death gyven them." Look at St. Paul, he argues, who rejoiced and gloried in his pains, in the "contynuall deathe" which was his life, because "he was gladde to remember howe ones he shoulde dye, and thereby passe to Christes presence, whose quarell he defended in this worlde with all his myghte and power." Or:

> Loke upon saynt Laurence, lyinge broylynge upon the burnyng cooles, as merye and as quiet as though he lay upon swete reed roses: When the turmentours tourned his body upon the fiery gredyernes, he bad the cruel tirant eate of his burned syde, whiles the tother parte was a rostynge. This saying declared that this holy marter feared no death. [p. 282]

"Howe manye thousande martyrs," he cries, suffered "incredyble peynes" from all the horrible tortures which tyrants could devise (eight of which he enumerates) rather than deny their allegiance to Christ. "This was a manyfest token, that feare of death hadde no maner of place with our blessed martirs, the whiche with a constante boldnes defied and dispised the myghty, cruell, and fierse emperours, theyr courage to dye overthrew the ragyng madnes of tyrantes."

Lupset's explanation for this "myrthe in so pitious martyrdomes" is, quite simply, that these men knew that Christ "nother could nor wolde deceive them, but that for theyr lyttel regarding of this lyfe they shoulde opteyne an other lyfe, where their joy shulde never have nother change, nor decrease, nor ende." And this explanation serves as a natural transition to his peroration, in which he urges Walker to welcome death fearlessly as a faithful Christian. "Mystruste you not Christe," he exhorts Walker, for the truth of his doctrine has been proven by "innumerable myracles," and witnessed to by the blood of the saints and the trembling and quaking of "the divels with all the damned spirites."

> Be not moved with the common ensample of the hole worlde: though both spirituall and temporall men, though the pope with all his cardinalles byshoppes and prestes, thoughe the princes with all theyr gentylmen and subjectes magnifye, esteme, love, noryshe, and by all meanes cheryshe this lyfe, yet beleve you the trouth, and thinke al the world false, where Christes sayinge agreeth not with that the world doeth. If it were possible, that you sawe the angels of heven lyve contrary to the preachynge of Christe, yet ageynste them all beleve the sonne of god, and love not to abyde in this lyfe, when Christe calleth you hense: make a smale valure of this present plesures, whan Christ sayth all be vanites, and may be torned to endles sorowes: Regarde no honour, no promotion here, when Christe sayth, the place of honour is in heven, and here is none advancement that is not both shame, and also may be cause of a perpetualle wretchednes. Dispice the ease and rest and that these riches bringeth, in as moche Christe saythe, that of them be taken many impedimenntes and lettes to enter into the sure quietnes of blessed soules. Thynke no place to be for your abydyng in this world, when Christe sayth, here is not your countrey, but your father and your dwelling place is in heven. Haast therfore hence. This is to saye, be wyllynge to forsake this straunge countray. And seinge the waye to your homewarde lyeth by deathe, take a couragious stomake to die: and dye gladly, that you may dye well. Beleve I say Christe, and you shall thynke it paynefull

to be in this lyfe. Beleve Christe and you shall be gredye to
be partaker of the hevenly joyes, wherupon wyll folowe a
plesante remembraunce of deathe, by the whiche you shall
departe frome your peyne to that joye, the whiche you desyre.
[pp. 283–84]

This climactic section of the *Waye of Dyenge Well* has been
quoted almost in toto for two reasons: first, in order to provide a
fair sample of Lupset's Christian eloquence at its finest; and second, to provide a sample large enough so that its elements may be
examined closely without our losing sight of their interrelationship in context. As a set-piece of hortatory rhetoric—studied,
lyrical, essentially conventional—its artistic merits clearly surpass,
in some respects, those of any comparable "Stoic" passage in the
treatise. Considered in detail, however, it seems to me demonstrably
inferior, as a whole, to the best of such passages.

On the one hand, Lupset presents the Christian answer to the
fear of death with all the artfulness at his command. The result
is a truly eloquent passage whose orderliness contrasts most effectively with the preceding jumble of classical dicta. It expresses
nobly perhaps the most distinctive article of the early Christian-
humanist creed: that the superiority of the Christian Revelation
and the Christian ethic is essentially quantitative rather than qualitative. The classical insights were of the same order; Christians
simply know more, and with more certainty. Thus equipped, they
can attain even greater heights of moral achievement than the
ancients—and have. Thus, the Christian martyrs were more fearless than the Stoics because (1) they suffered gladly not only death
but also horrible tortures, and (2) they not only suffered both
gladly, but even sought them out.[58]

Lupset's firm control of this argument is suggested by the ease
with which he employs a wider range of diction than usual. His
eulogy of the martyrs is surpassed only by his earlier argument

58. Seneca would scarcely be impressed by this argument, since—
quoting Epicurus, and anticipating modern psychologists and theologians—
he condemns the craving for death no less than the unmanly avoidance of
it. See, e.g., *Ep.* 24.

from necessity in its free and effective use of the verbal resources of both traditions. Furthermore, by piling up concrete details for their cumulative impact on the reader, he does communicate to some extent his admiration for those Christian heroes. And, finally, he even succeeds in imparting some freshness and vitality to his conventional otherworldly peroration by means of a variety of rhetorical devices. Not only is Christ quoted repeatedly as "one having authority," but his dicta are set up in balanced, parallel constructions; are dramatically opposed to antithetical worldly interests; and are arranged in climactic order. Here, too, as elsewhere in the passage, alliteration, hyperbole, triadic combinations, and so on, enhance the effectiveness of the message. There can be no legitimate doubt of Lupset's determination to do his best by the Christian position as he understands it.

On the other hand, the relative weakness of this passage is all the more apparent for precisely this reason. The impression it leaves with the reader is not, in the last analysis, one of power and exaltation: at most, it may de defined as one of willing acquiescence. One Christian eulogy after another, for instance, is artistically undercut by an anticlimactic exegesis of the obvious. Why, if the dramatic tale of St. Lawrence does in fact compare favorably with that of Canius, does Lupset feel it necessary to add the depressing truism that the former's dying words "declared that this holy marter feared no death"?[59] So, too, the very eloquence of the peroration draws attention to the fact that much of its material does not belong here at all, but in the next section under "love of life." Placed where it is, it testifies chiefly to the utter conventionality of the thought of this passage. Lupset's mind is, in this regard, medieval: promises of heaven are inseparable from denunciations of the world. He even uses here automatically the old distinction between *spiritual* and *temporal,* although he has repudiated it earlier in the treatise. Clearly his mind, once settled in the old, familiar groove, simply follows out the basic pattern set for centuries.

59. Cf. below, chap. 3, pp. 122–23; Lupset here seems to be anticipating the exegetical techniques—earnest, but unartistic—of a Reformation preacher.

Furthermore, if rhetorical skill is not able wholly to conceal the stock traditionalism of Lupset's thought, neither is it able to conceal the poverty of his verbal equipment when dealing with Christian concepts and attitudes. These he simply cannot communicate as effectively as his new, freshly realized material. Life must, inevitably, be referred to as "peyne" and "this straunge countray"; heaven, as "joye," "the sure quietnes of blessed soules," and "home"; hell, as "endles sorowes" and "perpetualle wretchednes." Martyrs are, almost without exception, "holye martyrs" or "blessed martirs." Not saints themselves, but "the bloude of [the] sayntes," witnesses to the faith. Moreover, redundant synonyms creep in here, as Lupset strives to revitalize tired notions. Paul defended Christ's cause with "myghte and power"; the joy of heaven has neither "change, nor decrease, nor ende"; both "spirituall and temporall" men "magnify, esteme, love, noryshe, and by al meanes cheryshe this lyfe"; "ease and rest" provide many "impedimenntes and lettes" to salvation; and so on. Even the obvious dramatic potentialities of St. Paul's tribulations and St. Lawrence's macabre wit *in extremis* are curiously smothered, by the use of indirect discourse; apparently Lupset's command of dialogue is somehow limited to classical material.

In summary, this would-be climactic passage witnesses eloquently to the transitional state of Christian thought in the early Renaissance. Because it is decisively Christian in intent, its weaknesses echo insistently those of the medieval tradition which it seeks to uphold. Lupset is still too close to this played out heritage, with its decadent stagnation of both thought and expression, to escape from even the dreariest of its clichés. The new blood provided by the humanists, and the ferment of the Reformation, will eventually revivify the basic propositions of the faith intellectually; and the deepening devotional experience of the Counter-Reformation period will ultimately revitalize them emotionally, and enable them to be imaged forth in a fresh way. In the meantime, the artistic impression created by this passage is of a faith not unlike that of a nominal Christian today who is "deeply moved" by a great Christian festival (Easter), or ritual (the burial service), or saint (St. Francis), or poet (Donne). The response is genuine, but conditioned and essentially superficial. "Beleve I say Christe," Lupset cries, as he draws to the end of his exhortation to Walker. "Beleve Christe and you shall be gredye to be partaker of the hevenly joyes . . . And hereof is made a glad dying, the whiche I styl name a good dieng." And then he adds, as a reluctant, perhaps, yet clinching, afterthought:

> It is a true sayinge, that who so ever feareth death, he shal never do a dede worthy for a lyvyng man. Therfore if hit were but onely for lyfes sake, it is our parte to despise the feare of deathe. [p. 284]

Here speaks the Christian humanist, in all his basic ambivalence. "Beleve Christe," yes; but, in any case, live well—if only "for lyfes sake"!

The second major hindrance to dying gladly—the love of this life—Lupset dismisses with striking ease (pp. 284–87). A consonance of Christ's sayings—"whom if you thynke to be god, you muste also thinke it all trouth that he saith"—suffices to overcome this temptation; the supporting ammunition of ancient vanity-literature is not needed. The conventionalism of the argument is modified only slightly by the new classicism, the new biblical scholarship, and the new interest in independent observation.

Thus, Lupset's emphasis upon the power of mind, and his definition of the kingdom of heaven partially in noneschatological terms, are less conspicuous than his use of hackneyed phraseology for the propagation of a thoroughly traditional message. Since the "remembrance of deth is a ever grevous thoughte" to those who value too highly this world's goods, he urges the reader to consider their true worth as determined by Christ's authority—and then to act in accordance with that evaluation: "let the truthe have in your stomacke his place." The "wylful povertie" of the Christian lies in indifference to material goods, as mere "instrumentes and toles to the pilgremage and passage of this strange countrey" which God will provide for those who care only for the "kingdom of heven, the whiche standeth in the clennes of conscience." Because Christ commands almsgiving, warns us of the rich man's spiritual danger, and depicts the pleasures of the two worlds as mutually exclusive, the Christian is to "kepe his minde in a due order to godward,"[60] and let his "treasure be . . . couched in heven." This done, he will "take no pleasure of taryinge in this lyfe, but rather it shal be werines and tediousnes to [him] to be here absente from [his] hartes desyre, the whiche alway stycketh and cleveth to [his] treasure in heven."

This depressing passage is enlivened in two significant respects. The concern of the early humanists with biblical studies and sound practical exegesis is reflected here with particular clarity, for the ideal of determining accurately the "plain sense of Scripture" controls the entire discussion of Christ's teaching—transmuting, for example, the "camel" of the warning about wealth into "a greatte caboull rope."[61] Notable, also, is the suggestion of contemporary reference in Lupset's description of the successful worldly man, with the "worlde at [his] wyll"—able to "avaunce his frende, and to undo his foo"—so hardened that it will not "synke in his brayne" to hope for heaven. Only the admirable Canius is portrayed with more colloquial vitality. In this slight tendency to particularize his discussion by reference to his own actual environment, as well as in his approach to the Bible, Lupset adumbrates an important

60. N.B. the characteristic substitution of "mind" for the *Crafte*'s "heart and soul," and "in a due order" for the less restrained "ever ready up."

61. On the historic significance of Colet's lectures on St. Paul, as a "landmark in literary and social criticism," see Adams, chap. 3. Such exegetical techniques derived not only from textual and historical scholarship, as Miles makes clear, but also from philosophical convictions that More, for one, could not accept. Believing, on Neoplatonic premises, that "Scriptural Truth, being the written revelation of God, cannot be other than one and undivided" (Miles, p. 183), Colet approached the Epistles "not as parts of an anonymous and timeless (and allegorical) Bible, but as letters written by a certain man in a certain historical milieu" (Bush, *Prefaces,* pp. 10–11). In thus striving to work out "one strictly unified sense consistent with the 'persons, places, circumstances, and times' surrounding the composition of the text in question" (Miles, p. 184), he was, of course, anticipating the methods of Protestant exegetes such as Thomas Becon (see below, chap. 3, pp. 121–22 and note 17); the Catholic humanist Colet, however, does allow for allegorical interpretations under some circumstances. See also Hunt, chap. 4.

development in the literary tradition of the ars moriendi. As found here, however, these new elements tend rather to intensify the dominant impression of meager and stale traditionalism. The "great Christian paradox," which Taylor will develop with complex sensitivity, continues to be interpreted with the simplism of a fifteenth-century ascetic.

In the final portion of the treatise, however, Lupset forcefully reasserts his best powers of analysis and organization (pp. 287–90). He opens it smoothly by reintroducing the image which prefaced the central discussion: now that the two chief "stones and blockes" on our way to a "gladde deth" have been "taken away," it remains for us only to consider briefly what aids may be available for our journey. And "nothynge" in Lupset's opinion, "shalle further us more . . . than shall an ordinate lyfe, that is to live in a just and a due maner after one rule and one forme." In thus placing the concept of a disciplined rule of life at the very center of his view of the ars vivendi, yet at the same time repudiating all extreme rules in favor of moderation, he signalizes the reemergence of his original modus operandi. Once again he strives for a true amalgam, rather than a mere mixture, of Stoic and Christian thought. Once again he develops his points with careful attention to literary structure, rather than merely assembling notions in sequence. The immediate result is an effective presentation of a threefold rule of life which will insure a glad death and certain salvation. The indirect result is a persuasive summary of the Christian humanist's final understanding of the deepest issues of life and death and destiny.

That his first rule should be "remember death" was inevitable. Both Christian devotional discipline and Stoic ethical discipline admonish Walker—in Seneca's words—to be "ever awake in a quicke remembrance of death, as though every houre were our last space of induraunce in this world"; both exhort him to resolve each morning "so to passe the day folowing as though at nyght a grave shuld be [his] bed."[62] So, too, Seneca's arguments on behalf of these commandments are universally applicable—as Taylor will

---

62. Cf., e.g., Seneca, *Ep.* 12, 49, and *De brevitate vitae,* vii, 9.

prove in making them the cornerstone of his argument in *Holy Dying*. Some die each day, and it might just as well be you, or I, or all of us.[63] In any case, each day that we live "is devyded and parted with death," since "some parte of our life, hath ben diminished. . . . Thus dyinge we alway be, though death be not alway upon us."[64] And, finally, both traditions agree that the remembrance of these facts will lead Walker to "bestowe well [his] lyfe."[65] It is the ethical rather than the devotional interpretation of this last phrase, however, which Lupset adopts instinctively; and he asserts with easy finality that this rule is really what Christ meant to enunciate when he urged his listeners to prepare for the Second Coming.

The second item in Lupset's rule is a vigorous adjuration to "be well occupyed." This choice is eminently suitable both philosophically and artistically. On the one hand, it is again a universal dictum: ethical in its implications, established as central by Christian tradition—in the catalogue of Deadly Sins and in the *regulae* of monastic orders—and supported by the Stoics' earnest denunciations of wasting time.[66] Sloth is condemned by all as "a kankerynge rustines" to body and soul alike, "an eatynge consumption [that] wasteth to naughte bothe vertue and strength"—the "grave of lyvynge men." Moreover, it is often the root of other vices even worse: "for it is an yvell ydelnes to do no thynge, but a worse ydelnes hit is to do not well." Into "suche an ydel felowe," says St. Chrysostom, "the dyvel entrith, as in to his owne howse by good right. . . . [and] claymith his rule." On the other hand, Lupset applies his theme directly and personally to Walker as the rather spoiled servant of Cardinal Pole. Hence his selection accords skillfully with two literary conventions as well: the traditional association of the sin of sloth with the calling of the servant (this vice, he generalizes confidently, "in servynge men most reyneth"), and the

---

63. Cf., e.g., *Ep.* 70.
64. Or, as Herrick so felicitously expresses it to Corinna, "we are but decaying." Cf. Seneca, *Ep.* 4, 12, and esp. 24; and *Ad Marciam*, xxi, 6.
65. See above, note 56.
66. See esp. Seneca, *De brevitate vitae*.

traditional reintroduction of the personal touch at the close of the moral epistle. And both these conventions justify the preponderance here of Christian and colloquial phraseology as against the dominant Senecanism of the first paragraph.

To show Walker *how* to be well occupied, however, "were a mattier inoughe for a nother worke." Lupset is satisfied for now if his reader understands

> that death is not to be feared, and that by contynuall remembraunce of death, you shall prepayre your selfe to dye gladlye with a good wyll: the whiche you can not do, onles you be in hope of the everlasting life, and this hope requireth some trust in the clenes of a good conscience, the which ever foloweth a gracious intent of living wel. So that if you live wel, you shal dye wel. And of the way to live wel you can not misse, if you arme your minde to be strong agaynst al suddennes of deth. [p. 289]

Although this recapitulation of his main theses as an interlude between his second and third rules interrupts the sequence of his argument a bit awkwardly, it serves also to underline the significance of the latter by setting it apart as a type of peroration.

Here—in a discussion of the duty of "unceasing prayer"—we find his conciliatory technique employed once again at its very best. On this topic the two traditions neither speak in one voice, nor even agree in substance. Yet the Christian must perforce include prayer in his rule of life, and the humanist must somehow discover this sine qua non in the life of the obviously salvable pagan. Lupset's resolution of this problem is no less, and no more, satisfactory—in terms of its contribution to the enrichment of Christian devotional literature—than his others have been. On the positive side, we must register his insistence that prayer cannot be divorced from life, and particularly from ethical behavior —and also, incidentally, his adroit exegesis of St. Paul's clear-cut, but impracticable, command (1 Thess. 5:17). The "sayinge of psalmes or axing with wordes of god his grace," he maintains, constitutes only "one fynal portion" of prayer:

the very praier is to be ever wel mynded, to be ever in charitie, to have ever the honour of good in rememberance, to suffre no rancore, none yre, no wrath, no malice, no syn to abyde in your delyte, but to be in a continual good thought, the which you maye kepe whether you slepe or wake, whether you eate or drynke, whether you feaste or fast, whether you rest or labour, and never paraventure you can pray better, than whan you must give your selfe to serve your maister, to whom the course of your life is due and bounden, specially when god hath given you suche a maister, whom your service can not plese without you be studyous to please god. [p. 290]

On the negative side, we find still further evidence of the tendency of humanism to depose a personal God in favor of some universal ideal such as "the honour of good." And a concurrent reinterpretation of prayer is of equal significance for devotional literature. As interpersonal communion with God—as adoration, thanksgiving, meditation, penitence, dedication, intercession, contemplation, and love—it disappears, leaving behind only the meager residue of the "sayinge of psalmes,"[67] simple petition, and obedience to his moral law.

Taken as a whole, however, these three disciplines as Lupset describes them do indeed make up a general rule to which all "good men and wyse men" could subscribe as valid and profitable. And the rule of prayer is itself so ethically inclusive that it may properly be separated from the other two as virtually an epitome of what it means to live well—and thereby to die well. On this note he closes his discussion, concluding with a benediction of singular interest because of its very traditionalism:

Nowe that by this I thynke my promysse fulfilled, I will at this poynte bed you farewel, and I pray god give you a stronge

67. Although it may be argued that the psalms embody every type of verbal prayer mentioned above, the point is that the connotations of "sayinge" suggest, not private and spontaneous, but public and formal worship —the "hours" of the religious, for example.

corage to passe valyantly through death, to come from thence
to everlastynge lyfe, by the helpe and grace of our mayster
and savyour Christ, to whome lette us for ever more render al
glory, prayse, and honour. Amen. [p. 290]

The contrast between this particular intercession and the argument which has preceded it is notable. Christ as Savior; grace as
strictly divine in origin, and bestowed upon man gratis; "glory,
prayse, and honour" as elements of worship; and the medieval
view of dying as in itself frightful—all these are included here *for
the first time.* Beliefs and attitudes distilled and expressed in
liturgical tradition are not easily dismissed, even in a new age. The
same forces which perpetuated them in the *Crafte* despite the
pressures of late-medieval thought are now operating to preserve
them despite the pressures of Renaissance vitality.

In summary, Christian humanism of the early Renaissance, as it
is reflected in the *Waye of Dyenge Well,* is still a far cry from
what may be called the "humanistic Christianity" of the seventeenth century. The rich resources of the classical tradition are
now available to the Christian author; but as yet he can no more
exploit their artistic potential to the full than he can restrain their
intellectual potential within the bounds of his Christian heritage.
For the purposes of this study, moreover, it is well worth observing
that even such a limited fusion of artistic material as does occur
here and there in Lupset's treatise is wholly absent in his handling
of death itself. Not only are his techniques bookish and derivative,
but they even fall short of their models. Except for two slight
references to the omnipotent tyrant of the *danse macabre,* he seeks
to communicate the reality of death solely by the rhetorical elaboration of its inescapability—by piling up synonyms to that effect
in complex sentences, rather than through imagery.[68] He contents
himself with the adjectives "sweet" and "bitter," ignoring or re-

68. See above, for example, pp. 90–91.

jecting not only the stale offerings of the medieval tradition,[69] but
the most striking metaphors of Cicero and Seneca as well. Death
as a harbor at the end of a long journey by sea; as the snuffing-out
of a lamp; as a "melting away"—such stock classical images of the
later Renaissance are still "unavailable" to him. The *Waye of
Dyenge Well* contains not a suggestion of that fresh vision of
death which will characterize the Elizabethan era.[70]

Even more significant for the development of the ars moriendi
is the extent to which the two traditions remain intellectually as
well as artistically disparate. Lupset's enthusiasm for Stoic thought
is by no means uncritical, as we have seen; in many ways it is discriminating and constructive. Yet his treatise abounds in dis-
crepancies and unresolved tensions between the two world views
which he is seeking to reconcile. The Christian humanist, as depicted indirectly in the *Waye of Dyenge Well,* reasserts his dignity
as rational creature and ethical idealist—and tends to lose his sense
of sin. Dismissing the glib traditional explanation of suffering as
purgatory in this world, he tends to ignore, temporarily, the problem of suffering altogether—not to mention the concept of *redemptive* suffering.[71] Rebelling against the extravagant claims of
the Church to intellectual and sacramental authority over his life,
he tends to reject also its claims, as the historic Body of Christ in

69. Theodore Spencer reports that in all the popular religious lyrics
and saints' lives of the fourteenth and fifteenth centuries, and seventy
metrical romances as well, he found only five adjectives applied to death:
"doleful," "horrible," "cold," "cruel," and "dreadful" (*Death and Elizabethan Tragedy,* p. 69 and n.).

70. The role played by the Stoic literary tradition in stimulating and
nurturing this vision is suggested by Bacon's essay "On Death." On the
one hand, he attacks the tradition explicitly in arguing against excessive
preoccupation with death: "Certainly," he remarks with a modern shrug,
"the Stoics bestowed too much cost upon death." On the other, he focuses
his argument on the weakness of fearing death; draws heavily on the
Stoics themselves for his arguments; and cites death scenes and "last words"
in defense of his points.

71. Lupset's failure to discuss this theme cannot be attributed wholly to
his quest for universality: Seneca, for example, says that Socrates chose to
remain in prison "in order to free mankind from the fear of two most
grievous things, death and imprisonment" (*Ep.* 24).

the world, on his loyalty; and to deny not only the coercive validity of sacramental discipline, but the sacramental view of life itself. And, finally, he renounces a socially indifferent private pursuit of holiness in favor of an unselfish ethical responsibility—but tends in the process to lose that spiritual sensitivity, grounded in worship, which is essential to great devotional literature. All these themes we shall find reasserted vehemently in Taylor's masterpiece. The burden of restoring historic Christian theology and revitalizing Christian spirituality will devolve upon the intervening generations.

# CHAPTER 3

## *The Sicke Mannes Salve:* A Calvinistic "Crafte"

The influence of the English Reformation in general, and of English Calvinism in particular, on the literature of "dying well" was exerted along quite different lines than was that of the English Renaissance. Marshall Knappen's thesis, that "early Puritanism represents rather an intensification and refinement of medieval attitudes than an attack upon them,"[1] is strikingly applicable to this particular field. Eminent Tudor Reformers, whatever their attitudes toward other significant human experiences, did indeed labor with godly zeal to instill in their benighted as well as sinful countrymen refined and intensified medieval attitudes toward dying.[2] The fruit of their labors is well represented by Thomas Becon's *The Sicke Mannes Salve* (1561)[3]—a Calvinistic "Crafte"

1. *Tudor Puritanism*, p. 451.

2. Gordon S. Wakefield observes in *Puritan Devotion* that recent studies of the Puritan movement have rendered obsolete such sweeping generalizations about its medievalism as those of G. G. Coulton: considered as a whole, it was *not* simply "the descendant of all that was most repulsive in medieval asceticism" (pp. 1, 5). Yet even Wakefield excepts from this argument the Puritan contributions to the ars moriendi, noting the "radical contrast" between the "philosophical calm" of a Socrates and the "medieval fear of the last things" which permeated Reformed thought and piety, regardless of theological persuasion, throughout the sixteenth and seventeenth centuries (p. 143).

3. *The Sicke mannes Salve. . . .* The edition used for this study is that of 1563, as found in Becon's *Worckes (STC #1710)*, vol. 2, fols. [ccxvii$^r$]–cclxxxiii$^v$. The copy in the Columbia University Library is bound separately. Although Becon apparently composed the treatise before 1553, the earliest edition extant is that of 1561; and it "cannot be ascertained" whether or not the latter has been revised. See D. S. Bailey, *Thomas Becon and the Reformation of the Church in England,* p. 144. See also below, note 6.

much more closely allied to its medieval prototype than to its humanistic predecessor. Once again we find a literary structure determined primarily by theological and practical, rather than artistic, considerations; an argument grounded solidly on traditional Christian premises about the nature and destiny of man; and an emotional orientation uncompromising in its otherworldliness, and hence basically devotional in its response to the challenge of death. Certain very important modifications, however, were the natural by-products of the Reformers' struggle to purify this heritage; and it is to these, also, that we must look for the Puritan contribution to the growth of the ars moriendi as literature. The *Sicke Mannes Salve* is no less clearly differentiated from the *Crafte* in content and tone than is Lupset's far more radical *Waye of Dyenge Well*.

Becon's work has been chosen for detailed examination for two principal reasons. In the first place, he was no more a brilliant original thinker than was Lupset, in spite of the far greater eminence he attained in the course of a full lifetime (1512–67). Rather, he was a sound interpreter and skillful communicator of the thought of his intellectual superiors. A "diligent hearer" of Latimer while a student at St. John's, Cambridge,[4] he set out after his ordination in 1538 on the troubled course which was common to all unusually able convinced evangelical Churchmen of his time: difficulties, recantations, and semiexile in the provinces under Henry; honors and respectability under Edward; imprisonment and continental exile under Mary; and, finally, upon acquiescence (after some scruples) to the Elizabethan establishment, restoration, preferment and peace. Throughout his lifetime the effectiveness of both his preaching and his writing was widely acknowl-

---

In quoting from this work I have rendered the pagination, for convenience, in arabic rather than roman numerals; normalized the abbreviations given for the names of Becon's characters, and expanded all others; adjusted the long *s, u* and *v, i* and *j* to conform to modern usage; and corrected a very few typographical errors.

4. Becon, General Preface to Folio of 1564, as quoted in Alexander B. Grosart, "Becon, Thomas," *DNB*. For a full biographical study, see Bailey.

edged by friend and foe alike,[5] while the appointments he received when Protestants were in power testify to the soundness
of his Reformed orthodoxy. The *Sicke Mannes Salve* merits our
attention as the only major treatise on "dying well" published by
one of the outstanding popularizers of the thought and attitudes
of mid-century English Calvinism.[6]

The second commanding reason for its selection is its astonishing popularity. Not only was it far and away the most popular of
all of Becon's forty-seven varied works, but it was one of the top
best sellers among Elizabethan devotional books in general. At
least eleven editions were printed between its appearance in 1561
and the end of the century, and at least another seven between
1600 and 1632. It is reasonable to infer, therefore, that this treatise
spoke to the condition of the times with unusual effectiveness—
certainly with a power achieved by none of the less traditional
devotional works of the humanists. Such a widely acclaimed book
is a noteworthy milestone along the way from the *Crafte* to *Holy
Dying*.

Both the complete title of Becon's treatise and its personal
introduction are as revealing as those of Lupset's. The title reads

5. The range of Becon's works is wide, although he is best known as
a devotional writer. As such, Helen C. White considers him second only
to John Bradford as "the most important and influential . . . of the time"
(*The Tudor Books of Private Devotion,* p. 166). All subsequent references
in this chapter to Miss White's work allude to this particular study.

6. Bailey argues persuasively that Becon mirrored his age not least
clearly in his very lack of a precise theological stance—that he knew which
side he was on, "but exactly where on that side he was never entirely
sure" (p. 117). Influenced as a boy by Lollards and Lutherans, and as a
collegian by Latimer, he came in maturity to revere and follow Cranmer
more than any single thinker (pp. 2–6 18ff, 54ff, 84–88, 117–18). Furthermore, the "thoroughly assimilated" Lutheranism of his earlier, Henrician
works (pp. 46, 137) is modified in *both* Zwinglian and Calvinistic directions during the following three reigns (pp. 33, 38–39, 46, 104–06). In
deference to Bailey's authoritative study, I have avoided labeling Becon a
Calvinist; but I have no such reservations about labeling this particular
work Calvinistic, in both argument and flavor.

as follows: "The Sicke mannes Salve, wherein the faithfull Christians may learne both how to behave themselves paciently and
thankefully in the tyme of sickenes, and also vertuously to dispose
their temporall goods, and finally to prepare themselves gladly
and godly to dye . . ." Underneath, on the title page of the 1563
edition, is a quotation from "Matt. xi": "Come unto me all ye that
are sicke and diseased, and I wyll comforte you."[7] Only the sheer
bulk of the treatise (more than seven times that of the *Crafte*)
suggests to the reader at first glance that this title promises anything more than a reworking of the old familiar conduct-book.
And the Dedicatory Epistle (fols.217$^v$–18$^v$), which corresponds
in function to Lupset's remarks to Walker, strengthens this impression of conservatism, for it echoes not only the stock medieval arguments themselves, but even their very arrangement and
phrasing. Becon reminds Master Basil Fielding of the "misery,
vanitie, and shortnes of our mortall time"; of our "bondage" to
death, which may "oppresse" us at any moment; and of the awesome Judgment which awaits us thereafter. He lauds the remembrance of the Last Things as the strongest "bit to brydle oure carnall affectes," the best "scholemaster to kepe us in an order." And
he bemoans the persistent tendency of sinful men to forget these
truths in their mad pursuit of material wealth; to "murmure and
grudge agaynste God" when they are duly punished with illness;
and, finally, to come to their spiritual senses too late, only to fall
into justifiable despair, and thence into eternal damnation. A brief
description follows of the persistent struggle against the world,
the flesh, and the devil which constitutes the good life of the
Christian, and which leads inevitably to a "good ende." However,
says Becon, he has discussed this topic fully elsewhere; the purpose of the present work is to teach "faythfull Chrystians, how
they ought to make provision for their latter end, that they may
departe in the fayth of Chryst." After specifying once more the
three sections of his treatise named in the title, he adds that he has
"enterlased many comfortable exhortacions unto the sicke, and

7. The emblem, though appropriate ("ARISE, FOR IT IS DAY"), is
irrelevant, since it appears on other title pages of Becon's work.

diverse godly and necessary prayers," some for the sick themselves and others for intercessory prayer by friends.

Like Lupset's, however, Becon's prefatory section displays significant modifications of thought and feeling in the very process of affirming its conservatism. Conspicuous even here are those distinctive aspects of Becon's religious orientation which are also, in greater or less degree, characteristic of the early English Reformation in general. By all odds the most important is the extreme scripturalism of his thought, expressing itself in an equally extreme scripturalism of style. Every point, however axiomatic or innocuous, is supported by a plethora of quotations and allusions, all carefully documented in marginalia. (Thirty-eight such references, drawn from twenty-two books of the Bible, are given within the two and a half pages of the introduction.) These, plus innumerable minor allusions and verbal echoes, create a scriptural texture so thickly woven that the reader often feels, as Miss Helen White expresses it, confronted by a "new piece of noncanonical Scripture" (p. 239). Closely related to this style is a tone new to the literature of the ars moriendi: that of zealous, even aggressive, didacticism. And both scripturalism and pedagogical energy are marshaled in support of themes equally unfamiliar to Becon's predecessors: a militant emphasis on the moral demands of the Christian life; a rigid focus on soteriology, at the expense of warm devotion to either the human Jesus or the living Christ; and a virulent detestation of Roman Catholicism. The Puritanism of his approach to the old material is unmistakable. And its effects on the body of the treatise are not unlike those of Lupset's humanism. Here, too, we find a new and appropriate form; an expanded argument enriched with suitable new material—and a similar failure to amalgamate old and new with complete success.

The structure of the *Sicke Mannes Salve* represents a most interesting refinement and intensification of the *Crafte's* liturgical movement. Instead of an implicit drama, we find an explicit closet drama; instead of an orientation to Everyman as obedient Churchman, an orientation to Everyman as independent Protestant; and instead of a five-part theological pattern tracing the way of reconciliation to God, a three-part combat depicting the way to triumph over the world, the flesh, and the devil.

The dramatic form chosen by Becon is a curious blend of Job, the classical dialogue, and perhaps genuine drama as well. Philemon (Becon himself) and three "approved frends" (fol. 219ᵛ) set out to visit their neighbor Epaphroditus in order to "comfort hym with the heavenly consolacion of the holy scriptures that he may bear this his sicknes both the more paciently and thankfully" (fol. 220). Like his biblical namesake, Epaphroditus turns out to be "sick nigh unto death"; but, unlike St. Paul's earlier "fellow-soldier," he is not spared at the last minute (Phil. 2:25–30). The mission therefore extends itself by several hours, and the Scriptures are called on for more than mere consolation. The friends do aid Epaphroditus in various concrete ways as time goes by— writing his will, moving him when he is uncomfortable, and so on; but above all, they talk. Or rather, they preach. They quote the Bible, the Fathers, and the Stoics with awesome ease and in overwhelming abundance; and when they do not quote, they paraphrase. Now and then Epaphroditus holds the floor himself— notably when he dictates his will, takes leave of his household, and makes his confession of faith. For the most part, though, it is Philemon who dominates the scene, reproving, exhorting, advising, encouraging, consoling, instructing, leading the prayers, and finally taking charge of the funeral arrangements.

Becon's preference for this name as a pseudonym[8] is readily explained by the high praise St. Paul gives his "dearly-beloved . . . fellow-labourer" for his "love and faith . . . toward the Lord Jesus and toward all saints," and also by the apostle's prayer "that the communication of [Philemon's] faith may become effectual by the acknowledging of every good thing which is in [him] in Christ Jesus" (Philem. 1:1–7). The identification is underlined by a reference to a servant named Onesimus, presumably forgiven and reinstated in obedience to Paul's request—though now, we note, working for Epaphroditus! (fol. 219). The fictional Philemon describes himself modestly as "no learned man, but a lover of

8. He uses it in other works as well.

learninge, and such one, as hath a good wil, wel to do, and envieth no man that can do better" (fol. 263ᵛ). None of the other visitors, however, claims even so much. All three content themselves with contributing occasional relevant stories or quotations, or with interjecting sympathetic questions or exclamations about the sick man's progress. As dramatis personae they are almost completely undifferentiated. Christopher is allowed to define "the crosse" and to explain "cross-bearing" (fol. 221); Eusebius is perhaps a shade more knowledgeable than the others about Church history; but Theophile is no more three-dimensional than the "most excellent Theophilus" addressed by St. Luke (Luke 1:3). All are equally well-read in the Christian classics and the "ethnicks"—and equally deferential to Philemon. On the whole, the names seem appropriate less for their historical references than because they all suggest types of godliness.

Becon's use of this artificial form cannot be attributed with certainty to any one source of inspiration. Echoes of the classical dialogue are obvious enough; indeed, the sequence of physical phenomena which heralds Epaphroditus's death is strongly reminiscent of that described in the *Phaedo*. At the other extreme, small, homely, colloquial interchanges scattered throughout the treatise suggest at least a sporadic interest in trying for an effect of genuine drama. Surely, though, the major inspiration for the form of the *Sicke Mannes Salve* is the biblical dialogue between Job and his four (counting Elihu) comforters. As Philemon and his "old familiars" approach the home of Epaphroditus (fol. 220), the rebellious and despairing cries which assault their horrified ears are chiefly those of Job—though Jeremiah naturally contributes some useful laments. "Now," Becon seems to say, "I shall show you how Job's so-called friends *should* have responded."

The ensuing drama does in fact follow the tripartite chronological division promised in the title, though without explicit demarcation of acts. The traditional argument serves as a framework for an extraordinarily full consideration of almost every conceivable facet of a Christian's proper response to illness and imminent death —several of them wholly new to the ars moriendi. Some of this material just elucidates, extends, or modifies the old; some, though tangential, appears logically relevant; but some, polemical or moralistic, is quite inconsequential to one about to die. Unabashed, the friends discuss such irrelevant matters with Epaphroditus just as enthusiastically as they do the state of his soul—producing some seventy-five thousand words of dialogue in the course of their pastoral call! Sister Mary Catharine's acid observation on the absurd impracticality of the *Sicke Mannes Salve* as a conduct-book is clearly justified.[9] But it misses the point. The key to the new orientation of the Puritan "Crafte" is given in a comment by Theophile just before Epaphroditus's death-throes. It is a "great joy and comfort," he declares, to be with one

> so godly mineded [*sic*]. For in you as in a cleare mirrour we behold our selves, and se what shall become of us heareafter. Of you as of a lively scholemaster do we learne, how we shall behave our selves, when God layeth the crosse on us. And we most humbly besech God to geve us the like pacience and thankfulnes. [fol. 279ʳ]

In brief, Becon is directing his treatise specifically at the healthy, holding up for their inspection the mirror of a "godly death" that they may learn from such a "lively scholemaster" to prepare themselves for a similarly blessed end. Like the dialogue form, this orientation springs naturally from his Calvinist premises, although it suggests humanistic influences as well.[10]

9. O'Connor, *Art of Dying Well*, p. 195.
10. An earlier treatise by Becon, on essentially the same topic, reveals an enthusiastic classicism that one would not suspect from reading the *Sicke Mannes Salve:* see "The Prayse of Death: set forth in a dialoge between Man and Reason . . ." in *Worckes,* 1563 *(STC* #1710), vol. 3, fols. [ccccx]–[ccccxxi]. Marginal citations are numerous to Boethius, Sallust, Herodotus, Plato, et al.—and relatively few to the Scriptures. Furthermore, "Reason" speaks not merely with colloquial vitality, but also with something of the irritable snobbery of the true humanist pedagogue: "Lord GOD," he exclaims (after some three folio pages of "Manne's" whining protests), "what meanest thou to use all these idle words: for as I perceave by thee, thou art very unlearned in Philosophy" (fol. [ccccxii]). Douglas Bush credits Becon with a reverence for "good Latin" worthy of Ascham:

The Puritan repudiated scornfully the notion that reason alone can ever discover the content of a moral law, still less establish its authority over man. He therefore challenged ecclesiastical authoritarianism with an even more radical biblical authoritarianism, predicated on his fervid assumpton that the Word of God could be "harmonized" in regard to any and every topic of human significance. At the same time, however, he was himself the final authority as to what that holy word really did command. It was incumbent upon his leaders to convince him that a given response in a given situation was in fact called for by divine fiat. Implicitly, then, he also assumed that acceptance of revealed truth and assent to revealed authority not only can be, but ought to be, grounded in reason.[11] This notion, though less optimistic than Lupset's, exalts Everyman's rationality well beyond the limits set by the *Crafte*. The *Sicke Mannes Salve* follows the earlier work in laying down a general devotional scheme to be followed when the time comes; but its primary purpose is to satisfy to the mind of the reader, while he is still "his own man," the validity of that traditional pattern of response. Hence the use of the quasi-dramatic

---

"Good Latin [they would agree], as the instrument of God-given reason, is the symbol of religious, ethical, and social solidarity" (*The Renaissance and English Humanism*, p. 77). Cf. A. G. Newell, "Thomas Becon and Literary Studies," *Evangelical Quarterly* 33 (1961): 93–101.

11. Cf. Knappen, pp. 346–47. "Puritan piety," as Wakefield notes, "was to be informed and in the widest sense intellectual . . . there must be understanding" (p. 63). For a useful summary of the principles of scriptural exegesis and homiletics which derived from this premise, see ibid., pp. 16–24; and see below, note 17. Protestant casuists, also, strove to protect the faithful from the "vagaries and perils of private judgement" (Wakefield, pp. 116–17); and even well into the seventeenth century private meditation was defined as an "earnest musing upon some point of Christian *instruction* . . . a bending of the *mind*" (italics mine) in order to strengthen the Christian "against the flesh, world, and devil" (Isaac Ambrose, quoted in Wakefield, p. 88). For a thorough discussion of this last aspect of "Puritan piety," see U. Milo Kaufmann, *The Pilgrim's Progress and Traditions in Puritan Meditation*, Yale Studies in English, 163, chaps. 6 and 8, esp. pp. 119–26, 175–87.

mirror technique, instead of authoritarian rubrics. And hence the tactless—and incredible—long-windedness of Philemon and his friends: their indulgence in hours of preachment and polemics, supported at every point with barrages of Scriptural citations.[12]

Furthermore, the secondary aim of the treatise is to prepare this healthy Christian even now for death, by moving him to pursue with godly zeal the given ideal of the Christian life. It was all very well for the Reformers to talk about good works as merely the signs and assurances of one's election; but the resultant moral pressure to "do good" and "eschew evil"—understood in terms of external behavior rather than, say, devotional "intention"—was stronger than ever. Emotionally speaking, the smashed idols of Roman Catholic legalism were promptly reconstructed according to new specifications. Even the most carefully orthodox Calvinists of later generations sometimes involved themselves in outright anomalies. Not surprisingly, therefore, Becon argues at some length that we shall be rewarded according to our works (fol. 218$^r$–18$^v$); and he states several times that a good life will *lead to* a "blessed end"—rather than, say, "betokening" it. On his own terms, his inclusion of a good deal of moralistic and hortatory material is no more impractical than his intense scripturalism.

Because of the essential oneness of the devotional life, as Miss White suggests, devotional works have a tendency to "grow by accretion," to fatten indiscriminately on interests and concerns of the moment (p. 33). The ars moriendi escaped this fate of the sixteenth-century Primer and other devotional miscellanies because Becon's didactic and moralistic fervor was counterbalanced by a rigorous sense of theological form. By reorganizing the drama of Christian dying into three acts only, and then identifying them with the traditional three arenas of combat in Christian living (in this case ordered as the flesh, the world, and the devil respectively), he imposes a pattern on his material which keeps his Reforming

12. Cf. Nathaniel Spinckes's *The Sick Man Visited,* written more than a century after Becon's treatise, which sets forth in detail *six* such "comfortable" visitations to a Puritan Moriens! (Cited in Wakefield, p. 147.)

"accretions" under firm control.[13] The result is that the ars
moriendi takes a long step toward reunion with the ars vivendi—
without thereby relinquishing its own integrity.

The first section of the treatise (fols. 220–35) discusses the
brevity and uncertainty of life, the role of friends in spiritual assistance to the sick, the nature and cause of illness, and the Christian's proper response to it (including the "works of faithful repentance"). Here a few sentences of the *Crafte* have been expanded
into almost thirty pages of careful discussion on the meaning and
purpose of suffering. "Deathbed suffering" has been extended to
include any illness, whether fatal or not; but the only accretions,
properly speaking, are two passages, tangential to the dramatic
situation, on the proper use of the Bible and the nature of prayer.
And these are as basic to the Reformer's argument as Lupset's
premises are to the humanist's.

The second section (fols. 235–54) incorporates much more material which would have seemed extraneous to the fifteenth-century work. Triumph over "the world," Becon teaches, is won when
a man "forsaketh and geveth over the world, before the worlde
forsaketh him" (fol. 243); and the climactic testimony to such a
victory will be the faithful recitation of the Christian Creed. So
far, so good. But the Puritan is also concerned about one's duties
to the world before renouncing it. After a brief discussion of the
doctrine of stewardship, therefore, he presents us with a sample
will.[14] Into this he manages to inject his views on the Christian's

13. Becon's use of a liturgical phrase for his structural framework is the
kind of minor detail which supports Bailey's thesis that he never renounced
entirely the values of the institutional Church as Cranmer had tried to
preserve them. William Perkins, per contra, built *his* medicinal tract on an
appropriate (?) scriptural text: "The day of death is better than the day
that one is born" (Eccles. 7:1). See *A salve for a sicke man: or, a Treatise
Containing the Nature, Differences, and Kindes of Death; as Also the
Right Manner of Dying Well* . . . Note also that Becon even makes use, in
this treatise, of a few liturgical prayers; see below, pp. 128–29 and nn.

14. Since the Puritans in general agreed with Perkins that "to die
intestate, or to leave earthly responsibilities untended, is a sin" (Wakefield,
p. 146), it is curious that Becon himself apparently died intestate (Bailey,
p. xv).

duty toward his family, his servants, his debtors, and the poor in general; on the ministry and the value of sermons; and on the true nature of death and the sub-Christian quality of the burial customs of his time. Equally detailed sample leave-takings follow.[15] These consist more of exhortations and admonitions to family and servants than of benedictions. Hence they serve Becon as vehicles for his opinions on the respective duties of a wife, a widow, a mother, and a mistress of a household; of children in general; of a son, a youth, a husband, a father, a master, a neighbor, a landlord, and a citizen; of a daughter, a young lady, and a "godly woman"; and, finally, of servants. The section concludes (fols. 246 et seqq.) with an elaborately complete sample confession of faith to be made in the presence of all by the dying man, just before he is left alone with his intimate friends to face the bitter agony of the deathbed. In this portion of the treatise, then, Becon goes far beyond the mere expansion and elucidation of traditional deathbed doctrine. Here he uses the barest suggestions in the *Crafte* as springboards for a host of sermonettes which belong, properly speaking, under the ars vivendi. All the same, they have been incorporated into the old pattern, not just tacked onto it.

The third and longest section by far (fols. 254–82) opens with prayers by the faithful friends that Epaphroditus may remain faithful to the end in spite of their bitter struggles which lie immediately ahead. There follow full discussions of the Christian answers to the fear of death itself, as "terrible and fearful"; the fear of death as "painful"; the temptation to cling to life for its material pleasures; and the temptation to cling to life for its richer pleasures, such as friendship. These comparatively elementary troubles disposed of, Becon moves to deeper levels of spiritual discomfort. He defines the Christian's weapons for overcoming the devil's temptations, then discusses with elaborate thoroughness the Christian answers to the temptation to despair in all its aspects (fols. 260$^v$ et seqq.). Here he includes quite naturally his views on the moot topics of deathbed repentance, the treasury of merits, and of

15. The word *sample* is used more loosely here and below, since only the will is cast in a form which might actually be serviceable to the reader.

course the doctrine of election—with particular emphasis on the seven signs which fully certify that one is predestinate to eternal salvation. The remainder of the treatise follows the *Crafte* rather closely (fols. 276 et seqq.). The interrogations, however, call on Epaphroditus to reaffirm only two points of faith: faith in the resurrection of the body and in the "blessed state of the godly departed, and . . . the immortality of the soule." As the final "extreme agony and conflicte" with the "infernal army" draws nearer (fol. 280), the dying man prays to Christ, gazes on his Lord with eyes of faith, and is assured of the presence of angels in his chamber to strengthen and defend him. The friends' commendations and intercessions alternate with their "comfortable exhortations" to faith and courage and with his own (weakening) signs of continuing faith. In the coda following his death (fols. 282–83$^v$), an unexpected eulogy of the deceased precedes the usual prayers of thanksgiving and petition; and the treatise proceeds as far as the first preparations for the funeral.

In this section, then, the humanistic concern with the fearful nature of death itself has been accepted as a valid and serious temptation, the temptation to avarice expanded, and the temptation to despair asigned a position of central importance. It is these shifts in emphasis which are really significant for our study, rather than the (relevant) accretions of polemic theology and a new "sample funeral eulogy." Unlike the more generalized, catchall devotional works of the period, the ars moriendi has by now established itself as a distinctive genre responsive to individual authorship, its basically traditional contents adaptable by a controlling mind to the needs of a specific time.

Becon's militant sectarianism not only modified the form of the ars moriendi and enlarged its area of concern, but influenced it in less tangible ways as well. The techniques he used to implement his Reforming purposes add little to the artistic effectiveness of the *Sicke Mannes Salve* itself; but they hold creative implications for the future enrichment of the tradition.

## SCRIPTURALISM

As used by Becon, for example, scripturalism adds rather more quantity than quality to the ars moriendi. Proofs for each and every point are deliberately marshaled in numbers calculated to overwhelm any but the most intransigeant. In theory, this procedure is amply justified by his premises. The ultimate authority of the Bible as God's word, and the equal validity of all its parts as inherently congruent in their teaching, are as axiomatic to Becon as the ultimate authority of the Church was to the author of the *Crafte,* and the ultimate authority of reason to Lupset. They are self-evident propositions. The proper use of God's scriptural revelation does, however, require elucidation; and this Becon provides in part early in the treatise, with a succinct application of the mirror philosophy of history to the "histories" found in the Bible. Here he says,

> as in most pleasaunt mirrors and godly glasses, we behold our frail nature, our wicked wil, our beastlike manners and synfull life. We se gods justice, punishment and vengance upon the disobedient and stiffnecked transgresses [*sic*] of his holy commaundements. Againe we behold his tender mercy and loving kindnes toward penitent synners, and howe ready he is to forgeve, whansoever we tourne unto him. Moreover in holy histories, we consider what our duty is toward god, after we have received benefytes of him. Verely to labour unto the uttermost of our power, to be thankful unto him, and to lyve worthy his kindnes. These and such like things must the godly reader consyder, when he readeth the histories of the holy scripture. [fol. 229]

Approached in this straightforward way, entire narratives "clearly" support Calvinist dogma just as effectively as do those individual texts beloved of the polemicist. In short, Becon renounces those devices for the multilayered interpretation of the Bible by which the medieval Church explained away difficulties, and commits himself—along with all evangelical exegetes of this period—to the plain sense of Scripture.[16] And it is in obedience to these principles that he constructs a mosaic of biblical story and precept around each detail in his argument.

The technique is certainly impressive, and, to a point, entertaining as well. Like Lupset's illustrative anecdotes, the stories of David, Job, Lazarus, the Prodigal Son, and other vivid personalities of the Old and New Testaments provide intervals of welcome contrast to his abstract argumentation. From an artistic viewpoint, however, the principle is overworked in practice. To give only one example, God's merciful restoration of those who accept his just punishment in faithful penitence is illustrated, not by one or two obviously relevant histories, but by a retelling of the stories of Joseph, David, Job, Tobias, and—after some intervening argument—Moses, Manasses, the Prodigal Son, the man who took up his bed and walked, the Penitent Thief, the man rescued by the Good Samaritan, and finally the Lost Sheep (fols. 228–31ᵛ). The modern reader may be forgiven a gasp for breath. It is difficult to make due allowance for the historical circumstances that made such a style, not just minimally palatable, but in fact immensely popular.[17]

Worse yet, even the best stories lose much of their effectiveness by being explicated with solemn care, in a homiletic style as

16. See Kaufmann, pp. 27–41; and cf. Knappen, p. 357; Wakefield, pp. 13 n. 16, 21; and above, chap. 2, note 61.

17. It should be noted that Becon had developed his technique during the so-called Catholic reaction of 1543–47, when the newly won permission to own and read the vernacular Bible was withdrawn once more from most of the people. (See Craig R. Thompson, *The Bible in English: 1525–1611,* p. 10.) Under these circumstances, his dense scripturalism served to familiarize his readers not only with the main outlines of Reformation theology, and their "validation" in the Word of God, but also with the Bible itself. (Cf. Bailey, pp. 39, 44–45, 116). No doubt this secondhand reading was valued even more highly under the Marian regime, after the inspiriting permissiveness of Edward VI's government. By 1563, when the folio edition of Becon's works appeared, the inexpensive Geneva Bible was already gaining wide circulation; yet to read the Scriptures in the vernacular was still something new and therefore exciting. Furthermore, as Wakefield reminds us, the privilege had been "bought by martyrs' blood" (p. 15)— a point not yet dulled by time.

traditional in essence as it is barren of literary effectiveness.[18]
This may take the form of a running exegesis, such as Becon employs for the story of the Prodigal Son:

> Blessed Luke telleth, that a certain man had two sonnes, and
> the yonger of them said unto his father: father geve me the
> porcion of the goods, that to me belongeth. And he devided
> unto them his substaunce. Hitherto have ye hard of the fathers
> liberality toward his sonne. It folowed: and not long after, . . .
> he wasted his goods wyth ryotous livyng. Here se we the
> wickednes of the sonne. Now behold the plage of God. . . .
> Thus se ye into how great misery he is fallen for the misusyng
> of his goodes. Behold now agayn his repentant and sorowful
> hart. . . . Now mark also the pitifull compassion and tender
> mercy of the father toward his sonne. . . . In thys history do
> ye se the exceding great mercy of God toward penitent syn-
> ners most lively painted and set forth. [fol. 230]

At other times the didactic application of the story is reserved for
the end. A (short) legend about St. Ambrose, for example, is told
by Christopher without such interruptions; but Philemon has no
intention of letting the patient (or the reader) draw his own conclusions. "A notable hystory," he comments promptly, "declaryng
that God is not there present, where the crosse is absent" (fol.
226ᵛ). If the illustrative tale is complex enough, a running exegesis
may be combined with a more elaborate recapitulation than that
which concludes the story of the Prodigal Son. Thus, the history of
Manasses is explicated at every point, yet elicits a long commentary
from Philemon in the set style approved for popular preaching:
"In this history many notable thynges are to be learned. First, . . .
Secondly, we learne. . . . Thirdly it setteth forth unto us. . . . Forthli,
we learne of this history . . ." (fols. 228ᵛ–29). The rather meager
effectiveness of such passages is not enhanced by the fact that the
lesson mirrored in all such instances is virtually identical: God's
just punishment of the wicked, and his merciful restoration of the
penitent.

18. See Owst, *Preaching in Medieval England,* pp. 309–11, 313; and
cf. Wakefield, pp. 23–25.

Becon's citation of authority in other ways is equally overfull and hypercautious. A harmony of the teaching of the Psalms, Christ, St. John and St. Paul on any point might well be thought sufficiently convincing even to a sixteenth-century Protestant; but Becon leaves no scriptural stone unturned in his determination to establish Calvinist doctrine as in truth God's Truth. The result is epitomized in his exegetical expansion of the creedal statements about the nature and work of Christ (fols. 247–51). The 131 words of the Nicene Creed are here transmuted into some 4,000, with the aid of not only 13 references to the Psalms, 28 to the Gospels, 5 to John's Epistles and Revelation, and 46 to St. Paul's Epistles—92 in all—but also 41 others to Genesis, Job, Isaiah, Jeremiah, Daniel, Hosea, Zachariah, Ecclesiasticus, Acts, 1 and 2 Peter, Jude, and, of course, Hebrews.[19] The use of 133 scriptural quotations and allusions in support of 131 words is extreme even for Becon; but his treatment of less crucial topics is only proportionately less thick in its scripturalism. One short speech of Philemon's, chosen at random from many on the subject of humbling oneself before God, compresses 16 references from 11 books of the Bible into 285 words (fols. 224ᵛ–25). Another, chosen from many on the "Way of the Cross," contents itself with only four references, but quotes them all in full: "For whom the Lord loveth, he chasteneth, they are Bastards and no sonnes, that somtime fele not the Crosse. . . . By many tribulacions (sayth thapostle) must we enter into the Kingdom of God. Here unto pertaineth the saying of the vertuous woman Judith: . . . Blessed is the man, that suffreth temptacion, sayth S. James" (fol. 226ᵛ).

Becon's method of controlling such densely scriptural argumentation is less obtrusive than his narrative technique, but no less monotonous in the long run. Each point in a sequence is concluded by a summary which incorporates all that has gone before. In the first section, Epaphroditus's progress toward victory over

19. I have followed for the sake of convenience the sixteenth-century Calvinist's acceptance of the Pauline authorship of all the Epistles except Hebrews.

the flesh is marked by three such cumulative prayers.[20] In the last, his resistance to the devil grows in much the same way, though the successive states are less logical, and not always crystallized in prayers. The process is seen at its clearest, however, in the expanded Creed of the second section. Here Epaphroditus defines his belief in "one God," then "one God the Father," "one God the Father Almighty, Maker of heaven and earth and of all things visible and invisible"; "one Lord," "one Lord Jesus Christ"—and so on (fols. 246ᵛ et seqq.). For all its hoary respectability in the pedagogical realm, this ponderous technique can scarcely be called effective in an artistic sense. Psychologically, it does have a certain validity as a way of suggesting Everyman's growth in Christian understanding and commitment; but its crudeness in this respect is obvious, even without reference to Taylor's subtle and intricate treatment of the same theme in *Holy Dying*. Its one real virtue is that it allows Becon to multiply his scriptural citations indefinitely: he can—and does—exhaust the major texts and supporting histories for each point in his argument without ever obscuring the pattern of the whole.

We should not, however, dismiss Becon's use of Scripture as merely exhaustive and uninspired collation. The piecing together of intricate amalgams such as we find in the *Sicke Mannes Salve* is a delicate operation if the plain sense of each unit is to survive the process. Granting as a matter of course that his selection of proofs reflects his Reformed position, one must, I think, credit Becon with a notable fidelity to his principles of scriptural interpretation. The histories he chooses do in fact mirror the points under discussion without being distorted for the purpose. The contexts of sentences quoted in isolation do support his use of them in a given

20. He learns first to humble himself before God's righteous will, and prays for a patient and thankful heart (fol. 224ʳ–24ᵛ). He learns next to confess his sinfulness, and prays for true repentance—this time with humility *plus* patience and thankfulness (fol. 229ᵛ). Eventually he comes to make a really full and Christian confession—now including humility, patience, thankfulness, heartfelt repentance, and faithful trust in God's mercy for Christ's sake (fol. 234).

argument. With perhaps two or three exceptions, even his most
sectarian passages are entirely devoid of that finicky, querulous
textual hairsplitting which mars so much sixteenth-century religious literature. In sum, the new intellectual firmness which
characterized the mind of the Renaissance as exemplified in Lupset's *Waye of Dyenge Well* characterizes Becon's thinking also,
obscured though that strength may be by his religious authoritarianism.

As Knappen points out (pp. 355, 361–66), the Puritan faith in
the inerrancy of Scripture was to collapse before long under the
weight of its own intrinsic weaknesses; but the *Sicke Mannes Salve*
is a star witness to the power of such argumentation during the
early years of the Reformation. At the same time, it testifies to the
major role played by such literature in incorporating the diction
and imagery of the Bible into the very substance of the English
language. The literary effectiveness of passages such as those cited
above depends almost entirely upon the literary power of the
originals. Yet in a period when vernacular Bibles were still rare,[21]
and biblical clichés not yet shopworn and meaningless like those
of ecclesiastical tradition, this power was far greater than the
modern reader can easily understand. Later, when the impact of
the original text had been dulled by familiarity, writers such as
Milton, Bunyan, Baxter—and Taylor—would use it freely as an
incomparable literary source. In the meantime, the reverent literal-
ism of pedagogues like Becon helped to swell the ranks of knowledgeable and responsive readers for the masterpieces to come.

## DIDACTICISM

Becon's aggressive didacticism is the second by-product of his
theology with significant implications for our study. Again he
provides us with a rather extreme example of an orientation, and
a tone, thoroughly characteristic of the devotional literature of his
time—and new to the ars moriendi. As Miss White shows so

---

21. Louis B. Wright states emphatically that "the abundance and cheap-
ness of printed Bibles placed them within reach of every Elizabethan citizen" (*Middle-Class Culture in Elizabethan England,* p. 236). But cf. above,
n. 17; and White, p. 180.

clearly, each theological faction seized every opportunity to inculcate its own doctrinal viewpoint in the intellectually passive layman by doctoring such aids to private devotion as psalters, primers, and other, more specialized types of treatises.

Frequently Becon argues forthrightly on behalf of Calvinist beliefs and practices. His discussions of the meaning and purpose of suffering, of the proper form for Christian funeral rites, of the Christian's true weapons against Satan's temptations, of the remedies against deathbed despair, of the resurrection of the body and the immortality of the soul—these and many others are elaborated far beyond the layman's need for basic instruction. More often still, he follows the customary subtler procedure of simply assuming the rightness of his position and insinuating it into the very fabric of his work. Thus, for example, his expansion of the traditional role of Moriens's friends transmutes them into representatives of the priesthood of all believers;[22] and his editing of prayers transforms even the most traditional into vehicles of sectarian instruction. One way or another, he seizes every occasion, however inappropriate, to explicate with careful precision the theological presuppositions or implications of every point, however minor. The dominant concern of the *Sicke Mannes Salve* may be to convince Protestants of the duty of a (purified) traditional response to illness and death; but its author must keep one eye on the Romish enemy at every instant.

Once the fundamentals of Christian doctrine, as understood by the medieval Church, had themselves been called into question, it is understandable that this habit of theological explication should have grown upon the Reformers particularly, and even the Roman Catholics to some extent.[23] But that Becon was addicted to it is

22. Citing Perkins's similar emphasis on the "priestly nature of the whole society," and the consequent duty of "callers" on the sick to be "more than casual, worldly comforters," Wakefield makes the interesting point that this teaching of the Reformers—wholly persuasive though it be to the Protestant mind—led ultimately to the "revolting sentimentality" of Evangelical deathbed scenes in the following century (pp. 146–47). He is speaking, be it noted, as a Methodist scholar and pastor, to an audience of Methodists.

23. See White, pp. 228, 224–25.

only too obvious from addenda such as his preposterously elaborate version of the Nicene Creed. The effects of this habit upon his prose may be seen in the very first sentence of his Dedicatory Epistle:

> Christ our Lord and Savioure, considering what and how great carnal securitie and fleshly quyetnes reigneth in mortal men of al ages, yea and that in them, that professe godlynesse, that is to saye: Christians, which by their profession are dead unto the world, and have their life hydden with Christ in God, insomuch that they being occupied about worldly and transitory thyngs, which sone perish and come to nought, do utterly neglect the things that appertaine unto the salvacion of their soules: in many places of his holy gospel admonisheth us to watche and to make provision for our latter ende, least we be founde unready whan we shall be called out of the world. [fol. (217ᵛ)]

Stripped of its parenthetical definition of the Christian profession and its redundant admonition that "transitory" things "sone perish and come to nought," this sentence would be some twenty percent shorter and rather more than twenty percent smoother and more effective. In brief, Becon's pedagogical zeal often clogs the movement of his prose.

More fundamental still, it clogs the inner movement of passages which are explicitly devotional. The breath of the Spirit is smothered by the weight of insistent didacticism. Because the *Sicke Mannes Salve* identifies Epaphroditus primarily with Everyman, and his friends with the faithful bystanders of the *Crafte,* its prayers are semiliturgical to the extent that they are relatively short, centered on one theme, and generalized in reference.[24] In fact, at least

24. Their traditionalism is particularly striking because Becon's anthology of prayers entitled *The Pomander of Prayer* (1558) marks "the beginning of a development of socially specific prayers which Becon was to carry to its full-blown perfection in a later work, *The Flower of Godly Prayers* [1560]" (White, p. 167). Here, there are no prayers for specific degrees or estates even in the second section.

the *commendatio* "Depart, O Christian Soul" (now much abbreviated) is wholly liturgical (fol. 281$^v$).[25] About a dozen others are Puritan prayers only in that their wording is entirely scriptural, in accordance with a devotional fashion of mid-century Protestantism.[26] The overwhelming majority, however, strive with ponderous Reforming earnestness to inculcate both right belief and right attitudes in their user.

Sometimes the doctrinal instruction intertwined with devotion is almost as casual and straightforward as that of liturgical (or scriptural) prayer; in this case, its obstrusiveness comes from its being so much more thickly encrusted on the skeletal obsecration.[27] More often, it is aimed at the worshiper not only for its own sake, but also for its value in controlling his devotional response. In its own way, that is, it is designed to be affective. One group of such prayer meditations reminds God of the central affirmations of Reformed doctrine at some length, in order to "comfort" the worshiper's own "weake and synful conscyence" (fol. 271$^v$). Doctrinal polemic and a rather basic type of comfort-casuistry are here inseparable. Thus, Epaphroditus reviews in two separate prayers his total dependence upon God's mercy and asserts firmly his trust in Christ alone. At least one prayer of this sort so far forgets itself as to refer to God, about halfway through, in the third person (fol. 283). The other important pedagogical-pastoral group reminds God of his past mercies, as recounted in scriptural histories which mirror the present situation:

25. See also, for example, the intercession on fol. 254. And cf. above, note 13.

26. White, p. 139. Becon includes several in their original form, a goodly number constructed of two or more psalms alone, and a few which combine psalm material with prayers found in the New Testament. By the seventeenth century, if not earlier, this fashion was grounded solidly on familiar principles: citing Lewis Bayly's *Practise of Pietie* (*STC* #1602, the earliest extant edition [1613] is the third, "Profitably amplified"), Wakefield explains that "the Christian should be so familiar with Scriptural phrases that he can speak to God 'as well in his (God's) own holy words' as in his native tongue" (p. 69).

27. See, for example, the prayer of confession on fol. 234.

> O Lord Jesu Christ . . . we most humbly besech the, deliver
> this sick and weake parson . . . from all ugsome and terrible
> assaultes and temptations of the devil, synne, and hell. Deliver
> him (O Lord) as thou deliveredst Noe from the raging
> waves of the sea. Lot from the destruction of Sodom. Abraham
> from the feare of the Chaldes. The children of Israel from
> the tiranny of Pharao. David from the hand of Goliah. The
> thre men from the violence of the firy fornace in Babilon.
> Daniell from the mouth of the Lions. Jonas from the belly
> of the whalefishe, and Peter from the prison of Herod: even
> so, O gratious Lord God, Deliver the soul of this parson,
> both now and whensoever he shall depart hence from al
> pearel and daunger. [fol. 275]

Even without knowing the stories in detail, the frightened sufferer
(or, more commonly, sinner) gains from such a list a vague assurance that God will live up to his past performance.

Nonetheless, Becon's instructional prayer obviously leaves something to be desired as prayer. The acknowledgment and reexami-
nation of basic convictions is no doubt necessary from time to
time, if the devotional life is not to atrophy; but an ability to take
them for granted most of the time is equally necessary, if one's devotional life is not to become paralyzed through spiritual self-
consciousness. The *Sicke Mannes Salve* professes itself to be
essentially an "aid to devotion" in the traditional sense, and exhibits its many prayers in support of that claim. Yet it illustrates
to perfection one of the major weaknesses of mid-century devotional literature. We are not surprised to learn that private devotion was nourished, throughout this controversial era, primarily
by Catholic aids carried over from the medieval tradition with
only minimal revision to ensure their doctrinal acceptablity.[28]

It is the tone of urgency—of dynamic conviction and missionary
zeal—informing the driest arguments as well as the prayers which
reminds us of their positive contribution to the ars moriendi. The
tumult and the shouting of this period resulted in something more

28. White, passim. These were not supplemented by the rich devotional
literature of the Counter-Reformation until the following generation. See
below, chap. 4.

than a mere stalemate, as divergence of opinion stiffened into irreconcilability on many issues which seemed fundamental. It resulted also in a fervent recommitment to those affirmations of historic Christianity which all disputants agreed *were* fundamental. For the first time, perhaps, since the thirteenth century, dogma became in and of itself affective.[29] Thus, Becon's preoccupation with the motifs of sin, Judgment, penitence, and Atonement reflects a new sensitivity to man's actual, as distinct from theoretical, sinfulness before the God of righteousness. The loving Father of medieval thought in its trusting moods? The gracious God of humanistic optimism? Certainly; but only after we acknowledge our sin and bow down to him in faithful repentance. It is important to note, however, that the concept of the *imago dei* is as yet unrecovered in Protestant thought as represented by the *Sicke Mannes Salve*. Man's sin lies in the extent to which he offends God by denying his lordship, breaking his commandments, and violating his righteous will. There is no suggestion of man's also offending God by denying his own highest creative capacities, betraying his own human standards, and violating his own integrity. The sense of sin which permeates the literature of the turn of the century will be the richer and more poignant for the addition of the latter viewpoint; but there is something impressive, even awesome, in the single-hearted conviction with which the mid-century Puritan declares his need for redemption. Once again the creeds—even Becon's—become dramatic proclamations of living truth. The new tone, with its suggestion of cosmic issues impinging on the quiet world of private devotion,[30] imparts to the Puritan "Crafte" a dynamic vitality missing in both the ecclesiastic's conduct-book and the gentleman's essay.

## ANTI-CATHOLICISM

Becon's anti-Catholicism is, however, more than a theoretical position to be defended with the energy of conviction: it is a

29. Cf. Wakefield, speaking of Puritan sermons: "like St. Paul . . . they dealt with the great and numinous themes of the Faith and of their own experience, and this often fills with power their tedious paradigms" (pp. 24–25).
30. Cf. White, pp. 135, 161, 182.

passion. As Knappen puts it, the Tudor Puritan "never forgot or forgave the Catholic; yea, he hated him with perfect hatred" (p. 352). It is this virulent detestation of papistry, expressed in diatribes throughout the treatise, which leads Sister Mary Catharine to refer to it as "the bigoted Becon's" (p. 10). Yet even this least attractive facet of his sectarianism has a significant contribution to make to the development of the ars moriendi.

Becon is rarely content simply to rebut the Catholic position: he must also indulge in denunciations of those "enemies of the crosse of christ, depravers of the holy scriptures, and corruptours of christen souls" (fol. 241). Among the epithets which he spits out are "idle Papists," "wily wicked Papists," "purgatorirakers," "superstitious Massemongers," "monkish hypocrites," and even "devils incarnat" (fols. 243, 274, 236$^v$, 243, 249, 274). The theoretical justification for even the most extravagant of these epithets becomes apparent when we turn to his equally venomous attacks on Roman doctrine. For example, their teaching that "all men even the most godly and faythfull must doubte of their salvacion" is a doctrine "both wicked and damnable," "a devilish errour," because it "maketh god false of his promise, quencheth faith, blotteth out hope, destroieth love, disquieteth the conscience, filleth the hart with whole seas of unrestfull and wycked imaginations, and so driveth the doubtful parson unto desperation and finally unto dampnation. O murtherers. O soul slears" (fol. 273$^v$). Professed religious leaders who lead their followers down the "very path unto hell" (fol. 272$^v$) not only by teaching wrong belief, but even more by inculcating wrong attitudes, surely merit "godly hatred" from Becon's point of view. As for their religious practices, no faithful Puritan can consider without revulsion such "beggarly superstitious, popysh, and divelysh Ceremonyes" (fol. 260$^v$)—for the same basic reasons. The "most wycked and abhominable popysh Masse," a daily sacrifice "divised" by the papists "for lucres sake," denies the full redemptive efficacy of Christ's Passion and seeks to make Christ "(as they use to say) Jacke out of offyce" (fols. 240$^v$, 249, 250). And masses for the dead, along with pilgrimages, trentals, diriges, and all other intercessory practices developed "for the mayntenaunce of [the papists'] idle bellyes" are worse than useless, since they presuppose the existence of purgatory, which Becon refers to as the "firy fornace of the Bishop of Rome" (fols. 240$^v$, 277). They are "all newe contrefaict and straunge sacrifices, devised . . . by the crafty conveyance of man through the subtile suggestion of slye Satan" (fol. 249). At best, "mumbling Massemongers . . . promise with their Massing mountaines of gold, but performe molhilles of glasse" (fol. 263); at worst, they delude men with the vain expectation of obtaining forgiveness of sins *after* death through the sacrifices and good works of others, and thus, again, lead them the "right way to hel fire" (fols. 240$^v$, 273). After such passages as these, one is not surprised to find, in the eulogy of the dead at the end of the treatise, praise of Epaphroditus for the specific virtue of having "abhorred all Sectes, Papistes, Anabaptistes, Libertins, etc." (fol. 282$^v$).

In the light of these sentiments, two other weaknesses in the devotional literature represented by the *Sicke Mannes Salve* become readily comprehensible. In their revulsion against the sacramental system of the Roman Church, the Reformers tended at first to jettison sacramentalism altogether. The faith which they retained in the efficacy of Baptism and the Eucharist was "badly attenuated," as Knappen puts it (p. 346).[31] And any sort of sacramental approach to life in general seems to have disappeared entirely. That sensitive devotional awareness of divine interpenetration in daily existence which is one of its fruits—and one of the glories of *Holy Dying*—is simply nonexistent in the Calvinistic "Crafte." Similarly, in their revulsion against late-medieval piety the Reformers tended also to repudiate Christ as a comforting

31. This generalization, which seems to me irrefutably valid for Becon's age, should not, of course, be extrapolated to encompass the entire Puritan movement, as it so often is. On the other hand, the great Puritans cited by Wakefield—those who followed Calvin in urging frequent Communions, who "had no doubt of a real presence of Christ in the Supper," who were "moved to intense rapture by the sacramental theme" (pp. 43–44, 50, 52–53)—would surely have been astonished at the inadequate treatment of this topic in *The Sicke Mannes Salve*. Whatever his positive views may be, Becon keeps them to himself, only observing in the most incidental way that a godly Christian is of course a faithful communicant. (See below, note 38.)

person immediately accessible to the devout sinner. Instead, they preached soteriology endlessly, emphasizing what God *had* wrought in Christ, and the conditions for participating in that historic transaction, and the joys of knowing oneself among the redeemed, and the damnable sinfulness of despair no matter how great the offense. There are few pages indeed in Becon's treatise which do not contain some mention of one of these four specific points; and he allots some seventeen thousand words—almost one-fourth of the entire treatise—to the subject of deathbed despair alone. Yet his Christology is forbiddingly cold. For all his assurances that the certitude of redemption is "sweet and comfortable," he communicates no sense of personal trust in, still less personal interrelationship with, a Redeemer. It is the *doctrine* of the Atonement which is to evoke an emotional response from the reader. Becon, like his fellow Reformers, is quite willing to discard, along with the sacraments, all that intimate devotion to the human Jesus and the ever-present compassionate "Lord and Friend" which warms the *Crafte*—and will warm devotional literature again.[32]

Nevertheless, we must not ignore the artistic effectiveness of Becon's impassioned attacks themselves. Certainly the vitality of such passages enlivens the work considerably, providing still

32. Wakefield argues vigorously against this "misunderstanding" of Puritan devotion to Christ (pp. 94–101, 156–60, and passim); most of his arguments, however, seem to me merely to strengthen the position he is attacking. See esp. pp. 59, 96, and 100–01 for specific instances of Puritan focus on "our *whole* redemption . . . and not some fragment"; "the *whole* work of Christ from Creation to the last day"; "the *universal* purpose of God in Christ"; the inseparability of the "human Jesus" and the "Eternal Son of the Father," whose "Heart" is "His *eternal* disposition" (all italics mine). Wakefield's own conclusion summarizes effectively the very argument I have tried to develop: "Puritan devotion, then, is Christo-centric, but Christ is always seen in His relation to God and to the Purpose of God . . . everywhere He is transcendent, and His sway is cosmic. . . . But there is no lack of ardour" (pp. 159–60). Miss White, far from "misunderstanding," actually warns against exaggerating this shift in devotional orientation, and points to the survival of such traditional prayers as the *Fifteen Oes* for evidence (chap. 13). "But in general they [the Protestant devotional writers] put their trust in the efficacy of theological reminder" (p. 226). Certainly Becon does.

another type of relief from didacticism. Just as Lupset's classical enthusiasms raise the Senecan portions of his *Waye of Dyenge Well* to a higher literary level than that attained by his traditional material, so, too, Becon's lyrical hatred of papistry expresses itself with much greater skill than most of his doctrinal convictions. Rhetorical devices are used with much greater freedom than elsewhere. Even though simple alliteration carries most of the burden of his righteous wrath, his employment of double alliteration, parallelism, climactic order, and dramatic exclamations as well can be illustrated from the quotations above. It is in such passages, too, that lively colloquialisms creep in, albeit apologetically. Even rhyme may be used, as in his discussion of the superstitious funeral customs carried over by the Church of England from Roman practices. The solemnities to be discussed he itemizes as "solempne singyng, devout ringyng, holy censyng, priests pattering, candles lightening, torches brennyng, Communions saying, and such like" (fol. 240). Even though "solemn singing" is immediately set apart, as acceptable, from the other items on the list, the rhyme which it provides starts one reading in precisely the right light tone of satirical scorn, so that we are prepared to accept his dismissal of everything else as "things superfluous and unprofitable." The most conspicuous advance of the *Sicke Mannes Salve* over the earlier treatises studied, so far as literary substance is concerned, may therefore be attributed primarily to the intensity of Becon's narrow sectarian passions. The treatise offers the reader not only an authoritative pattern of conduct and a collection of useful devotional material like the *Crafte;* not only a reflective "consideration of death" and an ars vivendi like the *Waye of Dyenge Well*—but also numerous passages, of merely tangential relevance to the argument, whose major function is to communicate emotion by means proper to art.

THE QUASI-DRAMATIC FORM

The last technique we shall consider is also the most successful in furthering the immediate aims of the treatise: the dramatic form itself. Despite its awkwardness, it does support to a notable degree Becon's appeal to both the mind and the emotions of the reader. And therefore it marks a long stride toward the goal of a form which shall be completely satisfactory for the ars moriendi.

The dialogue of the *Sicke Mannes Salve* is extremely uneven in tone, though chiefly artificial, as we should expect. At the one extreme are those long passages, incredible as speeches, which are yet wholly acceptable in terms of the formal dialogue. In this group belong, for instance, Philemon's opening meditation on the uncertainty of life (fol. 219ʳ–19ᵛ); almost all his didactic speeches; and above all Epaphroditus's dictation of his will, farewells to his household, and confession of faith (fols. 235ᵛ–40,ᵛ, 243ᵛ–46ᵛ, 246ᵛ–53ᵛ). At the other extreme are occasional brief conversational exchanges which startle us by their realism in comparison with their contexts. For example, although Philemon is usually able to quote Scripture at any length he chooses, Becon represents him at one point (fol. 229ᵛ) as unable to remember the penitential prayer of Manasses, King of Judah: "*Phil.* Is there not a Bible here? *Eus.* Here is one." Epaphroditus, too, though blessed with an awesome memory and fluidity of expression, is not infallible. In the course of dictating his will, he pauses now and then out of consideration for his scribe; but once we find a more dramatic interchange: "*Epaph.* Have ye done. *Phil.* Yea forsoth sir. *Epaph.* Let me se, what now remayneth. *Chris.* Sir, wyll it please you to remember the pore?" (fol. 236ᵛ).[33]

Between these two extremes are ranged all those passages of pseudodrama whose stiffness and psychological absurdity are sometimes irritating, sometimes amusing, but on the whole curiously appealing. The largest group in this category consists of those set pieces in which Epaphroditus as a dramatic identity is ruthlessly sacrificed to Becon's pedagogical enthusiasms.

In the first section, the dying man is identified fairly consistently with Mortal Man, who must struggle, under godly tutelage,

---

33. Similarly, his expressions of physical suffering are usually no more than punctuations of the dialogue; but his lengthy leave-taking from family and servants concludes as follows: "*Epaph.* Well, the blessyng of God be wyth you, I am very faint. *Phil.* No marvell. For ye have talked a great while" (fol. 246ᵛ). Such tidbits, however, scarcely support Bailey's contention that Becon's "conversations . . . are natural and spirited" (p. 121).

to achieve the appropriate response to illness. Because of Becon's scriptural and didactic orientation, his characterization is amusingly implausible, but no worse. Thus Epaphroditus laments even before his friends enter his room that his "memory is past" and his "senses fayle" (fol. 220), and bemoans these and other equally drastic symptoms at regular intervals until his death; yet he is from the first as unrelentingly scriptural in his speech as anyone else. Periodically, on the other hand, he is transmogrified abruptly into a biblical and doctrinal ignoramus so that Philemon may share his own encyclopedic knowledge with the reader. We find the sick man making such awkward pleas as the following: "But I pray you rehearse unto me out of the holy scripture, for the quietnes of my conscience, some histories which may declare unto me, that god punishing sinners for theyr disobedience, doth afterward whan they repent and turne, forgeve them and receyve them again into his favour" (fol. 228). And later, when Philemon asks him, reasonably enough, "Ye remember the history of the prodigall sonne, written in the Gospell of blessed Luke?", this godly Moriens whose speech is saturated with biblical quotations and allusions replies, "What is that, I pray you" (fol. 230). His other friends profit, too, from such timely mental lapses. When reminded by Christopher that "the way to enter into glory is the Crosse," he asks obligingly, "What meane you by the crosse?" (fol. 221).[34]

In the second section, Epaphroditus gives up altogether his pretense of being Everyman. Now, as a vehicle for Becon's moralistic precepts, he reveals himself as a prosperous and complacent Puritan burgher who knows better than his wife, his son, his two daughters, or his servants what their duties are to God and their

34. Christopher wastes no words on friendly naturalness in his answer: "Temporal affliccion, as penury, hunger, evyll report undeserved, persecution, enprysonement, losse of goods, sycknes, and whatsoever mortifyeth the olde man." And soon afterwards he reminds Epaphroditus that "Abel, Jacob, Joseph, Moses, David, Helyas, Zachary, Jeremy, Myche, Job, Toby, John Baptist, Stephen, Paul, James, Peter, wyth many other whych were the chosen people and frends of God, were not fre from the crosse." Such coldly precise defining of terms and careful marshaling of biblical illustrations at every point in a "conversation" does not enhance its verisimilitude.

fellowmen. Moreover, he embodies dramatically as many of the virtues he preaches as possible. As a family man, his behavior has clearly been exemplary. As a businessman, he has pursued his calling with diligence and thrift—and amassed a fair-sized fortune as a result.[35] Some of this he has already distributed among causes both patriotic and virtuous: helping young men without capital to get started in business; furthering the "studies of good wites" and hence the cause of an educated ministry;[36] and relieving the needs of "pore sainctes" (fols. 282$^v$, 236$^v$). Still more of it he earmarks in his will for these lifelong interests; and he adds a sizable amount for highway improvement—a bequest, we are told, "commendable . . . before God" (fols. 236–37). In short, his relationships to his fellowmen have, as he himself admits, left nothing to be desired: "If thou dost resemble me," he tells his son, "as in countenance and lineamentes of body: so like wise in manners and conditions of lyfe and conversation, it shall not repent me to have begotten such a sonne. . . . Take hede therfoe that thou dost not degenerate and growe out of kynd" (fol. 244$^v$). Since his confession of faith is also unexceptionable, his relationship to God is apparently no less ideal. From now on, we assume, Epaphroditus will pursue the instructive role of Puritan Saint.

In the final act, however, his dramatic identity disintegrates altogether. Now, on the very threshold of death, he is transmuted

35. His estate as he distributes it in his will amounts to well over eleven hundred pounds aside from reality and personalty. In an England of economic transition and prosperity, Epaphroditus vacillates between the accepted view of the lowly as God's poor and the emergent feeling that poverty is the deserved lot of idle lubbers. He simply assumes that his servants can increase the value of his estate if they only renounce sloth and avoid waste (fols. 237, 246).

36. Bailey reminds us that after the dissolution of the monasteries, and the schools attached to them, the sons of the "gentry and nobility" rapidly displaced those of the "small tenants and yeomen" at the universities; the study of divinity naturally fell off; and the Reformers' ideal of developing a truly learned ministry for England seemed more remote than ever (pp. 60–61). Hence there is more immediate relevance and urgency in Epaphroditus's bequest than mere generalized good will toward higher education.

abruptly into an addlepated straw man, offering all sorts of incompatible reasons for his supposed despair so that Philemon may explain the appropriate remedy for each.[37] Once again we find him acknowledging himself a sinner, repenting with faith, accepting his redemption through Christ, and thanking God for his triumph over Satan's temptation to despair (fols. 261$^v$–64). So far, so good —at least if we postulate that all his earlier declarations of penitence and faith must be reaffirmed in the fact of Satan's fiercest deathbed assaults (fol. 261$^v$). But this leaves too many doctrinal details unexplained; so the dying man confesses his fear "least than Sathan wil shortly returne unto me, and assaile me with new temptations" (fol. 264). He is afraid of being condemned by the Law; by his own sinful life; by the tardiness of his deathbed "repentaunce and conversion"; by his total lack of merits and good works; and by God's eternal reprobation (fols. 264, 265$^v$, 268, 269, 270$^v$). As a dramatic character, he has by now disgusted the reader with the transparent feebleness of his Christian convictions, not to mention the willfulness of his stupidity. Worse yet, he then proceeds to describe himself, in stiffly parallel statements of fact, as one who has been godly all his life: faithful in attendance at Holy Communion, diligent in hearing sermons, earnest in his efforts to live in accordance with God's Word, and instant in prayer (fols. 271$^v$–72). These points are introduced logically, since they constitute—together with baptism, repentance, and faith— the evident testimonies of one's election, and are therefore elicited from Epaphroditus in order to answer the last of his fears.[38] Their

37. Wakefield observes that this concern for determining one's "standing with God" was the unique Puritan contribution to the literature of casuistry—and insists that such "desire for assurance" is psychologically entirely normal for any believing Christian, not a "dangerous mental aberration" to be treated, as it is in Roman Catholic manuals, among "eccentric scruples" (pp. 124–25). Possibly so; but for some twelve folio pages out of sixty-six? The proportion does seem suggestive.

38. Dent's *Plain Man's Pathway to Heaven* (the work immortalized as one item in Mrs. Bunyan's dowry) lists *eight* "infallible tokens" of election. Curiously enough, these include *neither* baptism nor regular attendance at the Lord's Supper. On the other hand, they do suggest in a bit more detail what "efforts to live in accordance with God's Word" might entail—so

effect, however, is to make him out not only a muddle-headed weakling, but also an unconscionable hypocrite. Even though he now perseveres triumphantly to an end which wins admiring exclamations from his friends, his dramatic character has been shattered beyond repair—and with it, much of his effectiveness as a mirror.

For all its defects, however, this quasi-dramatic form contributes much to the *Sicke Mannes Salve* that is really constructive. In the first place, the very fact that it chops up the argument and slows down its development is a positive value on Becon's terms. His ear for convincing conversation may be poor, but his ear for the limits of the average reader's tolerance to pure didacticism is very keen. There are relatively few passages which tax the powers of concentration of anyone with enough interest and educational background to start the treatise at all. Normally a general topic— the purpose of illness, say—is outlined carefully, and then treated segment by segment, with some sort of dramatic transition from each point to the next.[39] The absurdities of the work as drama are thus more than counterbalanced by the enormous increase in its readability as doctrinal handbook. Given such interludes, the general reader whom Becon is addressing is far more likely to absorb the doctrinal teaching as it comes up, and hence to accept as normative the pattern of devotional behavior which the author wishes to establish. He is also far more likely to remember, and perhaps follow, rules of conduct mirrored forth in an individual case, however awkwardly dramatized, than those laid down in impersonal instruction. And, finally, he is far more likely to read prayers with close attention and appreciation when they are placed in appropriate contexts than when they are merely assembled in an anthology under general headings. Thus, for example, Becon

---

perhaps Dent is simply taking for granted that anyone concerned about his election is necessarily a baptized and communicating Christian. Token No. 1, for example, is "A love to the children of God"—a virtue scarcely mentioned by Philemon & Co. See Wakefield, pp. 126–27.

39. Becon is following, of course, the normative homiletic method of Puritan preaching.

includes only three prayers directly relevant to illness, whether mortal or not, in each of his two most famous books of prayers (*The Flower of Godly Prayers* and *The Pomander of Prayer*); but he is able to work some twenty-two such prayers into the third section alone of his quasi drama. The pedagogical value of the *Sicke Mannes Salve* is, in sum, much the greater for its more verbose, but less intellectually demanding, form.

In the second place, this form tends to increase its evangelical value as well—to challenge and motivate the healthy, as well as instruct them. Above all, it reaffirms the traditional understanding of death as existential fact rather than intellectual topic. The uncertainty of life is underscored dramatically by the unexpectedness of Epaphroditus's illness. "It is not yet two daies," Philemon exclaims,

> synce I saw my neighbour ... well and lusty, yea and in perfect health, and behold he sent unto me even now his servaunt Onesimus, that I should come unto hym, wyth all expedition, all other busynesses set a part, if I ever entend to se hym a lyve: oh good god, what a world is thys! Ah most lovyng Chryste, what a sodeyn chaunge is this! . . . Ah Lord God, not yet two dayes past whole and strong, and now sicke and weake! O the unstedfastnesse of mans life. Whom wold not this provoke to watch and to considre his latter end? [fol. 219$^r$–19$^v$]

Furthermore, the immediacy of death's challenge is not dissipated by the many abstract discussions which follow. Even as Philemon and Epaphroditus discuss the fear of death and remedies therefor in terms reminiscent of Lupset, death itself is drawing nearer.

So, too, the Puritan conviction that every moral choice is invested with cosmic and eternal significance is emphasized through dramatic illustration. Becon has already described life, in the preface (fol. 218$^v$), as "knighthede or warfar," fought "valeantly and mightly" by prayer under "our graunde captayn Christ" to triumph and "a gloryous spoile of our enemyes," the world, the flesh, and the devil. And he has praised the remembrance of the Last Things chiefly for the incentive it gives to moral behavior.[40] Now he offers us a dramatic picture of one whose sudden death is blessed and his salvation certain because he has been obedient to these principles all his life. The moral—"Go thou and do likewise"—is clear; and it has the added force of being couched in dramatic, rather than homiletic, terms. Actually, the medieval attitude toward death and the Puritan attitude toward life are in a sense but two sides of the same coin. For the Reformer's dynamism—the urgent awareness of the dramatic moral implications of his mortality—represents just such an intensification and refinement of the medieval response to death as Knappen traces in other areas of Tudor Puritan thought. The dramatic form of the *Sicke Mannes Salve* represents a crude but significant advance toward a form which shall be completely suitable for the communication of both. By involving the reader vicariously in the experience of dying, it aims at shocking him into a full—a truly Christian—response to the facts of his existence. The technique has far-reaching implications for the development of the ars moriendi.

Although the interpenetration of old and new in the *Sicke Mannes Salve* is more successful in many ways than in Lupset's *Waye of Dyenge Well*, the two are still far from fused. Both strengths and weaknesses derive ultimately from the author's ambiguous characterization of Epaphroditus—or, by extension, of the reader whom Epaphroditus is to instruct and inspire. In so far as Becon identifies his protagonist openly with a limited and definable audience of devout middle-class English Puritans, his "Crafte" enjoys the notable artistic advantages which such a restricted focus provides. His acceptance of this limitation is only intuitive and halfhearted, though; and his gains are therefore relatively few. In many respects, as we have seen, he persists in treating Epaphroditus—and hence, indirectly, the reader—as Everyman re-

40. For even a moderate Calvinist to encourage this discipline is obviously inconsistent, but Knappen's comment is pertinent: "Even tough Calvinism was bent backward when it met the irresistible force of the Puritan conscience" (p. 341).

incarnate. But Everyman simply cannot die as Everyman within the context of Calvinist theology: even in the face of death, he is not "more simply human than otherwise," in the phrase of Harry Stack Sullivan. At the very least, the pastor—and the pedagogue—must consider such basic categories of humanity as "the elect" and "the unregenerate," and provide aid for both.[41] Hence the spiritual schizophrenia of Epaphroditus, as he oscillates between the roles of Persevering Saint and Belated Penitent. Becon's attempt to preserve the universality of the devotional tradition while imposing on it this incompatible view of man is necessarily futile; but the defects and dislocations which result have important implications for the future development of the ars moriendi as a literary genre.

On the positive side, much of its content is now selected and weighted with reference to a specific audience, like that of any other literary work. Socially and economically, for instance, Becon aligns his protagonist frankly with the successful bourgeoisie, rather than mankind in general. He is therefore clearly justified in placing a new emphasis on the temptation to too much love of life. Even if the theoreticians have not yet worked out an interpretation of the doctrine of "stewardship" which is fully valid for the new age, he must do the best he can to define what it really means to be "not rich in the world, but in the lord" (fol. 235$^r$–35$^v$). As a result, we find in the *Sicke Mannes Salve* a forceful presentation of mid-century Puritan economic theory in all its inconsistency.[42]

On the one hand, Becon reaffirms eloquently the conservative tenets of the institutional Church. The world remains a "stinckyng sinck of evils," the body a "vile and wretched carcasse," and all pleasures disgustingly corruptible; life is "miserable," in short, and the faithful Christian leaves it with a "good and glad wil" (fols. 255, 280$^v$, 257, 275$^v$, 275). Furthermore, if Becon's reader doesn't see it in this way, he'd better. "It is not possible," says Philemon,

41. "The reprobate," of course, he need not worry about; and yet, since these are unidentifiable to all but God, Christians are to pray in charity for the salvation of every individual—even the Pope! (Wakefield pp. 75–76). A Calvinistic writer in particular might well assume that any reader should be approached as—sooner or later—one of the elect.

42. See Knappen, chaps. 22, 23.

"that a man may lyve here pleasantly wyth the world, and afterward reigne gloriously wyth Christ." Indeed, "it is a most certain
signe of everlasting dampnation, where a life is led without
afflictyon" (fols. 222, 226ᵛ). The tale of Dives and Lazarus is one
of his favorites. On the other hand, this otherworldly Calvinist
preaches with equal eloquence—though less explicitness—the
anomalous notion that there must be a positive correlation in
God's world between godliness and material success. In particular,
those who accept material affliction in the right spirit are promised
material as well as spiritual rewards. Philemon stresses the concrete aspects of the happy endings of his histories (such as David's
"greate honor, glory, rytches, quietnes, and al kind of wealth");
and he points the moral emphatically: "And whan so ever we
repent and cease to synne, the Lord straightwais removeth and
taketh away the crosse that he hath laid upon our backes, and
poureth his blessyng agayn plentously upon us" (fols. 222ᵛ–24,
227ᵛ). The concession which the author of the *Crafte* makes, almost
apologetically, to man's sinful need for practical motivation, Becon
refines and intensifies into an article of faith.[43] The reader may
respond to the double incentive of ascetic stick and materialistic
carrot in any proportion he chooses, depending on the state of his
soul.

On the whole, The *Sicke Mannes Salve* displays the same effectiveness in all those arguments roughly classifiable as belonging to
the ars vivendi. Directed at a homogeneous group, they merely
establish the *principles* which *ought* to govern its behavior; and
in such theoretical discussions, the individual reader's status before
God is simply irrelevant. As an exemplar of the ars moriendi, however, the treatise seeks to trace out—and to justify—a definite
*pattern* of behavior, and one which *shall* be valid for "all sorts and
conditions" of Morientes. In this regard, the individual reader's
spiritual status is obviously of crucial relevance. The new understanding of man therefore exerts its most destructive influence on
precisely those aspects of the *Sicke Mannes Salve* which are most
firmly traditional in essence: its form, its expository and devo-

43. Cf. White, p. 177; and Wright, p. 167.

tional styles, and its treatment of the death scene iself. Generally speaking, the more successfully Becon adapts the medieval tradition to the needs of the Protestant faithful, the less effective his work becomes as a truly comprehensive devotional treatise.

From any point of view, it is apparent that the ars moriendi as a devotional genre has still not found a form adequate to its potentialities. The structure of Becon's quasi drama is, as we have seen, an intensified variant of the dynamic and universal form of the quasi liturgy. If Epaphroditus could be treated analogously, as no more than an improved Moriens, the result would be a treatise whose increased dramatic values served the old devotional purposes of the *Crafte* as well as the didactic and hortatory purposes of the Reformer. But such is not the case. There is no longer any clear-cut pattern of faithful response for Everyman to follow; and to this extent Becon's argument is weakened, rather than supported, by the form he has chosen. The single line of its dramatic action is interrupted and confused by his moralistic interlude of the second section, and utterly shattered by his discussion of despair in the third. Here, not even the two roles of Godly Puritan and Frightened Worldling suffice for Epaphroditus: he must also play Devil's Advocate, and be convinced of the satanic untruth of the Roman Catholic teaching on every moot point related to death. Clearly, any single intelligible line of progression is impossible under such conditions. Rigorous (and static) analysis is of the essence here; and it is only handicapped by being presented in pseudodramatic form. The dramatic dialogue serves Becon's purposes better than the relatively sophisticated form of the moral essay, in that it makes his instruction more palatable and even stirs the lethargic to pay attention. Basically, though, it is still unsatisfactory. Its simplicity is inappropriate for any arguments more complex than authoritarian pronouncements; for any appeals—devotional or moralistic—more directly affective than generalized patterns; and for any view of man which takes account of individual differences as well as common mortality.

Becon's adoption of an expository technique which demands

nothing of the reader, intellectually or imaginatively, is one of the more unhappy by-products of his attempt to write for Everyman. Intellectually, Epaphroditus is willing, even eager, to learn, but his background is severely limited (he knows almost no Latin, for example)[44] and his mental processes rather slow. The pedagogue's determined insistence that he shall understand fully every detail of his Reformed faith has two fallacies from the point of view of devotional literature. In the first place, one corollary of instilling thorough understanding in the stupid is the boredom and alienation of the intelligent. And in the second, the heavy-handed, unembellished statement and restatement of doctrinal theses is affective only in so far as the reader is already a committed Christian, emotionally predisposed to respond to dogma itself—and Calvinist dogma at that. However efficiently instructed, the unregenerate will remain outside the pale. In either case, or both, the treatise is no longer reaching Everyman; and the more earnestly it struggles, the less likely it will be to succeed.

So, too, the prayers of the *Sicke Mannes Salve* distill the devotional spirit of Tudor Puritanism, but offer little to one not already imbued with it. The distinctive quality of this new spirituality is that of paradox. On the one hand the sixteenth-century Protestant is keenly sensitive to the reality of a righteous God: that is, he encounters God at every turn—a God who confronts him in glory and condemns him in truth. And in this light, Puritan prayer is indeed communion with God more personal than Lupset ever dreamed of. On the other hand, and simultaneously, the instructional prayers discussed above suggest the tendencies of Reformed devotion toward doctrinaire impersonality. The key to the paradox seems to lie in the very unbridgeableness of the gulf between God and man. So depraved is man, so wholly other is God, that— metaphorically speaking—only doctrine can truly heal the breach. Certainly not Jesus of Nazareth; to a lesser degree, not even the living Christ. The early Calvinist depends on the total complex of

---

44. Only three quotations are given in Latin, all three extremely simple, and all translated promptly (fols. 242, 252ᵛ).

Christological dogma for his reconciliation with his Creator.[45] And his prayers therefore take their rise in doctrine, since God would be overwhelmingly unapproachable otherwise; they dwell on doctrine, since right belief is in soberest truth "saving health" —and they express and evoke emotion only to the extent that the worshiper can himself enter into this intense relationship with the abstract formulations of the Christian faith.[46]

It is the *Sicke Mannes Salve* at its best, artistically speaking, which reveals most clearly the far-reaching significance of Epaphroditus's split personality for the future of the ars moriendi as a devotional genre. And that best is indubitably the traditional death scene which climaxes Becon's quasi drama. The rest of the treatise, as we have seen, consists of an imperfect fusion of just two elements, medieval tradition and Reformed dogma. When we turn to the discussion of dying itself—to the material which constitutes the hard core of the tradition—the contrast is striking. Here old and new are amalgamated much more successfully; and the old now includes the humanistic tradition as well as the Christian. Medieval notions and attitudes, that is, have been intensified in some respects by those of the humanists, and *both* purified in accordance with the doctrine of the Reformation. Moreover, this portion of the work evinces a harmony of thought and tone which goes far beyond that of Lupset's few effective passages. Here Epaphroditus is really abstracted and universalized just as far as is doctrinally possible. Here, too, Philemon's lectures do fuse, as they do not elsewhere, all the available thought of the age into a truly

45. Cf. Philemon's exclamation: "God graunt us the *true knowledge* of hys sonne Christ, so may we be sure to be justified, saved and glorified" (fol. 251, italics mine). Wakefield's explanation is helpful: contrition and confession (and thence forgiveness and reconciliation) arise precisely from "adoration, and [from] the consciousness of the infinite gulf between God and man. 'Nothing', says Owen, in his *Sacramental Discourses,* so much 'brings God and man together as a due sense of our infinite distance'" (pp. 73–74).

46. Cf. Epaphroditus's cry: "God be praised for that true joy and singular comfort, which the faithful find *in his holy word"* (fol. 279, italics mine).

integrated Christian whole. Yet even here, the Calvinist view of
man not only complicates the argument and destroys its universality, but also vitiates its essential purpose of "comforting" the
dying—in the traditional, unsentimental sense of that corrupted
word.

The traditional framework of Becon's teaching on death is
strong and clear. Death is to be seen as the "departure" of the
"pilgrim" from this "vale of miserye" (fols. 257, 282$^v$, 255$^v$) to
Judgment and an eternity of bliss or torment (fols. 250$^v$, 253,
255$^v$-57$^v$, and passim). Dying itself is agonizingly painful (fols.
263, 275$^v$, 276), not only physically but spiritually, since it includes
a crucial battle (fols. 272, 281$^v$) to resist the "horrible assauts and
temtacions" of Satan (fol. 261$^v$), who then is "most busy," laboring
"unto the uttermost of hys power" with the aid of "al the infernal
army" to win man's soul for hell (fols. 263$^v$, 260$^v$, 261$^v$). Nevertheless, the true Christian, while meditating often upon these Last
Things for the good of his soul (fols. 217$^v$, 219$^r$-19$^v$), does not
dread death as "fearfull and terrible," but rather anticipates it as
"pleasaunte and amiable" (fol. 256). For, the "extreme agony and
conflicte" once over (fol. 280$^v$), he shall have exchanged

> lead for sylver, copper for gold, transytory mortal and cor-
> ruptible things for certen, immortal, and uncorruptible thing
> [*sic*], earth for heaven, sinne for godlines, darknes for light,
> fear for security, travel for quietnes, sicknes for helth, death
> for life, the company of men for the company of the most hie
> God, his heavenly angels and blessed spirits, the vyle pleasures
> of this world, for the inestimable joys of the glorious kyng-
> dom of God. [fol. 279$^r$-79$^v$]

To "make a good death" as a final expression of his faith is
therefore a spiritual duty[47] which the Christian has strong incentives for performing. Moreover, he is supported in "these extreame
necessities" by friends, by angels, and by Christ himself. The
friends supply godly aids, including "comfortable histories," to

47. Fols. 218$^v$, 256, 257. Becon calls it a "Christen and godly end" (fol.
282$^v$) or a "blessed end" (fols. 223, 224).

strengthen him in temptation; interrogate him not only to ascertain his faithfulness but also to encourage it (fols. 276–77ᵛ); and pray for him continuously.[48] The angels pitch their tents in his chamber and defend him from the "hellish army" (fol. 281ʳ–81ᵛ). And, above all, the contemplation of Christ provides that assurance of God's forgiveness and acceptance of the sinner without which he would surely despair and fall prey to Satan's "devouringe teth" (fols. 261, 281ᵛ–82). Indeed, God's saving grace in Christ is assured him, no matter how grievous his previous sinfulness, just so that his conversion be "accompanied with true repentaunce and unfained faith" (fol. 268ᵛ). In sum, we find in the *Sicke Mannes Salve* the same basic approach to death as in the *Crafte:* a similar *descriptio mortis;* a similar approval of the spiritual discipline of meditation on the Last Things; a similar assumption that a given technique of dying is universally valid; and, above all, a similar pastoral orientation.

In so far as humanistic notions about death may be fitted smoothly into this traditional framework, they are. Becon's blending of the classical tradition with the Christian in this instance is the more significant because humanistic influences are in all other respects general or indirect. the dialogue form, validated by scriptural usage; the use of illustrative histories and occasional spurts of rhetorical eloquence; the ideal of solid argumentation; and the suggestion of the humanistic doctrine of reasoned virtue which lurks in the Puritan emphasis on the necessity for understanding the faith. Direct echoes of classical culture are virtually nonexistent in the first two sections, except for a rare hint that playing the *man* might be in itself a value, though not an extremely important one.[49] Yet the third section of the treatise finds humanistic thought supporting medieval doctrine in just that role of easy subordination which Lupset sought in vain to assign to it.

48. The dying man is presumed to be more grateful than Moriens: "one faithful preacher," he says, "which is able with the swete promises of the holy scriptures to comfort the weake and desperate conscience is better than ten thousand mumbling Massemongers . . . yet chiflye in the time of sickenesse."

49. See, for example, fol. 220.

The hackneyed medieval metaphors for death are now joined
by the classical image of the quiet haven after the dangerous voyage;[50] and the inevitability of death is now underscored with the
familiar Senecan reminder that "so sone as we be borne, so sone
begin we to die. This our life is nothing els then a very passage
unto death" (fol. 254ᵛ). Becon follows Lupset rather than *traditio*
in asserting confidently that the "bitter agony" of death is actually
but "a little and short paine"—and in any case far lighter than
those "intollerable paynes" and "grevous torments" suffered by
the prophets, the apostles, and the martyrs for Christ's sake (fols.
256ᵛ–57). Like Lupset, too, the Puritan considers the remembrance of the Last Things spiritually valuable largely for its incentive to moral effort; and he, too, reiterates vehemently that "of a
good lyfe commeth a good death" (fols. 219, 282ᵛ; see also 218ᵛ,
224). Nonetheless—again like the humanist—he faces somewhat
more realistically than the author of the *Crafte* the intrinsic fearfulness of death, and stresses the Senecan argument from necessity,
though in a Christian form (fols. 254ᵛ–56ᵛ). The traditional reminder of man's necessary mortality through Adam is first strengthened by a paraphrase of Seneca and an adaptation of the *ubi sunt*
motif:

> There shall none other thing chaunce unto us by death, than
> that hath hearetofore chaunced unto our predecessours, and
> shal likewise chaunce unto our posterity. Who hath lived,
> that hath not died? . . . All the holy Patriarches, Judges, Kings,
> Priestes, Prophets, and al other which lived before the com-
> ming of Christ, died. Jhon Baptist, Christes mother, and all
> the Disciples of Christ dyed. Yea, christ him self . . . suffred
> death. [fol. 254ᵛ]

The inference is clear: "It is naturall to dye, whi then labour we
to degenerate and growe out of kind? Our auncestours the most
holy and most perfect have dyed, why disdayne we then to folow
their stepes?" Why "beare so impaciently thys comon chaunce?"

50. Fols. 237ᵛ, 280. See also fol. 255ᵛ, where Becon gives a whole series
of images from the *De Senectute* which parallel Christian ones.

Moreover, this rather cool Stoic sentiment gains in forcefulness in its own turn by being subsumed under the Christian motif of *imitatio Christi:* "Is the servaunt greater than his Lord? Or the disciple above his master? Our Lorde hath troden the way afore us. . . . Our master hath geven us an example to die." Also, sheer *necessity* gains in meaning when interpreted as the "good plesure" of a loving God. In trusting submission to his (personal) will, rather than in Stoic acquiescence to Fate's impersonal decree, is our peace. And yet, in spite of all this subordination of Stoic *apatheia* to Christian certitude, Becon's final expression of assurance is realistically muted: "Whoever is a true Christian . . . shall not *greatly* be afraid of death; but he shall rather triumph over death" (italics mine).

Even the discussion of the deathbed struggle itself exhibits humanistic influences. Lupset's virtue of "lusty courage" is again specified as a spiritual prerequisite for dying well (fols. 255$^v$, 256$^v$) ——but now made to fit smoothly into the medieval interpretation of the experience of dying. More interesting is the extension of the temptation to avarice to include "thought taking for departing from frends" (fols. 257$^v$–59$^v$). Philemon's first remedy against this is to remind Epaphroditus with conventional pessimism of the inconstancy of worldly friendship—i.e. to contradict flatly, by implication, the classical exaltation of this relationship. Interestingly enough, though, the sick man is not, in this particular instance, so tractable as usual. He continues to protest as if Philemon's instruction had made no impression at all: "But I shal nevermore se them, nor have the company of them, that we may rejoyse and be glad again together." His mentor's second remedy —that all true Christian friends shall be reunited in heaven—is amplified at far greater length than his first, and with a rhetorical eloquence which suggests far more fervent conviction. Eusebius is even allowed to quote pertinent remarks of Cato the elder and Socrates (as they are found in, respectively, the *De Senectute* and the *Tusculanae disputationes*).

Both medieval and humanistic thought are not only worked in smoothly with Reformation theology, but also informed with its spirit. Considered individually, the arguments which result seem genuinely fused. Becon's treatment of death's intrinsic fearfulness is characteristically effective. On the one hand, his use of classical materials enables him to communicate more forcefully man's ineluctable bondage to death. On the other, this very emphasis on death's frightfulness tends to underscore his teaching on the all-sufficiency of Christian faith: a faith which can meet *this* challenge, one feels, is a faith to be reckoned with. More simply, the "ethnicks" are called on to enhance his own (purified) description of that other world to which death is the passage. Their suggestions that death may be itself ultimate are of course unusable; but their more hopeful descriptions of a possible afterlife support directly his "comfortable" rejection of purgatory and his assurance to the elect of their immediate reception into paradise (fol. 255$^r$–55$^v$).

Still a third way of handling the classical tradition is to modify it radically whenever necessary to bring a specific insight into line with Calvinist doctrine. This technique is well represented in Becon's adaptation of the Stoic encouragement of *memento mori*. Lupset considers the renewed emphasis on moral living which it inspires a step in the right direction because it enables the good man to work out his own salvation without excessive fear and trembling. The tone of the humanist's discussion is therefore cheerful and encouraging. Becon, too, considers it a step in the right direction—but now interpreted as one which forces every man, however good, to recognize his inability to work out his own salvation, and hence leads him to acknowledge his dependence on God's saving grace alone. The tone of the Churchman's discussion is therefore penitential and admonitory.[51] In all three cases, then, classical notions, images, and attitudes are incorporated freely into Becon's own thought, but definitely subsumed under his theological convictions.

51. Cf. The theme of the funeral sermon for which Epaphroditus leaves ten shillings in his will: "a Sermon, wherein the people may be admonished of their mortality, and be taught, how they ought to dispose them selves in this life, that when the time come, they may yeld up a good soule into the hands of the living God" (fol. 237).

In much the same way, he makes full use of medieval material on the actual deathbed agony, but adapts it freely to his own interpretation of Moriens's needs. Accepting the notion of a universally effectual technique of dying "unto salvation," he denounces in vehement polemic the inclusion in that technique of funeral rites and other post mortem works of intercession justified by the doctrine of purgatory (fols. 240–43). He also realigns the forces supporting Moriens. Friends become immeasurably more important because they represent the true Church; supernatural intervention is minimized, but Christ's readiness to save even more heavily stressed; and all sacramental help is rejected in favor of the all-sufficiently of "faith... prayer, and... the word of God" alone (fols. 268–69, 279$^v$–82$^v$, 260$^v$). Lastly, his handling of the temptations themselves is similarly modified. The temptation to spiritual pride, inconceivable to the good Protestant, does not even merit his attention. The temptations to worldliness and despair, on the other hand, merit very close attention indeed. And the temptation to fear of death itself—now a truly formidable weapon of Satan—must be remedied with almost equal care. Hence Philemon refutes formally the proposition that "death is terrible and fearful" (fol. 256); and the friends interrogate Epaphroditus at length (fols. 276–78$^v$) to underscore his faith in the unconsciousness of the body in the grave, the instantaneous departure of the soul to glory, and the ultimate resurrection of the body in a "far better state" (fol. 253)—"immortal, uncorruptible, whole, stronge, precious, and in all poyntes lyke to the gloryous body of our Lord and Savioure Chryst Jesus."

Underlying all these modifications and adaptations of traditional material, both classical and medieval, is a basic orientation very close to that of the *Crafte*. Becon, too, would instill in his reader a pious trustfulness strong enough to carry him triumphantly through the naturally fearful experience of death to the "unspeakable joys" of everlasting life. And in many respects the author's Calvinism does refine and intensify medieval doctrine in such a way as to further this aim. The doctrines of election, of salvation by faith alone, of the priesthood of all believers, of the perseverance of the saints—these, together with the rejection of purgatory, are indeed "comfortable" teachings to anyone certain of his own faithfulness. For the dying Christian may then face life's final challenge with an apostolic assurance that his victory is certain, and that his imminent departure will be "unto glory."

Nevertheless, it is precisely this pastoral aim of reassurance and support which the *Sicke Mannes Salve* fails to realize. Even as it solves for some readers some of the problems posed by death, it is creating new ones for many others. Becon's view of man, like Lupset's, simply does not allow for the total fusion of the varied elements with which he must work. The essence of his dilemma as a pastor lies in the fact that the fear of his parishioners now takes its rise in his "comfortable" doctrines themselves, instead of in aberrations or corruptions of those doctrines, as in the fifteenth century. In the absence of any doctrine of purgatory, the drama of the death scene is now invested with literally eternal significance, and its emotional intensity therefore much increased. This pitch of intensity is raised still further by the minimizing of heavenly intervention, and the repudiation of all sacramental help, *in extremis,* so that the burden of responsibility for the Protestant's eternal destiny rests squarely on the human participants in the drama. It is small wonder that accounts of "good" and "bad" deaths make up a considerable proportion of Puritan literature of the sixteenth and seventeenth centuries.

Now, then, what of the protagonist of this drama? If he is in truth confident of his election, all is well, as shown above. If he has any doubts whatever, for any reasons whatever, in any degree whatever, his spiritual situation—not to mention his emotional state—is well-nigh desperate. Doubt is, we are told emphatically, damnable (fols. 273–74). Now the selfsame "comfortable" doctrines assure him that his defeat is certain, and hell his eternally predestined home. An individual trapped in this downward spiral toward despair and consequent damnation[52] may be able to break

52. Philemon traces the sequence explicitly in one of his attacks on Roman Catholicism: "Is this [the teaching that men should doubt their salvability] any other thing then to say, despair, dye, be dampned? o devils incarnat" (fol. 274).

out of it with the aid of remedies directed to his personal needs: that is, he may be induced to recognize a particular proof of his own election, or moved to a genuine repentance for the sin of doubt—and thus be led to an assurance of reconciliation. But the Everyman to whom Becon addresses himself cannot be merely argued either into "harty and unfained repentance" or into "mighty and strong faith," no matter how often and how convincingly he is told that without them "none can be saved" (fols. 255$^v$–56$^v$). Indeed, the more earnestly the author strives to protect his godly reader from unwarranted fears inspired by Satan, the more likely he is to frighten the troubled and uncertain. He expands his list of the "sure tokens" of election, for example; or he dwells on those "certain swete mocions of true and inward joy" which accompany the recognition that God has indeed saved one in spite of his own total depravity (fol. 263$^v$). Simultaneously, the man unblessed by a conversion experience and unsupported by a plethora of good works finds himself implicitly condemned, and his sense of alienation from God thereby intensified.

In sum, the *Sicke Mannes Salve* necessarily fails to communicate pastoral comfort to Everyman—just as it necessarily fails to achieve unity and coherence—simply because of its rigidly dichotomous view of man. For the Calvinist saint, such a treatise exorcises both natural fears and those inherited from fifteenth-century superstition; and it inspires renewed devotional and moral efforts by means of doctrinal instruction which is itself, as we have seen, affective. For the Calvinist sinner, on the contrary—possibly elect, possibly reprobate, but in any case troubled in mind and spirit—such a devotional aid may well do more harm than good. Certainly a generalized authoritarian treatise of instruction can no more answer the spiritual needs of both groups effectively than could an authoritarian conduct-book worked out on such principles.

The further development of the genre of the ars moriendi depends, therefore, upon men's healing the dislocations created by the Reformers' lopsided emphases on man's depravity as against his capacity for response to grace; and on his duty to understand as against his need to feel. For the first, devotional writers will either reject Calvinism's radical doctrines of total depravity and irresistible grace altogether, in favor of a somewhat less gloomy view of man; or they will accept them, but seek new and distinct ways of comforting the weak and reaching the unregenerate. As for the second, they will come to adopt once more a fully pastoral orientation in their work, renouncing polemics as the essential lines of Protestant theology gradually become established. Concentrating less energy on instruction and disputation, they will be free to expend more on developing the affective elements in Christian faith and devotion.

## CHAPTER 4

## Parsons, Bunny, and the Counter-Reformation "Crafte"

The development of the English ars moriendi moved into its final stage in the last quarter of the sixteenth century, as soon as the Counter-Reformation made its influence felt on English devotional literature in general. By this time the practice of methodical religious meditation had become an important spiritual discipline for Roman Catholics on the Continent, as Jesuit reformers and missionaries administered the *Spiritual Exercises* of St. Ignatius to believers wherever they went, and preached the religious duty and value of regular meditation of the same type. Continental devotional literature was therefore flourishing vigorously in response to the popular demand for guidance along the lines of the precise but flexible system developed by Ignatius.[1] Protestant England received the impact of this vital devotional and literary movement both directly and indirectly: directly, through the underground activities of the Jesuit missionaries, and indirectly, through the cordial reception accorded such continental works by Protestant leaders.[2] In these treatises they found just those affective elements

1. Between 1522 and 1541; the Society of Jesus was approved by the Pope in 1540, the *Exercises* in 1548. For the historical background the underlying principles, and the general procedure of Ignatian meditation, see Louis L. Martz, *The Poetry of Meditation*, pp. 4–10, 13–20, 25–38, 46–47, 112–15. See also John R. Roberts's useful introduction to *A Critical Anthology of English Recusant Prose, 1558–1603*, Duquesne Studies, Philological Series, esp. pp. 21–28. For specific reference to the *Exercises* themselves, the edition used in this study is St. Ignatius Loyola, *The Text of the Spiritual Exercises of St. Ignatius,* trans. John Morris, 4th ed.

2. See Helen C. White, *English Devotional Literature [Prose], 1600–1640,* University of Wisconsin Studies in Language and Literature 29, chaps. 4–6. For an intensive study of the significance of this movement for English religious poetry from Southwell to Vaughan, see Martz, *Poetry of Meditation.*

most conspicuously lacking in comparable Protestant works. Here, then, was the solution to the major Calvinist problem outlined in the preceding chapter: how to inculcate in the unregenerate an emotional predisposition to respond to that doctrinal instruction which the godly found so moving in itself. The first generation of Protestants had managed to preserve the devotional classics by purifying them quietly of distinctively Romish teaching; now the same technique was applied to contemporary Catholic works of recognized merit. "Purged" of "wrong belief," they were circulated just as eagerly among Protestant flocks as the originals were among Catholic cells.

The *locus classicus* of this form of enthusiastic plagiarism is the celebrated work known as "Bunny's *Resolution*" (1584),[3] remembered today less for its enormous popularity at the turn of the century than for its decisive impact on one reader, Richard Baxter.[4] This is a Calvinistic adaptation by the Rev. Mr. Edmund Bunny— sometime itinerant evangelist, at this time chaplain to Edwin Sandys, the Archbishop of York, and a minor theological writer (1540–1619)—of *The First Booke of the Christian Exercise,*

3. The edition used for this study is R[obert] P[arsons], *A Booke of Christian Exercise Appertaining to Resolution,* "perused" by Edmund Bunny. I have expanded abbreviations; adjusted the long *s, u* and *v, i* and *j* to conform to modern usage; and omitted the italicization of biblical quotations and paraphrases.

4. "a poor Day-Labourer in the Town . . . had an old torn Book which he lent my Father, which was called *Bunny's Resolution* (being written by *Parsons* the Jesuit, and corrected by *Edm. Bunny.* . . . And in the reading of this Book (when I was about Fifteen years of Age) it pleased God to awaken my Soul." Richard Baxter, *Reliquae Baxterianae: or, Mr. Richard Baxter's Narrative of his Life and Times,* p. 3.

Somewhat less familiar, perhaps—and a good deal less convincing—is Robert Greene's attribution of his own "deathbed repentance" (in 1592) to a work which he refers to only as the *Booke of Resolution,"* although the context identifies it clearly as Bunny's Protsetant version; see "The Repentance of Robert Greene," in *The Life and Complete Works . . . of Robert Greene,* ed. Alexander B. Grosart, Huth Library Series, 15 vols., 12: 165–70. See also John Driscoll, S.J., "Robert Persons' *Book of Resolution:* A Bibliographical and Literary Study" (Ph.D. diss., Yale University, 1957), p. 7.

*appertayning to resolution,* a small volume published in 1582 by the famous Jesuit Robert Parsons.[5] The Catholic original, designed ostensibly for English Christians of all religious persuasions,[6] was to be the first of three books "containinge . . . what so ever is necessarie to a Christian after he hathe once receaved the faithe" (p. 8). Having persuaded the "Christian by name, to become a trewe Christian in deed, at the leaste, in resolution of mynde" (p. 11), the author would then teach him how "to begynne a right," and how "to persevere unto the ende" (p. [ii]). This comprehensive project however, he never carried out. Instead, he became embroiled in feuding with Bunny over what he termed the latter's "foule and false dealing" with Book I,[7] and in issuing a revised edition thereof which would be more clearly distinguishable from the "punished and plumed" Calvinist version.[8]

What is of particular interest for our study is the fact that Bunny's revisions are, almost without exception, doctrinal *only*[9]

5. *The First Booke of the Christian Exercise, appertayning to resolution.* Unless otherwise noted, all subsequent references to Parsons's work are to this edition. I have expanded abbreviations; adjusted the long *s, u* and *v, i* and *j* to conform to modern usage; and omitted the italicization of biblical material.

6. Parsons's preface "To the Christian Reader" pleads with some fervor for a mutual effort by all Christians to lay aside "all hatred, malice and wrathfull contention," and to "joyne together in amendment of our lyves, and prayeng one for an other" (p. 4).

7. This phrase is incorporated in the subtitle of Parsons's preface to a second, much enlarged edition of the *First Booke of . . . resolution,* now entitled *A Christian Directorie Guiding Men to their Salvation.* This preface will be referred to hereafter simply as Preface, 1585.

8. Preface, 1585, fol. 5. Also, of course, he became increasingly preoccupied by, and involved in, plans for the invasion of England. For a temperate and judicious account of Parsons's career, see John E. Parish, "Robert Parsons and the English Counter-Reformation," Monograph in English History, *Rice University Studies* 52 (Winter, 1966). For a briefer, informal study see Denis Meadows's apologia for Parsons in *Elizabethan Quintet.* In the same vein is Evelyn Waugh's *Edmund Campion.*

9. He does indeed, as Robert McNulty points out in "The Protestant Version of Robert Parsons' *The First Booke of the Christian Exercise,*" *HLQ* 22(1959):294, tend to "improve" Parsons's diction and phraseology from time to time; but not in the passages relevant to this study.

—and, with but few exceptions, as unobtrusive as possible.[10] Far
from displaying that virulent, all-pervasive hostility to papistry
in and of itself which characterized mid-century Reformers such
as Becon, he joins "R. P."[11] in deploring the extent to which
incessant controversy has undermined the spirit of devotion and
the practical service of God, and in pleading that all Christians
lay aside malicious contentiousness and join together in amendment of life and mutual intercession. Indeed, he goes so far as to
commend this work to Protestants not merely for its "good perswasion to godlines of life," but specifically—and especially—
because it comes from their "greatest adversaries . . . in the cause
of religion."[12] A close examination of the two versions of those
passages which employ traditional deathbed themes will therefore serve a double purpose. Parsons's use of his conventional material exemplifies, in a small and tentative way, the influence of the
Ignatian method of religious meditation on Catholic devotional
literature. And Bunny's handling of those pages illustrates vividly
the way in which this influence was promptly made available to
English Protestants as well: through adaptations which preserved
—and now and then, as we shall see, actually enhanced—the new
formal, imaginative, and affective elements in Counter-Reformation literature even as they censored its doctrinal content. The impact of this process upon the ars moriendi was to provide it at last

10. Cf. Bunny, "Preface to the Reader," p. [vii], quoted in part below.
McNulty emphasizes this point, arguing that "there is no attempt to steal
Parsons' glory or even the prayers of his readers" (pp. 275–76). Fr. John
Driscoll, S.J., per contra, notes that the "unacknowledged changes far out-
number the marginal notes and contain significant revisions"; see "The
Seconde Parte: Another Protestant Version of Robert Persons' Christian
Directorie," HLQ 25(1962):139 n. 1. True—and understandable: "Insofar
. . . as Parsons intended The Resolution as a missionary work for Roman
Catholicism, Bunny deliberately inverted that intention" (McNulty, p. 276).
The editorial procedure was common throughout the period; see Helen C.
White, Tudor Books of Private Devotion, passim.

11. Bunny professes not to know the identity of "R. P." See his
"Preface to the Reader," fol. 5$^v$.

12. Ibid., fols. 7$^r$, 7$^v$.

with a structure ideally suited to its purposes, and to complete its transmutation from pious tract to literary genre.[13]

Parsons's original intention, as he explains in his "Advertisement to the Reader" (pp. [iii–iv]), was merely to issue a second and expanded English edition of a continental devotional treatise of the Ignatian type: Gasper Loarte's *Essercitatio della Vita Christiana,* originally translated in 1579 by "James Sancer," but now out of print.[14] Finding, however, that the new material which he had contributed did not fit well with his fellow Jesuit's, he decided to issue it independently. The two books to follow, he assures us, will incorporate the work of Loarte and others into his own scheme of organization; this one is entirely his own.[15] The incompatibility between the *First Booke of . . . resolution* and Loarte's work which Parsons so justly observed is of the utmost significance. It stems from the fact that the earlier treatise is an authentic handbook for the devout, while the intended supplement is an evangelistic appeal to the comparatively indifferent. The former offers, therefore, practical materials and suggestions for systematic meditation, in a straightforward, useful manner; the latter employs the same materials and techniques *indirectly,* as literary tools for the furthering of its own purposes. The projected sequels will be reconcilable to Loarte in content and tone because they, too, will be addressed to committed Christians; but Parsons sees, as Becon did not, that the uncommitted and the halfhearted must be approached in another way. Hence a comparison of the use of traditional death-

13. The *STC* lists some forty eds. of the *Booke of . . . Resolution* (or parts thereof), including both Roman Catholic and Protestant versions. For a full bibliographic listing of Parsons's English works, see A. F. Allison and D. M. Rogers, *A Catalogue of Catholic Books in English . . . 1558–1640,* pt. 2, entries 611–42. Allison and Rogers correct and supplement the *STC* listings of Recusant publications, but explicitly disclaim any definitiveness for their own survey of these elusive works.

14. The edition used for this study is Gaspar Loarte, *The Exercise of a Christian Life,* trans. Stephen Brinkley [James Sancer]. I have expanded abbreviations. Brinkley, the "production manager, technical expert, and personnel chief" of the Jesuits' underground press in England, later helped Parsons in France with his *Christian Directorie.* (Meadows, pp. 135, 146).

15. Cf. Preface, 1585, fols. 5$^v$–6.

bed material made by the two Jesuits, Loarte and Parsons, will elucidate the beginnings of the process by which a specifically devotional technique came to contribute richly to the artistic equipment of seventeenth-century religious writers.

Loarte, an experienced spiritual director,[16] states explicitly that his treatise is intended for all committed Christians, whether "better learned" or of the "simpler sort,"[17] who wish to lead truly Christian lives, and who are therefore in need of one compact treatise containing all the "principal exercises which every Christian man is bound to use."[18] However, the very comprehensiveness of his survey, as well as the simplicity and clarity of his treatment of each topic, suggests that his "little labour" was indeed "principally framed for the . . . more ignorant sort" (p. 295), whether this slightly inconsistent comment near the end of the treatise be his or his translator's. In a directive tone of kindly but firm pastoral authority, he instructs the devout reader in the correct technique for virtually every religious practice of the Christian life which is in any sense "private,"[19] and therefore a "spiritual exercise."[20] The meditation on death with which we are exclusively concerned in this study is thus only one "direction" in a rather elaborate spiritual conduct-book for the pious.

16. Parsons, "To the Christian Reader," p. 1. Somewhat surprisingly, perhaps, there is evidence that Fr. Parsons himself had real "gifts of tenderness and wisdom as a director of souls" (Meadows, p. 113; see also pp. xiii–xiv).

17. Table of Contents, title of chap. 10.

18. "The Authour to the devout Reader," p. [v].

19. The treatise sets forth the correct sacramental and practical procedure for entering upon his new, Christian life; outlines the spiritual exercises which he should use both daily and on holy days; explains the nature and value of "mental prayer," and provides him with directions for meditating on all the accepted, standard topics; discusses the sacraments of Penance and Communion, and the value of receiving them frequently; and concludes by warning him of the temptations which beset those who attempt to lead a spiritual life, and suggesting the proper remedies against them.

20. St. Ignatius defines a spiritual exercise as "any method of preparing and disposing the soul to free itself from all inordinate affections, and after it has freed itself from them, to seek and find the will of God concerning the ordering of life for the salvation of one's soul" (p. 1).

More specifically, it constitutes one meditation in a sequence of seven (a "week")[21] on sin, death, and Judgment—the "purgative" sequence which St. Ignatius recommends particularly for those "of limited understanding and naturally of little capacity" (p. 9). In his own series, however, Ignatius omits all the Last Things but hell, remarking only in passing on the value of "calling to mind death and judgment" in general (p. 30). The meditation supplied by Loarte (pp. 83–86) is nevertheless fully as Ignatian in spirit and execution as the immediately derivative meditation on hell which follows two "days" later.[22] The exercitant first prepares himself reverently for meditation, in accordance with general instructions given at the beginning of this section of the treatise (chap. 6). He then prepares himself imaginatively, according to the Ignatian principle of the "composition of place"—of seeing with "the eyes of the imagination the corporeal place where the thing I wish to contemplate is found."[23] Loarte's directions are analogous, though less vivid: one should meditate on death, he says, "even as though that houre were nowe arrived. Imagining therefore it is so, and howe thou art nowe come to that latter time of so great feare and grief, discourse upon these articles folowing."[24] "These articles" consist, as is customary, of a precise number of points—in this instance, the most popular number of three: "First

21. The Ignatian scheme organizes the individual meditations into four "weeks," consisting ideally of five exercises daily; but great flexibility is permitted in the chronological interpretation of a "week." Loarte, writing specifically for those occupied with mundane affairs, sets his sights lower, at one or two exercises daily, but is somewhat more rigid in his system.

22. Loarte's "week" is divided as follows: on Monday, the subject for meditation is past sins; on Tuesday, present sins; on Wednesday, death; on Thursday, Judgment; on Friday, hell; on Saturday, heaven; and on Sunday, the exercitant's gratitude to God.

23. St. Ignatius, p. 20.

24. An earlier description of the technique he advocates reveals more explicitly its Ignatian nature: the details of the Passion "are in suche wise to be meditated, as though they happed even in that instant before thine eyes, in the selfe same place where thou art, or within thy soule: or otherwise imagining thou wert in the very places where suche thinges happed, if haply this waies thou shalt feele better devotion" (p. 67).

.... Consider secondly .... Thirdly thinke ...."[25] The meditation ends as the exercitant draws three "right profitable lessons," and gains new incentive to live now as he will wish to have lived when he comes in fact to die.

The two departures from the precise schemes laid out in the *Spiritual Exercises* are noteworthy: the elimination of the second preparatory prayer between the composition of place and the meditation proper, and the substitution of a concluding moral exhortation for the recommended colloquy with the crucified Christ. The first omission simplifies the mechanics of the exercise, and thus helps the beginner to maintain his concentration on the imagined scene, whatever it may be. The second modification is more suggestive, since Loarte does, in another instance, direct the exercitant to complete his meditation with a prayer to Christ which is, in effect, a colloquy: "Being then stirred up with . . . considerations [of past sins], and moved with compunction . . . prostrate thy selfe at our Saviour's feete . . . and with great sorowe and humilitie pray him to pardon thee those . . . abhominations which thou haste committed" (pp. 79–80). Assuming that the exercitant were indeed moved with compunction, his prayer would probably conform instinctively to Ignatius's description of a colloquy as informal in style, "made properly as one friend speaks to another, or as a servant to his master" (p. 23). In the meditation on death, however, such a devotional response—which issues only indirectly in moral action—gives way to one directly moralistic. Like Lupset and Becon, Loarte encourages the discipline of *memento mori* primarily because it is "a very profitable thing to eschewe sinne" (pp. 83–84). Partly for this reason, this meditation lends itself more readily than others in the series to direct adaptation by Parsons.

In spite of this minor deviation from the Ignatian formula, the

25. In his treatise on *How to meditate the Misteries of the Rosarie,* [trans. John Fen], Loarte explains his preference for three as deriving from "the perfection and devotion of this number, as also, that each one may meditate them more amply, and with less confusion." Quoted by Louis L. Martz, "John Donne in Meditation: The Anniversaries," *ELH* 14 (1947): 251.

meditation remains faithful to its spirit and purpose. The devotional exercise, as worked out by St. Ignatius, seeks not only to instill in the exercitant a clear intellectual understanding of the real nature and value of anything in the light of God's truth, but also to excite in him an emotional response to this particular truth intense enough so that he will be moved to live out its implications. For "it is not to know much," writes St. Ignatius, "but it is to understand and savor the matter interiorly that fills and satisfies the soul" (p. 2). And spiritual exercises in general, according to Loarte, are the means whereby the soul grows "more zealous and fervent in the love of God, with newe purposes and inflamed desires [to know and to serve him]" (pp. 29–30). Meditation, in particular, is a "savourie and fruitful" exercise (p. 34).

The specific "spiritual motion" which the purgative sequence of meditations seeks to arouse is that of "confusion for sins." The exercitant applies his senses, memory, understanding, and will to the consideration of sin, death, and Judgment "in order to put [himself] to the blush, and to be confounded."26 Thus, in meditating on death under Loarte's direction, he does not merely remind himself on an intellectual level that life is short and uncertain; that worldly possessions are valueless in the light of eternity; and that the agony of dying will be much eased if through a good life he shall have earned the friendly succor of Christ, Mary, saints, and angels in that crisis, and the right to hope for eternal salvation. Such specific truths are not assumed to be in themselves affective, as they were by Becon. Instead, the exercitant is taught to invest them with emotional power by first projecting himself imaginatively onto his own deathbed. All the physical, mental, and spiritual agonies conventionally associated with dying are now evoked by the three articles which he is directed to consider: first, the anguish of imminent separation from relatives, friends, and possessions; second, the "ineffable griefe" of death itself, and the horror of the temptations and visions which accompany it; and third, the torment of anxiety about the soul's future, as one realizes that the body is about to "yeelde foode to wormes, neither shal any one

26. St. Ignatius, pp. 3, 28, 21.

jote of al the riches rest with it, but only that poore peece of clothe wherin it shal be wrapped, and that smal circuit of earth wherin it is interred." Having duly considered these points "even as though that houre were nowe arrived," the exercitant is at last ready to "understand and savor . . . interiorly" the abstract lessons with which Loarte concludes the meditation; and to feel "confusion for sins," through fear if not through shame.[27] Such a response is not, as yet, the true repentance, or contrition, demanded by theologians of all parties; but whereas the Puritan simply lectures his reader on its crucial importance, the Jesuit guides the exercitant personally in the direction of that spiritual turning point.

It is important to note that the handbook of directed meditations avoids specific image-making, *on principle.* St. Ignatius warns those who administer his own exercises against imposing upon the exercitant their own opinions and advice; they are to "allow the Creator to act immediately with the creature, and the creature with its Creator and Lord" (p. 6). By extension, they will also minimize their personal imaginative contributions to a given

27. Cf. St. Ignatius's second prelude to his meditation on hell: "to ask for an interior sense of the pains which the lost suffer, in order that if I through my faults forget the love of the eternal Lord, at least the fear of punishment may help me not to fall into sin" (pp. 26–27). Greene's professed reaction to the comparable chapter in "the booke of *Resolution*" exemplifies the ideal: "After that I had with deepe consideration pondered upon these points, such a terrour stroke into my conscience, that for very anguish of minde my teethe did beate in my head, my lookes waxed pale and wan" (p. 165). The two pages of soliloquy that follow may be summarized adequately in Satan's two lines: "Mee miserable! Which way shall I fly / Infinite wrauth, and infinite despair?"

Baxter's more critical comment on his mental and emotional state after reading "Bunny's *Resolution*" is suggestive: God showed him, he writes, "the unexpressible weight of things Eternal, and the necessity of resolving on a Holy Life . . . But even at *that time,* I had little lively sense of the *Love of God in Christ to the World or me,* nor of my special need of him! For *Parsons* and all Papists almost are too short upon this Subject" (p. 3; and see below, n. 36.) Martz, however, demonstrates that this emphasis on God's fearfulness and the *"weight* of things Eternal" (italics mine) was characteristic of Jesuit spirituality in particular (*Poetry of Meditation,* esp. pp. 145–49).

meditation. Loarte therefore encourages the reader to make the preliminary composition of place with the eyes of his own imagination; and, even more important, to "propose" his own "examples" (i.e. images)[28] whenever it is necessary to "visualize" an invisible topic of meditation, such as one's sinfulness. St. Ignatius does suggest several images for this particular subject: one might, for example, "see" oneself "as an ulcer or abscess whence have issued so many sins and so many iniquities, and such vile poison" (p. 24).[29] Nonetheless, these images are included only to exemplify his principle of "abasing" oneself "by examples." Loarte's directed meditation on death is the better from the viewpoint of devotional theory because of its artistic limitations.

Parsons, on the other hand, was able to write unhandicapped by this artistically crippling duty of self-effacement. For the *First Booke of . . . resolution* is directed to readers still far from being pious would-be exercitants—readers "so carelesse, or so carnallie geeven," that they possess only the minimal interest necessary to make them glance at his opening pages (p. 8). These unregenerate cannot, of course, be expected to cooperate with him by making any imaginative effort of their own to appropriate inwardly the truths of which he will remind them. All he can ask for is that they should "conquer theyr myndes to so much patience, as to goe throughe to the ende of this booke" (p. 14). From there on it is his task alone—with "the assistance of God, and helpe of consideration" (p. 24)—to convince them of the error of their ways, and to move them to the "necessarie resolution, of leavinge vanities to serve God . . . according to [their] profession" (p. 9).

The "helpe of consideration," we soon learn, is of crucial importance in Parsons's scheme for realizing this goal. His general introductory remarks are followed immediately by a chapter warn-

28. See St. Ignatius, esp. p. 28.
29. The exercitant might also imagine himself as literally enchained by sin; or as a knight before his king whom he has offended; or simply consider the soul "imprisoned in this corruptible body, and [one's] whole self in this vale of misery, as it were in exile among brute beasts" (pp. 28, 20–21).

ing the nominal Christian that "earnest consideration and meditation of our estate" is necessary to salvation (pp. 15–24). As this
quotation suggests, *consideration* as Parsons defines it is very
roughly equivalent to *meditation* in the Jesuit sense, and the two
terms are used interchangeably most of the time. Simply as a mental discipline—the careful and attentive application of the mind
to spiritual matters—it is the "very eye of our soule," for it leads
us to "chue . . . well" Christian truths and duties, "direct [our]
waye aryght, and . . . understand the same." But without "the
*heate* of meditation" (italics mine) we "are not moved . . . but
doe beare the knowledge thereof locked uppe in [our] breastes,
without any sense or feelinge." Potentially, therefore, meditation is
also the "keye whiche openethe the doore to the closet of our
harte." Parsons's scheme for converting "blynd worldlinges" is,
quite simply, to persuade them to "consider," in the modern sense,
the traditional subject matter of Christian meditation—and then
to guide these considerations in such a way that they may become
affective as well, and hence really fruitful. And the technique he
uses for this indirect guidance is to force the reader, by artistic
means, to meditate approximately according to the highly effective
system developed by St. Ignatius.[30]

Parsons's use of the traditional material on the horrors of the
deathbed epitomizes this adaptive technique at its best. Whether
taken directly from Loarte or not, his chapter on the "daye of
deathe"[31] does in fact employ the same material to the same end:
the bringing of the exercitant to "confusion for sins." The crucial
difference lies in the fact that the reader of the *First Booke of . . .
resolution* would never choose voluntarily to be confounded. Hence
he must be led through his meditation with a subtlety, as well as

---

30. Parsons had better reason than some of his fellow Jesuits to trust
in this system as an efficacious tool for reaching those not yet wholly committed to the Faith: he himself, only ten years earlier, had been reconciled
to Rome after making a ten-day retreat at Louvain—using, under skilled
direction, the *Spiritual Exercises*. See Meadows, p. 108.

31. Part 1, chap. i. The full title is: "Of what opinion and feeling we
shalbe touchinge these matters, at the time of our deathe"; the shorter form
of the running title will be used for convenience.

an explicitness of imaginative direction, totally foreign to the conventional handbook. It is extremely interesting to note that in spite of these peculiarly difficult circumstances Parsons's chapter (pp. 98–117) is much more tightly Ignatian in structure than its equivalent in *The Exercise of a Christian Life.*

Following the Ignatian precept that the purgative sequence of meditations is easier and more profitable for the beginner,[32] Parsons introduces the traditional topics of sin, death, and Judgment soon after the preliminary discussion of the duty and value of meditation; only the necessary considerations of the ends for which man was created intervene. His chapter on the deathbed therefore assumes that the reader is as yet wholly unmoved, if not, indeed, hostile. Not only does Parsons ask nothing of him in the way of knowledge or interest, but he is even artfully cautious about introducing the conversational I-thou style so natural to the devotional handbook.

Thus, the preparation for meditation (pp. 98–102) which corresponds to the Ignatian preludes of prayer, composition of place, and prayer is similarly tripartite, but the prayers have become homiletic generalizations, and the whole passage is couched carefully in the third person. For the general preparatory prayer, Parsons substitutes his thesis: that worldlings and reprobates who simply will not listen to prophetic truth will find in themselves "a straunge alteration in judgement and opinion" on their deathbeds, when God "begynneth to doe judgment." The composition of place consists of a general description of the great change which will then take place, as mirth turns to sorrow, stoutness to despair, and so on—a scene partially dramatized by a quotation from the Apocrypha, in which the worldly-wise bemoan their folly and iniquity and denounce themselves as "senseless men" (Wisdom 5). And the final petition for grace to make the present meditation aright—the prayer omitted by Loarte—becomes a rhetorical plea: "Oh that men would *consider* these thinges *now!*" (italics mine).

---

32. Cf. St. Ignatius, pp. 8–9. Loarte prefers the Passion as the basic subject of meditation, "as being a thing verye acceptable to [Christ], and of great devotion and profite for our soules" (p. 40).

A transitional passage maintains carefully the polite use of the generalized "men." Worldly possessions, says the author, are not only no help at this time, but even an affliction and torment to the dying. "For better understanding wherof, it is to be considered, that three thinges will principallie molest these men at the daye of their death."

The meditation proper (pp. 102–12) treats the same three traditional agonies that Loarte considers, but in a revised and still more precisely schematic way that is thoroughly Ignatian in its inspiration. The very first of the original *Spiritual Exercises* is a "meditation by means of the three powers of the soul upon the first, the second, and the third sin" (p. 20); and St. Ignatius elucidates what he has in mind as follows: "The first point will be to apply the memory to the first sin, which was that of the angels: and then immediately to employ the understanding on the same by turning it over in the mind: and then the will, desiring to remember and understand the whole, in order to put myself to the blush, and to be confounded" (p. 21). Making the usual allowance for the noncooperation of the reader, we find precisely this sequence in Parsons's treatment of each of the three deathbed "points." Each pain is summarized explicitly, and thus introduced into the memory if it was not there before. Each is then brought home to the understanding by means of either general discussion or, better, imaginative comparisons (the Ignatian "proposing" of "examples"). And, finally, the application of each to the reader's own conduct of his life is made explicitly, in a moral exhortation urging him personally to the appropriate "acts of the will."[33]

The first point, in Parsons's sequence (pp. 102–05), consists of the "deadlye torment" which attends the separation of body and soul. Even though he agrees with all his predecessors that these "excessyve paynes" are inexpressible, the Jesuit author is able to suggest three images which may help us "partlye" to "conceave" and "imagine" them. The result is a startling revitalization of a cliché so hoary and enfeebled that even Epaphroditus's groans could not breathe real life into it. The soul and body are compared,

33. See St. Ignatius, p. 2.

not to the dualistic opposites of bird and cage, or prisoner and prison, or breath and clay, but to two intimate friends forced to separate after living together for many years. The physical pain involved is suggested by the "raginge greefe" one feels at the death of only a little finger when it is killed by a surgeon. In general, the "cruell conflict" between death and the soul, which embraces more than the merely physical, is to be understood by reference to the suffering of a powerful and popular prince successfully besieged by his mortal enemy. The extended simile which follows exemplifies clearly the way in which disciplined meditation operates to revive and enrich hackneyed imagery. Lupset, having noted that death is an omnipotent tyrant, could do nothing more than amass synonyms expressive of man's (futile) struggles to evade him. Parsons, having meditated on the identical metaphor, works out a dramatic vignette, grounded in contemporary life, in which every detail contributes something to the spiritual truth which he is trying to communicate. "Imagyne" such a prince, he commands the reader, driven from "one holde after an other, one wall after another, one castell after an other," until he is cornered at last in one "litle tower," and

> his men slaine in his sight: what feare anguishe and miserie woold this prince be in: how often would he looke owt at the windowes and loope holes of his tower, to see whether his friendes and neighboures would come to help hym or no? and yf he saw them all to abandone hym, and his cruell enemye even readie to breake in upon hym: would he not be in a pityfull plight trow you? And even so fareth it with a poore soule, at the hower of death. The bodye wherin she raigned lyke a jolye princesse in all pleasure, whiles it flourished, is now battered and overthrowen by her enemye, which is death: the armes, legges, and other partes where with she was fortified, as with walles and wardes duringe tyme of health, are now surprised and beaten to the grounde, and she is driven onlye to the harte, as to the last and extremest refuge, where she is also most fearcelye assayled in suche sorte as she can not hold owt longe. Her deare frendes which soothed her in tyme of

prosperitie, and promised assistance, as yowth, physicke, and
other humane helpes, doe now utterlye abandone her: the
enemye will not be pacified or make any league, but night
and daye assaulteth this turret where in she is, and whiche now
begynneth to shake and shiver in peeces, and she looketh
howerlye when her enemye in most raginge and dreadfull
maner, will enter upon her. [pp. 103–04]

The second-person address of directed meditation has now in
fact been introduced, but cautiously. "Imagyne . . ." is a general
imperative, one which neither assumes nor establishes a personal
relationship between author and reader. Other isolated words and
phrases ("I", or "trow you?", for example) have gradually furthered
the development of an informal, friendly tone, but only in the
same casual, literary, "dear reader" sense. The conclusion to this
"example" moves in a little closer:

What thinke you is now the state of this afflicted sowle? It is
no marvaile yf a wise man become a foole, or a stowte world-
linge most abject, in this instant of extremitie, as we often see
they doe. [p. 104]

But Parsons is not quite ready to drive home the moral application in his own person. Instead, he quotes a sermon to the same
purpose, thus letting St. Augustine exhort the reader to repent
*now,* for the deathbed is at best frightful.

The second point (pp. 105–07) consists of the pain which ac-
companies the separation of the worldly soul from all that it
loved "most dearely in this lyfe"; "oh what a greefe, what a torment
will this be!" The consideration is only mildly imaginative, though:
to such a man the thought of his possessions wi'l be particularly
painful because he is about to be judged for his getting of them,
"whiles in the meane tyme other men in the world do lyve
merylye and plesantlie uppon that he hath gotten, litle remembringe
and lesse caringe for hym, which lyeth perhapps burninge in un-
quencheable fyre for the ryches left unto them." Now, however,
Parsons appeals to the reader for the first time in his own role of
pastor and preacher, asserting his personal concern for the spiritual

well-being of the latter *as an individual:* "What wilt thow saie,
(my frende) at this daye? . . . What are thow the better now to
have lived in credit with the world? in favour of princes? exalted
of men? feared, reverenced, and advanced, seinge now all is ended,
and that thow canst use these thinges no more?" Although he
withdraws again immediately, this tentative appearance in propria
persona operates skillfully to prepare the reader for the directive
blast which is to climax the chapter.

The third point (pp. 107–12) is the most elaborately developed,
since it comprehends all the agonies evoked by one's deathbed
thoughts of what lies beyond death. In defiance of the *Crafte* (as
well as of Calvinism), Parsons does allow some room for the
theme of putrefaction; but he subordinates it to that of Judgment,
about which the casual Christian may be presumed to need more
instruction. The fact that the body "must inherite serpentes, beastes
and wormes" is not enforced imaginatively, as we might expect,
by a meditation on that unpleasant destiny. Instead, the emphasis
is laid ironically on the elaborate care which the worldly expend
on something which is ultimately valueless. That which "must be
cast out to serve for the foode of vermen" is

> that bodie . . . which was so delicatelie handled before, with
> varietie of meates, pillowes, and beddes of downe, so trymlye
> set foorthe in apparell, and other ornamentes, where uppon
> the wynde might not blow, nor the sunne shyne: that bodye
> (I saye) of whose beawtie there was so muche pride taken,
> and wherby so greate vanitie and sinne was committed: that
> bodie, which in this world was accustomed to all pamperinge,
> and could abide no austeritie or discipline.[34] [pp. 107–08]

From this thought it is only a short and easy step to the dying

34. It is interesting to note, however, that Parsons's modifications in his
1585 edition include additions to this section which emphasize the mortuary motif: for example, "in steed of sweet savours, stinch; in place of rich
girdles, a rope; for curld heare, a bauld scull, &c." (*Christian Directorie,*
p. 430). Slight revisions such as this are only straws in the wind, yet they
do indicate the way in which the new devotional movement will contribute to an intensified preoccupation with *réalisme funèbre.*

man's "dreadfull cogitations" about the uncertain future of his soul. The reader knows, of course, that his soul must render its account at Christ's tribunal; but does he really apprehend the effect that this knowledge has on one as death approaches? "And now (deare brother) begynneth the miserie of this man." Because Parsons is citing these traditional terrors not to prepare the godly, but to stir up the impenitent, he is not inhibited by any fear of leading his reader to damnation through despair. On the contrary, he becomes the devil's advocate, presenting the usual case for the prosecution without the rebuttals we have come to expect. For the benefit of those whose knowledge of the Bible is weak, he offers fourteen sample texts to prove that Scripture condemns the dying man before the bar of his own conscience; and he assures us that Satan does indeed support the indictment with a bill of particulars, "urginge everie pointe to the uttermost." Like the pain of dying, the terror of this moment can only be suggested to the understanding. This time Parsons recounts two anecdotes which stress the fear of even "good men and saintes" at death's approach, and then asks the reader to imagine by himself the horror of those who "scarce have served God trewlie one daye in all their lyves." St. Augustine supplies the concluding exhortation once again: another sermon, even more dramatic, which contrasts the attitudes of the worldly soul and the just soul as they meet their angelic escorts, and then adjures the reader to fear death now, so that he need not fear it later.

A final point is now introduced which is definitely parenthetical, and subordinate to the preceding three (pp. 112–13). Even so, the reader is led to consider it in the same tripartite meditative order. Its purpose: to remind us that God does sometimes permit visions, or apparitions, of good and evil angels at the deathbed, partly to give the dying a foretaste of their destiny, but chiefly to edify the living. How faint the shade of the mighty block book! The major premise of the medieval pastor has become a minor supporting postscript of the Counter-Reformation evangelist.

Parsons's conclusion (pp. 114–17), like both preparation and meditation proper, follows more faithfully than Loarte's the structure proposed by St. Ignatius. Moralistic it must be, since his reader is far from ready even to participate vicariously in a devotional response to the meditation, much less speak to Christ himself. At the same time, though, Parsons invests it with more power than Loarte's by means of an ingenious device: he transmutes the impractical colloquy with Christ on the Cross into an imaginative soliloquy of the reader on his deathbed. The importance of his gradual establishment of personal rapport with his reader as an individual now becomes clear. He has not repelled the casual Christian by preaching *at* him as a sinner before he was prepared to recognize that fact for himself. While St. Augustine has been exhorting the unregenerate to fear death and repent, Parsons has maintained a conversational tone of well-bred restraint—comparatively light even in his expression of pastoral concern for the reader's welfare. One more quiet, generalized question introduces this section: what "man of discretion would not learne to be wise by other mens daungers?" And now, at last, the trap is sprung.

The final truth which the nominal Christian is to consider is—that all these prospects do in fact apply to him *personally*. Now Parsons leans heavily on the second-person pronoun: "thow must ... be enforced to thy bed, and there after all thy strugglings with the dartes of deathe, thow must yelde thy bodie, which thow lovest so muche, to the baite of wormes, and thy sowle to the tryall of justice." Now his affective elaboration of the point is no proposed example or anecdote, but a straightforward composition of place which projects the reader onto his own deathbed:

> Imagine then (my frende) thow I saye which art so freshe and froelicke at this daie, that the ten, twentie, or two yeres, or perhaps two monethes, which thow hast yet to lyve, were now ended, and that thow were even at this present, stretched out uppon a bed, wearied and worne with dolour and paine, thy carnall frindes aboute the weepinge and howlinge, the phisitions departed with theire fees, as havinge geeven the over, and thow lyinge there alone mute and dumme in most pitifull agonie, expectinge from moment to moment, the last stroake of death to be geeven the. [pp. 114–15]

And now, finally, the application of the point is made by the author personally, in a new tone of pastoral sternness:

> Tell me in this instant, what would all the pleasures and commodities of this world doe the good? what comforte would it be to the, to have bene of honour in this world, to have bene ryche and purchassed muche, to have borne office, and bene in the princes favoure? to have left thy children or kynred wealthye, to have trodden down thyne enimies, to have sturred much, and borne greate swaye in this lyfe? what ease (I saye) or comfort would it be to the, to have ben fayre, to have ben gallant in apparell, goodlie in personage, glytteringe in golde? would not all thes thinges rather afflict than profit the at this instant? for now shouldest thow see the vanitie of thes trifles. [p. 115]

Both the inclusiveness of this section and the demands it makes on the reader's own imagination set it apart from the points of the meditation proper. Considered cumulatively, the passages quoted above correspond to the total scene which the devout exercitant envisages in preparation for a colloquy with the crucified Christ: a scene not only visual, but pregnant with the worshipper's newly sensitive awareness of some truth about his existence. Parsons's final, comprehensive point is at the same time an introduction to a final, intensive assault on the reader's spiritual inertia.

The latter is now made to recognize and bewail, too late, the damnable futility of his lifetime of worldliness. For the evangelist's purposes, this soliloquy is in every respect the appropriate equivalent of the Ignatian colloquy. Its content, though in no sense prayerful, is still the "cogitations and speeches" of a responsive heart—and, indirectly, a quasi-dramatic review of the lessons of the preceding meditation. Its style, too, follows the colloquy in being loose and informal, in striking contrast to the stiff exclamations of Becon's Epaphroditus.[35]

35. Cf. Greene's soliloquy expressing his "despairing humour" ("Repentance," pp. 165–68). Not only are its contents *precisely* the cogitations one would expect from a "lifelong reprobate" who realizes—too late (?)—the horrifying destiny awaiting him, but its style is a most curious and

The chapter concludes with a brief summary preaching the same moral as Loarte's: live now as you will wish to have lived when you come to "that sorowfull daye." Once more Parsons's version relates artistic form to the psychological needs of his chosen audience. It begins with a final warning in direct address to his "deare brother," but then moves immediately into a generalized coda recapitulating the contrast between the deaths of good and bad men. The impersonal tone of the beginning of the chapter is thus reasserted, the tension of direct challenge relaxed, and the reader allowed to take a breather. Parsons is less interested in frightening him into a premature and inadequate "resolution" at this point than in having him move on to the still more jolting considerations which lie ahead. Simply by reading he has made a spiritual exercise, whether he knows it or not; now let its effects sink in gradually.

The invaluable contribution of methodical meditation to the artistic development of religious literature in general is well illustrated by its influence on the ars moriendi in particular. In the first place, the meditative structure provides an ideal solution to the difficulties inherent in every form considered so far. Like the quasi-liturgical structure of the *Crafte,* it is basically dynamic, guiding the reader from the first point to the last in sequence, and with the expectation that he will participate actively as he goes along. Within this framework, moreover, it organizes its points in a similar schematized appeal to memory, understanding, and will. Yet unlike the *Crafte,* it allows the author to pause whenever he wishes to— to reflect, to analyze, to elaborate affectively—without impeding or confusing the inner movement of the treatise. Thus, whereas the classical moral essay subordinates dynamic to static, concrete to abstract, and particular to general, the meditation inverts the relative positions of the two categories.

---

suspicious mixture (not a fusion) of Parsons's colloquial diction and tone ("Oh that my last gasp were come . . . ") and the earlier Protestants' clumsy biblical interpolations ("Now I remember [though too late] that I have read in the Scriptures . . . ").

The result is a structure much less intellectually demanding and much more adaptable to varied audiences. The humanist's concern is above all to prove himself worthy of a place among men of reason: he stands under judgment by his peers according to the lucidity, the artistry, and to some extent the originality of his discussion of an inevitably timeworn moral theme. For such a restricted audience, and such restricted purposes, the intellectual demands of his traditional structure are neither excessive nor inappropriate. The devotional writer, on the contrary, is concerned only secondarily with his own intellectual and artistic talents. Above all, he must help the individual reader to appropriate personally and effectually the inner significance of an equally timeworn religious theme—and must do this regardless of the latter's position on the social, intellectual, and cultural scale.[36] In this situation, the more flexible meditative structure is ideal, for the author may use it with as much or as little intellectual and artistic embellishment as he thinks appropriate to a given audience.

Of equal significance is the compromise achieved by this structure between the values peculiar to Becon's pseudodramatic form and those inherent in the expository literary essay. Parsons's essay becomes, in a sense, a one-sided colloquy with his reader, as he gradually permits the self-address of religious meditation to emerge in modified form: "Think, my soul" becomes "Think, dear brother." No more artificial than the classical dialogue, this technique is decidedly more immediate in its appeal. As in the *Sicke Mannes Salve,* authoritarian doctrinal instruction is relieved at regular intervals—but now by affective material that is integral to the structure. Hence the argument can be tightly schematized without undue awkwardness, besides being elaborated as fully as the author sees fit. The slight dramatic action which remains implicit in the

36. Cf. the young Baxter's response to "Bunny's *Resolution*": "I had before heard some Sermons, and read a good Book or two, which made me more love and honour Godliness in the General; but I had never felt any other change by them on my heart. . . . I had no lively sight and sense of what I read till now. . . . The same things which I knew before came now in another manner, with Light, and Sense and Seriousness to my Heart" (p. 3).

dialogue is the reader's imaginative participation in the concealed spiritual exercise. Parsons's use of the second-person pronoun reminds us even more forcefully than Becon's mirror technique that the spiritual points at issue are not merely academic. It is *your* relationship to God, *your* death, and *your* destiny which are the stuff of his colloquy. That is, the meditative structure allows, as pure drama does not, for just that direct personal contact between author and reader—that continuing pastoral relationship—which is indispensable to effective devotional literature.

Since the *First Booke of . . . resolution* is addressed to the widest possible audience of nonpracticing Christians—all those for whom the *Sicke Mannes Salve* is meaningless or even spiritually dangerous—Parsons elaborates his themes accordingly. He must avoid any obtrusive artfulness which might distract or alienate the man in the street—splendid rhetoric, for example, or cultured allusiveness. Once again the "help of consideration" leads him to an ideal compromise: a style hailed by Swift (together with Hooker's) as a model of "that simplicity which is the best and truest ornament of most things in life."[37]

In the first place, the rhythms of speech replace those of the formal classical essay, varying in the degree of their colloquialism in accordance with Parsons's tone of the moment. Even the more

37. *The Tatler,* No. 230, Sept. 27, 1710. Parish describes his "best style" as "eloquent, lucid, and uncontaminated by euphuism" (p. 2), but notes that "the *Directory* appeals to the mind more than the emotions" (p. 27). Pierre Janelle, whose critique is based on the *Christian Directory* alone, agrees that Parsons "appeals less to feeling than to reason," yet characterizes his "descriptive passages" as "of great force and beauty. . . . at times almost lyrical"—those of the "joys of Heaven and the pains of Hell" having an "extraordinary intensity"—and concludes that Parsons's work is "one of the greatest English literary compositions of all time." ("English Devotional Literature in the Sixteenth and Seventeenth Centuries," in *English Studies Today, 2d ser.,* ed. G. A. Bonnard pp. 161–62. The chapters of dry apologetic and "abstract demonstration" to which both Parish and Janelle presumably allude were added by Parsons in 1585—and dropped again in his revised edition of 1607, as "fitter to goe in some worke of that argument a part." (See Driscoll, *"The Seconde Parte,"* p. 146.) Cf. A. C. Southern, *Elizabethan Recusant Prose 1559–1582,* pp. 186–88.

formal and restrained passages of general exposition and discussion are far looser in their sentence structure than Lupset's, and suggest that he is speaking to the reader—or reflecting aloud. At the other extreme are the passages of immediate, personal exhortation, direction, and so on, which seem, comparatively, very colloquial indeed. In the latter passages especially, rhetorical devices are handled with notable ease and freedom. Parsons's use of parallel constructions, of repetition for cumulative effect, of climactic order, and so on, is almost invariably "casual"—that is, sufficiently inexact so that it might arise naturally in meditation or in speech. It is in the deathbed soliloquy of the worldly man, appropriately enough, that we find this technique used most richly and effectively. This speech which Parsons gives him is neither strict enough in its rhetorical development to suit an earnest classicist like Lupset, nor precise enough in its theological pattern to suit even an early Calvinist like Becon; but it is rhetorical and doctrinal in its organization. Rhetoric and religious allusions are now used with deliberate *imprecision,* and thus made to communicate more effectively the muddled and miserable thoughts of the dying man:

> o follye and unfortunate blindenes of myne, Loe, heere is an end now of all my delytes and prosperities: all my joyes, all my pleasures, all my myrth, all my pastymes are now finished: where are my frindes whiche were wont to laugh with me? my servantes wont to attende me, my children wont to disporte me? where are all my coches and horses, wherwith I was wont to make so goodlie a shew, the cappes and knees of people wont to honour me, the troupes of suters followinge me? where are all my daliances and trickes of love? all my pleasant musicke, all my gorgeous buyldinges, all my costlie feastes and banquettinges? and above all other, where are my deare and sweete frindes, whoe seemed they would never have forsaken me? but all are now gone, and hath left me heere alone to aunswere the reckoninge for all, and none of them will doe so muche as to goe with me to judgement, or to speake one worde in my behalfe.

Woe worthe to me, that I had not foreseene this daye rather, and so have made better provision for the same: it is now to late, and I feare me I have purchased eternall damnation, for a litle pleasure, and lost unspeakable glorie, for a flootinge vanitie. Oh how happie and twise fortunate are they whiche so lyve as they maye not be a fearde of this daye! I now see the difference betwixt the endes of good and evill, and marvaile not though the scriptures saye of the one, the deathe of sainctes are precious: And of the other, the death of sinners is miserable: Oh that I had lyved so vertuouslye as some other have donne, or as I had often inspirations from God to doe: or that I had done the good deedes I might have donne: how sweete and confortable woold they be to me now in this my last, and extremest distresse! [pp. 115–16]

The almost total absence of alliteration in this passage is as note-worthy a realistic touch as its (nostalgic?) enumeration of those delights and prosperities now recognized as will-o'-the-wisps. Else-where, alliteration is fairly common—usually in colloquial phrases such as "trouble and toyle," "weryed and worne owt," "beate their braynes," "strugled so sore," or "freshe and froelicke." Indeed, with the single exception of a reference to the reader as "gallant in apparell, goodlie in personage, glytteringe in golde," it appears only in the simplest form exemplified above. Yet Parsons uses even these simple pairings so appositely that they constitute an effective literary device in his work rather than an intrusive nuisance, as in the *Crafte*.

His imagery, too, is skillfully unliterary—comfortably within the range of the normally literate and imaginative middle-class reader. It is, in fact, restricted almost exclusively to the two types which spring most naturally out of the practice of systematic medi-tation: the brief biblical image, and the extended simile. Incidental metaphors are drawn from contemporary life and language ("beate their braynes," "strugled so sore," or "troupes of suters"), but these are probably at least half-fossilized already. The overwhelm-ing majority are firmly rooted in the Bible or in traditional imagery regarding death. The worldly have "hard" hearts, and are "chayned" by worldly pleasures despite the "bytter" remembrance of death, so they "purchase" damnation instead of "making provision" for that "last and extremest distresse"; then they suffer the agonies of the "dartes of deathe" until they receive the "last stroake" from their "mortall enymie" and "pass" through the "dore" to the heavenly "tribunall," where they "aunswere the reckoninge" at last, while their bodies become the "baite" of worms. The utter conventionality of these expressions is almost unnoticeable when they are read in context, however. They are widely separated from each other, and usually either radically transformed by colloquial elaboration, or imbedded in new and dynamic contexts. Above all, they impress the reader as strong and fresh because his attention is wholly absorbed by the author's dramatic appeals to his own imagination. The average exercitant will do most of his meditating in images dulled by overuse; but when he really turns the eyes of his imagination to a familiar theme, its timeworn clichés are more than likely to regain their original strength and sharpness. Even such a hackneyed metaphor as that of the "cruell conflict" of dying is endued with new life and power in this way. Since the anguish of dying belongs among those "invisible things" which must be visualized metaphorically, Parsons proposes this familiar example—and then explores it imaginatively and intellectually until it grows into a dramatic vignette whose essential triteness is scarcely noticeable. Similarly, he reinvigorates the old theme of deathbed horrors—damning memories, appalling visions, and overwhelming fears—by *visualizing an authentic deathbed,* in concrete and contemporary terms. The artistic gulf between this scene and Becon's is a measure of the contribution of sixteenth-century meditative methods to the imaginative power of the ars moriendi.

In its own way, therefore, Parsons's chapter on "the daye of deathe" represents an intensification and refinement of the medieval deathbed tradition as thoroughgoing as Becon's, and infinitely more creative in its artistic implications. Above all, it reasserts dramatically, without even Becon's few qualifications, the absolute medieval dichotomy between the deathbed drama and all the rest of life. The Jesuit's reader does not meditate on his mortality as such, still less comfort himself—albeit negatively—with the reflection that all life is a continuous dying. On the contrary, he focuses exclusively on the inevitable hour and its unique agonies, now restored to all their late-medieval horror, and more. Physical pain is once again excruciating; reason totters; and friends are not only of no particular value, but they are more faithless and hypocritical than ever.[38] Worse yet, these established torments—complete even to the possibility of deathbed apparitions—are only minimal: the degree to which they are intensified depends on the moral quality of the individual's past life.[39] In sum, all the fears implicit in the medieval tradition are now deliberately nourished as incentives to Christian living.[40] Stripped of every "comfortable" element, the ars moriendi is now restricted to a supporting role as commander of expeditionary forces for the ars vivendi.[41] And this limitation,

38. Even the traditional medieval interpretation of Aristotle's dictum reappears—also in intensified form—elsewhere in the treatise: the first reason not to delay repentance till death is that "the extreeme feare and paines of deathe, being (as the philosopher sayeth) the moste terrible, of all terrible thinges, doe not permitt a man, so to gather his spirites and senses [as to repent properly]" (pp. 387–88).

39. Ironically, the Jesuits followed personally quite another tradition of dying well—one that excluded even that minimal fearfulness postulated in their devotional exercises and published works. According to Meadows, Parsons himself died, following St. Ignatius, "in typically Jesuit fashion . . . quietly, undramatically, and in the midst of work" (pp. 173–74). A twentieth-century layman may perhaps be forgiven for finding *some* drama in Parsons's calling for the rope with which Campion had been hanged, and wearing it around his own neck during the recitation of the Prayer of Commendation, *"Proficiscere, anima Christiana"* (ibid., p. 175).

40. Parsons's 1585 revision consists largely of the intensification of the treatise's dynamic and forceful qualities by means of stronger verbs, descriptive phrases, adjectives, and nouns, in that order. Of the revisions made in this chapter, fully half (about thirty) serve directly to heighten the fearfulness of the death scene itself.

41. Note, too, that St. Ignatius warns the exercitant strongly "not to desire to think on pleasant and joyful subjects, as, for example, on the glory of Paradise, the Resurrection, *etc.,"* while he is occupied in the purgative sequence of the first "week," because "any consideration of joy and delight hinders the feeling of pain, grief, and tears for our sins" (p. 29). Cf. Lupset's recommendation of heaven as the appropriate topic for meditation (above, chap. 2).

or refinement, of its function, is still another factor contributing to its new artistic power.

In spite of Parsons's wrathful implication that Bunny's "foul and false dealing" with his work was somehow uniquely despicable, a close collation of the two versions' treatment of death indicates that Bunny's work actually follows quite faithfully the pattern laid down for such adaptations early in the Reformation. This he explains in some detail, both in his dedicatory epistle to the Archbishop of York (pp. [iii–ix]) and in his "Preface to the Reader" (pp. [x–xix]). He has "purged" the Roman work of "manifest error" and "other inconvenience" so that the "perswasion that it hath to godlines of life . . . might carrie no hurt or danger withall" (p. [iii]). In carrying out this project, however, he has been guided by earlier adaptations of the *Imitation of Christ*,[42] "altering no more than need required, and doing the same in quiet maner, without any grief against th' author . . . or disgrace to his doings (so much as might be, not betraieng the truth)" (p. [vii]). In accordance with this traditional approach, he leaves unchanged the Vulgate text and marginal chapter references, and claims to have overlooked also some of his opponents' moot opinions. The only alterations which need required were, as we should expect, strictly doctrinal: the retranslation of "abused" technical words, such as "penance" and "merit"; the omission of at least some "over venturous" opinions; and the ruthless excision of all "opinions and doctrines . . . such as are manifest corruptions" (pp. [xiii–xiv]).

Up to this point Bunny has been remarkably explicit and honest in his account of the conventional nature and purpose of his labors.[43] The fact that he now professes to have made other edi-

42. By *"Castalion* first, then also maister *Rogers,"* who "shew us, how such thinges maie rightly be used." Bunny himself apparently made still another "perusal" of this devotional classic.

43. His dishonesty is of that sort which evidently left even Puritan consciences untroubled during this controversial era: (1) he dismisses R. P.'s "false" teaching casually as the product of the "Schoole-men," although one citation after another is to a major theologian of the Patristic era; (2) he asserts with offhand assurance, and even condescension, that the Protestants have produced many such devotional treatises, so that he is propagating this

torial revisions without any reference whatsoever to doctrinal truth is therefore somewhat startling. Some cited passages, he asserts, have been omitted simply because they were not so directly relevant to the topic as Parsons's own discussions, or because they treated it *"more coldlie"* (italics mine). And such passages, we are told, might "discredit" the rest, or "let down the affections again which were stirred up before" (pp. [xiv], [xviii]). Curiously enough, though, this does not seem to be quite accurate. A collation of approximately one hundred pages in the two versions—all those passages relating to death, all those mentioned in Parsons's vociferous protests,[44] plus others suggested by the promising nature of their subject matter—revealed not a single omission devoid of "manifest error" or "other [doctrinal] inconvenience." Occasionally, the editor might plausibly argue that an excision was justified primarily by the irrelevance or dullness of the quoted passage; but in view of his hypersensitivity to sectarian implications elsewhere, such a defense would have to be dismissed as superfluous. *No* "error" or "inconvenience" from the Calvinist viewpoint is allowed to pass, whatever its context.[45] But Bunny's statement, at any rate, witnesses to the warmth of Protestant sup-

---

one chiefly from a charitable urge to encourage whatever is good in "our adversaries labors." This last, patently false, claim evoked from Parsons the famous challenge to name even one independent Protestant work comparable to the Catholic devotional treatises, classic and contemporary, which he lists (Preface, 1585, fol. 9).

44. Preface, 1585, fols. 7ᵛ–16. Page references in the text below alluding to Parsons's criticism of Bunny's version are to this satirical discussion. The majority of his illustrations are drawn from passages concerning the Last Things, including the problem of belated repentance. A collation of the two Tables of Contents supports the inference that Bunny's drastic revisions are fairly well restricted to this area of doctrinal disagreement. Otherwise, they function almost exclusively to assert man's total depravity in all ages, as against the Jesuit's position that man's negligence of spiritual matters is a phenomenon of the present decadent age only.

45. The spirit underlying these emendations of even the most trivial details is, as McNulty observes, one of "high seriousness": "Parsons many times reminds us that we must eventually give account of every idle and frivolous word; Bunny tests even adjectives, expletives, and connectives by that standard" (p. 277).

port for the affective purposes and techniques of continental literature. In effect, he does not merely alter, in time-honored fashion,
the theological frame of reference of an ordinary pious Catholic
treatise so that Protestants may safely read it; rather, he goes out
of his way to argue that the adaptation is even *more* affective than
the original, *and for that reason preferable.* In other words, he is
not only consciously enthusiastic himself about this particular
aspect of Catholic devotional literature, but he assumes a similar
enthusiasm in his audience.

Because not only his excisions, but even his pettiest emendations,
are theologically inspired and hence predictable, an exhaustive
tabulation of his revisions of Parsons's material on death is unnecessary. His treatment of the chapter on the "daye of deathe"
(pp. 101–20) will serve to illustrate his editorial methods; and his
version of another pertinent chapter, warning against "delaye of
resolution" (pp. 371–402), will illustrate the ways in which these
methods do sometimes serve to enhance the artistic values of the
original.

Parsons's brief essay on the "daye of deathe" undergoes some
forty revisions. First, the Catholic renditions of technical terms are
replaced by their Calvinist equivalents as a matter of course. As
Parsons puts it, Bunny makes him "speake after the phrase of
Protestantes"; indeed, he "frameth every mans speech (wher he
can) to such a stile as though he had bene trained up in John
Calvin's schole" (fol. 11$^r$–11$^v$). Thus, "our lord" becomes "the
Lord"; "doe penance," "repent"; and "good lyfe and vertuous actions," "amendment of life." Even "tribunall" is suspect, and becomes "judgement seat."[46]

Similarly, "over venturous opinions" are cautiously modified or
excised. The author of the Epistle to the Hebrews is not St. Paul,
but "the Apostle"; the author of a sermon attributed to St.
Augustine which seems to emphasize the importance to salvation of good works is not "S. Austen" but "S. Austen . . . (or some

46. This is one of the verbal substitutions cited by McNulty as purely
stylistic "corrections" of "mere Anglicized Latin" (p. 294); but it is argu-
able, in this instance, that the flavor of Parsons's choice is both more
Roman and less transcendently awesome than Bunny's older equivalent.

other under his name)"; and the identification of the fourth Psalm's "bed of his sorow" with the deathbed is modified, by the transposition of a comma, to "the bed of his last departure *especially*" (italics mine). Also, an extra marginal notation identified by the heading "B." reminds the Protestant that the "excessive paines" of dying are "especially to be restrained to the death of the worldly: for the godlie have for the most part a singular comfort therin" (p. 106). Presumably this one Calvinist explanation will counterbalance whatever heretical emphasis on good works may be implicit in Parsons's way of making precisely the same point. (The Jesuit's retort to all such didactic marginalia of Bunny's is that "certaine be idle and foolish, some be ridiculous and absurd, and other be wicked and tending to impietie" [fol. 12].) Most interesting of all changes in this category, however, is the disappearance in toto of Parsons's somewhat tentative discussion of deathbed apparitions, as well as his anecdote about Christ's appearance to a "godly bishop" afraid to die. Such visions, though attested to occasionally by respected authorities, run counter to the rigorous Calvinist understanding of the way in which God deals with his creatures. Bunny doesn't argue: he simply eliminates this fourth and subordinate point altogether.

When it comes to "manifest errors" and "other inconvenience," the Calvinist editor blue-pencils the text with a scrupulousness which verges, at times, on the ludicrous. A reference to sins of omission is necessarily cut, as is St. Augustine's dramatic picture of the soul's confrontation after death by its evil works. (Men like Bunny, snorts Parsons, "spare neither Fathers, Doctours, Prophetes, Apostles, nor Christ himself, when they stand in the way against their foolishe heresies" [fol. 15].) Just as predictable, though scarcely necessary, are the excisions of a mere mention of "saints" in the canonical sense, and of two uses of the colloquial "Marye yet..." But carefulness becomes literal-minded hypercaution when he refuses to let St. Augustine warn the reader to make his will "whyle thow arte whole, while thow art wise, while thow art thyne owne man." The stern doctrinal truth that there is no health nor wisdom in us must not be sacrificed to rhetorical eloquence; Bunny's Augustine limits himself to the single clause "while thou art thine owne man." So, too, the translations of biblical passages are corrected even when the greater freedom of Parsons's renderings is doctrinally inconsequential.[47] And any word is rejected which carries even the slightest implication that there might be a role for chance in human experience: "unfortunate" becomes "miserable"; "perhaps," "it may be"; and "happy"—in the one instance where the connotation of luck is faintly possible—"gracious." Above all, the use of hyperbole is not to be countenanced. Every instance of affective exaggeration, however insignificant doctrinally or successful artistically, is sacrificed to literal truth.[48]

Bunny's quiet but painstaking correction of any error, however minute, does sometimes result, therefore, in the destruction of an eloquent passage or a vivid image.[49] At other times, though, the same process results in the improvement of the artistic quality of Parsons's work. The several ways in which this may happen are, fortunately, well illustrated by Bunny's reworking of another chapter which includes traditional deathbed themes (pt. 2, chap. 5). Here, Parsons inveighs against "delaye of resolution . . . upon hope to doe it better or with more ease, afterward" (pp. 371–402). Inevitably, a large portion of his argument assumes the Tridentine position in regard to conversion and penance, and discusses from this viewpoint not only the dangers of delay in general, but also

47. E.g., Parsons loosely translates a verse from Luke 21: "When these terrible thinges begyn to come upon other men, doe you looke aboute you, and lyft up your heades . . ." The Calvinist gives the same Latin, but insists upon a literal translation: "When these things begin to com upon other men, do ye lift up your heades."

48. E.g., the dying man is no longer represented as physically alone (an unlikely contingency, in literal truth); and his soul is driven, not from the "extreamest parts" of his body, but simply from its "extreme parts."

49. One of the better examples of Bunny's ineptly pedestrian literal-mindedness in this respect occurs in a chapter irrelevant to this study. Parsons argues that God asks good works from us for our own sakes and will, moreover, "paye us home agayne with usury." The soberly conscientious Puritan substitutes "with advantage"—a dull phrase, and one not even justified as theologically necessary, since it implies with equal directness a positive correlation between good works and heavenly rewards.

the "insufficiency" of deathbed repentance in particular. Parsons refers to this one part of one chapter so often in illustrating Bunny's "foul and false dealing" with his treatise that the casual reader might well imagine that this discussion represented the major portion of the *First Book of . . . resolution*. We may infer that the Protestant version (pp. 423–56) at least exemplifies Bunny's most drastic adaptive techniques, and very probably represents as a whole the most radically modified section of Parsons's work.

It goes without saying that the Calvinist is rather hard put to it to revise such a chapter adequately by changing only details, as is his wont. In so far as he tries to abide by his policy of inconspicuous substitution, the results are unfortunate—sometimes meaningless, often awkward, and usually much weaker than their originals.[50] Occasionally, though, he is forced by his principles to adopt more drastic methods: to amputate where he cannot emend, or even, in Parsons's phrase, to "mangle" with high-handed freedom (fol. 14ᵛ). And it is in these instances that we find clearly exemplified the ways in which Protestant scrupulosity could, and did, further both the structural and the affective potentialities of Catholic devotional literature.

To begin with, the revised version is better proportioned than the original—an improvement directly traceable to the adapter's dutiful mangling of two long sections of the given text. Both instances are so extreme that Parsons uses them in his satirical elucidation of Bunny's editorial techniques. In the first, a long extract from an Augustinian homily is reduced to one short paragraph through the excision of all that cannot be unobtrusively corrected.[51] All that remains of St. Augustine's discourse is a protestation of ignorance as to the salvability of deathbed converts, and an exhortation to "repent" (instead of "doe penance") *now,* rather than risk eternal damnation. And Bunny deletes the

---

50. E.g., Parsons's straightforward admonition that "it is a privilege for a wicked man, to doe penance at his deathe" (p. 392) emerges as the following involuted statement: "It is as it were a priviledge for a wicked man, to have his repentance to bee begun, when he is to die" (p. 447).

51. Parsons, pp. 389–93; Bunny, pp. 445–46.

source of even this innocuous remnant, attributing it only to "one." Possibly he would have hesitated to name Augustine explicitly among those authors of "impertinent" and "less effectual" material that he felt free to eliminate? Whether or not this particular discourse is relevant or affective, however, it would be idle to pretend that Bunny's revision was motivated primarily by any such considerations. His editorial labors are directed only too clearly at the removal of words and notions and doctrines distasteful to the Calvinist—and of these alone. All the same, the resultant paragraph is in fact better proportioned to the chapter as a whole. In the second instance, Bunny revises and compresses in similar fashion a full discussion, complete with citations from Cyprian, Augustine, Jerome, and Ambrose, of the necessity for making satisfaction commensurate with the "weight and continuance" of one's sins. Again the verbal substitutions, the rephrasings, and the excisions all combine to eliminate only the inadmissible aspects of Catholic teaching on this subject.[52] The end result, nevertheless, is also—*incidentally*—preferable, in sheer conciseness, to the stodgily old-fashioned authoritarian original.

The revisions with the most far-reaching implications for devotional literature, however, are those which happen (1) to multiply the affective elements in the original, or (2) to extend and develop their potentialities. Both types occur in this chapter; and both arise from the most elementary sort of blue-penciling of Catholic "inconveniences." The implications of this simple fact are fascinating.

The first instance springs from Bunny's habit of erasing every reference to monachism, however innocent. In this case, Parsons is simply proposing an example in order to dramatize the absurdity of delaying one's repentance until it shall be easier, when actually such delay magnifies the difficulty by increasing the burden of penance which will be required. His illustrative anecdote, de-

52. Parsons, pp. 382–83; Bunny, p. 437. Parsons has a wonderful time pillorying Bunny for his rejection of the need for physical penance. Various ways of mortifying the body, he writes, "seem to be things nothing pleasant to the bodie of a Minister"; they are "to harde to this delicate doctour, and therfore he thrust them quite out" (fol. 15ʳ).

scribing a simpleton who seeks to lighten his load of wood by adding more to it, is introduced as follows: "It is written among the lyves of olde heremites, how that on a time, an Angel shewed to one of them, in the wyldernes, a certayne good felow" (p. 375). His tale is therefore a straightforward homiletic exemplum drawn from the approved corpus of Christian writings, with no less and no more dramatic impact than any scriptural incident might have if used in the same way. Bunny, however, will have none of hermits, visions, and such. So his version begins: "That were much like as if a good fellow" (p. 428). And the ensuing anecdote, shifted now into the subjunctive mood, becomes an *extended simile ostensibly born of the author's own imagination.* Indirectly, he has added to the treatise's store of images which may properly be called "meditative." (The hackneyed metaphor revitalized by consideration would in this case be that of the burden of sin.)

The second instance arises from the Calvinist's distaste for elaborate scholastic exegeses of Scripture, as well as from his fear of overemphasizing the dangers of belated repentance. Parsons climaxes his chapter with a vigorous and imaginative allegorical exegesis of Psalm 58 (pp. 393–96; [Psalm 59 in Protestant psalters]). The wicked who "turne at the evenyng"—i.e. who seek to return to God at the hour of death—shall be scoffed at by him: they shall "suffer hungar, as dogges" and "seeke by all meanes, for meate"—i.e. beg greedily for any penance which will prolong life or at least insure salvation; but they shall "runne aboute the citte" in vain, rejected derisively by the Lord. Parsons's detailed elaboration of the scene and its signification constitutes one of his more successful extended similes based on the composition of place. It is certainly neither impertinent nor cold; and anyway, it is the author's own, not "alleged out of others." Yet Bunny excises carefully every specific reference to the psalm and, necessarily, every specific application of those details to human experience (pp. 447–48). One's first impression is that he has destroyed the artistic quality of the passage altogether, retaining nothing but the central homiletic interpretation of the dramatic scene. On second glance, it becomes apparent that he has in fact preserved with great care *whatever imaginative elements could be separated from their biblical source.* The following clause, for example, does not depend for its validity on the meditative context of dogs returning to the city at evening, and is therefore retained: "When the beautiful summer day of this life is ended, and the boisterous winter night of death draweth on . . ." Bunny's adaptation of this one passage is not, to be sure, particularly impressive in itself; but in that it points the way forward to a freer use of meditative imagery, its artistic significance is immeasurable. Parsons's extended simile is one step removed already from images proposed by spiritual directors like Loarte because it provides explicitly the content of the spiritual exercise. Within a structure which is implicitly Ignatian, "Imagine . . ." leads to "Even so . . ." Bunny's version, by eliminating the given topic of meditation but preserving its spiritual application, removes the image one crucial step further from the devotional technique in which it is rooted. Now it stands alone as literary image. Its source—the biblical content of the consideration which produced and nurtured it—may be more or less discernible to the reader, depending on his familiarity with Ignatian devotional techniques and with biblical imagery; but its connotative richness is only intensified by that recognition. The devotional direction, utterly hollow and lifeless without the reader's own active participation, has been transmuted into the concrete meditative image.

On the whole, then, Bunny's contributions to the literary value of the *Book of . . . Resolution* are simply the by-products of his enthusiastic preservation of as much of Parsons's affective material as he possibly can. (It would be much easier, for example, to omit the exegesis of Psalm 58 altogether, instead of pruning it with such care.) One contribution, though, derives instead from his equally enthusiastic loyalty to Parsons's moralistic orientation in general. In this case, the indirect result of his Calvinist modifications is to intensify still further the Jesuit's concentration on the frightful elements in the deathbed tradition.

Parsons's work, as we have seen, subsumes legitimately both devotional techniques and the devotional spirit under his dominant purpose of moral reform. In terms of Catholic doctrine, the validity of a moral life does not wait upon a conversion experience; rather, the nominal Christian must be moved at least to moral resolution

and action, whether or not he is ever moved to that personal response to God which issues necessarily in such a commitment.
Hence the evangelist is quite justified in motivating his reader in
any number of ways other than love and gratitude—including fear
of the Last Things. The Calvinist disclaims fervently this approach,
and takes the greatest pains to revise every explicit reference, however minute, to such heretical notions. But his changes are in detail
only, in accordance with his editorial philosophy; the general tendency of the argument remains intact.

Thus, mindful of the Calvinist tenets that salvation is by faith
alone, and that deathbed repentance may therefore be true and
valid, Bunny dutifully revises subheadings in the Table of Contents: the "estates" of good and evil men at the day of death are
"indifferent," and conversion at the last hour is *"sufficient"* (pt. 1,
chap. 4, and pt. 2, chap. 5). Parsons's actual argument is virtually
unexceptionable in its details, so that his quiet editor only notes
that the custom of sin "is *seldom* removed upon the instant"
(p. 444), where the original reads *"can not* be removed . . ." (p. 388;
all italics are mine). Bunny is even moved to add a fifth reason of
his own for considering a last-minute conversion "doubtful" (p.
445).[53] In short, he not only sidesteps the usual battle on this
subject, but actually goes out of his way to support the opposition
as forcefully as he can. The results are formidable. It is true that
the Protestant reader is to envisage his own deathbed in slightly less
gruesome detail than the Catholic, since he need not people the
scene with monstrous apparitions; but he must contemplate it
with no explicit assurance that good deeds will guarantee divine
aid in that crisis, or eternal life thereafter. The power of Parsons's
limited approach to the traditional themes is intensified automatically by the new frame of theological reference.

On the other hand, Bunny does soften these implications to some
extent by preserving not only Parsons's moralistic orientation, but
also the legalistic *flavor* of his discussion. One illustration of this

53. Experience, too, teaches us to mistrust such conversions, since so
many of those who recover from illness return immediately to their former
sinful ways. (This argument, inadmissible on grounds of doctrine as well as
of authorship, Parsons excises in his turn.)

point will suffice, especially since it is drawn from that chapter
which Parsons accuses him of mangling most viciously. The original text reads as follows:

> Mark heere (deere brother) that this satisfaction [deferred
> until old age] must be bothe great and long, and also of
> necessity. What madnes is it then for the, now to enlarge the
> wounde, knoweing that the medicine must afterwardes be so
> paynfull? what crueltie can be more against thy selfe, than to
> drive in thornes into thine owne flesh, which thou must after
> pull owte againe with so many tears? woldest thou drink
> that cuppe of poysoned liquour for a litle pleasure in the
> taste, whiche wolde cast thee soone after into a burning fever,
> torment thy bowells within thee, and ether dispache thy lyfe,
> or put the in great joperdie? [p. 383]

Needless to say, Bunny conscientiously substitutes "the labour of
thine amendment" for "this satisfaction," and specifies only that
it be "verie great"; but he leaves untouched the remainder of the
passage (p. 437). The entirely non-Calvinistic implications of the
similes are simply ignored.

Logically, many Catholic treatises would in fact lend themselves
to valid Calvinist adaptation by means of such editorial techniques.
They would have only to be basically inspirational in nature: those
in which considerations of God and his redemptive work in Christ
moved the reader to wish to serve and imitate his Lord and
Savior. (They could also, of course, tell him how to do this.) Yet
Bunny chose deliberately to adapt a work which focuses unmistakably, even in the Protestant version, on the practical advantages
to be gained and evils avoided by resolving upon, and then exe-
cuting, a godly life. Moreover, he commends the substance of the
treatise specifically and earnestly to his readers. It seems reasonable
to infer, then, that Puritan leaders recognized by 1580, as Becon
had not, the futility of dealing with the morally insensitive in
terms of Calvinist doctrine in all its rigorous purity. They were
by no means prepared to modify their gloomy view of man's total

depravity; but they were perforce driven to modify their demands that the unregenerate repent and behave when motivated only by doctrinal instruction. Their concessions to his needs include not only an increasing emphasis on the affective elements in Christian devotion, but also an increasing tendency toward a legalistic interpretation of Christian ethics. Continental devotional literature (purged, of course) was therefore generally welcomed in England for its affective power; and a work such as Parsons's was no less welcome because its "persuasion to godliness" was directed to immediate moralistic ends. It might be permeated with implications which were "manifest corruptions"—but it got results. To the historian, the enormous popularity of "Bunny's *Resolution*" suggests the extent to which orthodox Calvinism capitulated within fifty years to the exigencies of an everyday world in which saints must do what they can with sinners, instead of consigning them gladly to hell. And for the student of devotional literature, it suggests the startling size of the English audience for religious treatises directed, *not* to the devout, but to the average nominal Christian. Today the latter contents himself with "religious"—i.e. inspirational —novels and magazine articles, if anything. In the sixteenth century, he subjected himself with apparent willingness to Parsons's moral exhortations—and hence, indirectly, to the influence of the Counter-Reformation version of the ars moriendi, in all its grim intensity.

And now, at last, we are in a position to appreciate the single greatest weakness of Parsons's essay as an exemplar of the tradition: that very narrowness of focus which contributes so much to its power. Parsons's denunciation of Bunny's edition as "punished and plumed" might well be applied to his own version of the *Crafte:* pruning it drastically in the interests of intensity, he has lost some of its basic devotional values at the same time. The ars moriendi has achieved artistic integrity at last, but lost temporarily its comprehensive pastoral orientation—its ability to quiet fears when necessary, as well as arouse them. The final need of the tradition, therefore, is an artist able to exploit to the full the potentialities of both the new form and the old matter: to subsume the art of dying into that of living without ignoring the valid claims of the former to independent consideration; to preserve the new structure, but expand it in such a way that it will encompass both aspects of this devotional theme; and to reconcile the new imaginative intensity with the old pastoral tone of quiet assurance. Jeremy Taylor will be that artist; and his *Holy Dying* will meet precisely these challenges.

## CHAPTER 5

# The *Holy Dying:* Artistic Climax of the Tradition

In Jeremy Taylor's finest work, *The Rule and Exercises of Holy Dying* (1651),[1] the religious and literary tradition of teaching man to die well and gladly achieved its apotheosis. Its genesis had been a determined protest on behalf of purified catholicity in Christian deathbed instruction; its artistic climax was reached under the same motivation. The result of Taylor's labors was a *Crafte of Dyinge* transmuted into a richly complex masterpiece of devotional literature. At its core is once again the old conduct-book, in which a sympathetic pastor guides Everyman to heaven through the straits of death by directing his behavior and ministering to his piety with the voice of authority. But this material is now modified and enriched with every resource of humanistic culture, of Reformation thought, of Counter-Reformation devotion, and of pastoral insight. Now the reader's mind and heart and will are all to be enlisted in the endeavor to die well—and the enlistment must be for life, not for one brief battle. The resultant treatise is an Anglican synthesis in the finest sense of the word. All the distinctive but limited insights of the preceding two and a half centuries are caught up and merged into a single luminous vision of the nature and the meaning of a Christian death.

The content of this vision has evoked curiously conflicting, even contradictory, reactions from Taylor's admirers. His nineteenth-century biographers, seeing the *Holy Living* and *Holy Dying* as a single work, characterized it as both conscience-quickener and "consolation,"[2] a masterpiece leading the Christian reader "through the

---

1. *The rule and exercises of holy dying.* The edition used for this study is the first, printed for R. Royston, a copy of which is in the Yale University Library. I have modernized *s*, and corrected a few obvious errors not in later editions.

2. W. H. Davenport Adams, *Great English Churchmen*, p. 328.

path of righteousness to a death of joy."[3] In the twentieth century, biographers and critics have agreed, in general, to consider the two works separately, but have agreed on little else. From Edmund Gosse, in 1904, to Canon C. J. Stranks, in 1952, one branch of critical opinion has extolled Taylor specifically for his supposed rejection of the old tradition, in favor of an (enlightened) "modern" attitude which sees death as negation or dissolution, rather than as "grisly horror."[4] In the same vein, though less enthusiastically, James R. King maintains that Taylor's treatment of death—far from being consolatory or joyous—is "oriented to stoic comfort rather than to a Christian faith in resurrection."[5] At the opposite extreme stand those who, following Logan Pearsall Smith,[6] dismiss the argument of the *Holy Dying* as *merely* traditional—as a hackneyed unworthy vehicle for the splendors of its author's style. Robert J. Nossen's position is characteristic: Taylor's "personal attitude toward death," he says, "is unaffected by the New Science, the changing world picture, and the upheavals within religion itself";[7] it is the *Holy Dying's* "imaginative quality, rhetorical beauty, and intensity of personal feeling" which transmute this essentially outmoded medieval treatise into an enduring work of art.[8]

3. Henry K. Bonney, *The Life of the Rt. Rev. Father in God, Jeremy Taylor,* p. 96; cf. George L. Duyckinck, *The Life of Jeremy Taylor,* pp. 77, 181–82. The current view is stated firmly by Raymond A. Peterson: *The Great Exemplar, Holy Living,* and *Holy Dying* constitute "three great devotional works, not two, as popularly supposed." See "Jeremy Taylor's Theology of Worship," *Anglican Theological Review* 46 (1964):211.

4. In order, Edmund Goose, *Jeremy Taylor,* English Men of Letters Series, pp. 91, 92; and C. J. Stranks, *The Life and Writings of Jeremy Taylor,* p. 112.

5. *Studies in Six 17th-Century Writers,* p. 192. King's discussion of Taylor (pp. 159–92) centers on *The Great Exemplar,* but this particular remark is a generalization.

6. Logan Pearsall Smith, ed., *The Golden Grove: Selected Passages from the Sermons and Writings of Jeremy Taylor.* Smith's introduction is a brilliant critical appreciation of Taylor's "aureate" style—and of virtually nothing else about his work.

7. "A Critical Study of the *Holy Dying* of Jeremy Taylor," in *Summaries of Doctoral Dissertations* 19, p. 37.

8. "Jeremy Taylor: Seventeenth-Century Theologian," *Anglican Theological Review* 42 (1960): 28.

As we shall see, however, Taylor's argument is neither radically modern nor blindly medieval. It is far more comprehensive and more tightly integrated than that of earlier treatments of the theme, using only those strands of the tradition which may be woven into the author's own larger pattern; but the pattern itself is no more— nor less—revolutionary than St. Paul's interpretation of the Christian life. Furthermore, an exploration of the intricate structural principles of the *Holy Dying* will lead us to recognize the organic relationship which in fact obtains between style and content. In the best tradition of English devotional prose, Taylor's style modulates purposefully in every respect "as matters do rise and fall."[9] Those who exalt him as a poet alone—whether a poet who alchemizes "pious platitudes" with a "limited and commonplace" brain,[10] or one who exploits his mastery of baroque style as a deliberate substitute for serious theological inquiry[11]—underrate him both as thinker and as artist. *Holy Dying*, at least, has other values than wealth of lovely imagery to justify its eminence among the masterpieces of devotional literature.

In truth, the traditionalism of Bishop Jeremy Taylor's approach to the ars moriendi went far deeper than mere source-hunting can validate—or refute. He was, quite simply but in the richest sense possible, T. S. Eliot's "traditional artist."[12] As perhaps the most

9. Roger Ascham, as quoted in Chambers, "The Continuity of English Prose from Alfred to More and his School," p. cxx.

10. Smith pp. xxvi–xxvii; cf. Gosse, pp. 70–72. Arthur Pollard assumes the same general critical position in his critique of Taylor's sermons; see *English Sermons,* in Writers and Their Work Series, 158, pp. 16–19. Ironically, it was Coleridge—one of the warmest admirers of Taylor's intellect—who coined the perfect metaphor for this interpretation of his genius: Taylor's teaching on original sin, he wrote John Kenyon (Nov. 3, 1814), was a *"Ghost* in marble" (quoted in Roberta F. Brinkley, ed., *Coleridge on the Seventeenth Century,* p. 264).

11. King, pp. 165–66; the entire chapter, entitled "Jeremy Taylor: theology and aesthetics," is relevant and stimulating. King's general conclusions, based on his analysis of the *Great Exemplar,* are at radical variance with my own.

12. See T. S. Eliot, "Tradition and the Individual Talent," in *Selected Essays,* new ed.

fully representative "central" Anglican of his time,[13] he committed
himself without reservation to a position that virtually forced him
to write with a "sense of the timeless as well as of the temporal,
and of the timeless and of the temporal together."[14] For the defense and propagation of this religious commitment, his gifts of
mind and temper were uniquely fitted; and they were developed by
training and experience well suited to his needs. The facts of his
life, as such, need not occupy us here, for adequate surveys
abound.[15] Rather, it will be useful to concentrate upon his personal
growth, as man and artist, in relationship to two distinctive facets
of the thought of Caroline Anglicanism: its understanding of the
nature of religious authority and its correlative interpretation of
the ideal Christian response to the dictates of that authority.

13. His one notable speculative deviation—in quest of a kindlier inter-
pretation of original sin—does not, I think, disqualify his claim to this
description. Raymond A. Peterson comes to the same conclusion; see "The
Theology of Jeremy Taylor: An Investigation of the Temper of Caroline
Anglicanism," *DA* 21 (1961):3178. Cf. H. Trevor Hughes, *The Piety of
Jeremy Taylor*, pp. 17–44; and James Thayer Addison, "Jeremy Taylor,"
*Historical Magazine of the Protestant Episcopal Church* 21 (1952):175–76.
In regard to the representative nature of his moral theology in particular,
see below, note 24.

14. Eliot, p. 4.

15. Aside from Taylor's admiring friend Bishop George Rust, whose
well-known funeral sermon (1667) is reprinted in the first vol. of the
Heber-Eden standard edition of Taylor's works (10 vols.), the following
have contributed more or less substantial studies: Henry K. Bonney (1815),
Reginald Heber (1822), Robert A. Willmott (1847), George L. Duyckinck
(1860), W. H. Davenport Adams (1879), Edmund Gosse (1904), George
Worley (1904), W. J. Brown (1925), Hugh Ross Williamson (1952), and
C. J. Stranks (1952). For an admirably full yet concise review of the his-
tory of Taylor biography, as well as criticism, see Paul Elmen, "The Fame
of Jeremy Taylor," *Anglican Theological Review* 44 (1962):389–403.
Unhappily, a mass of private papers and records disappeared—presumably
destroyed by fire—before Bonney and Heber could make use of them.
Canon Stranks's biography is therefore probably as full and accurate as
we shall ever have. Frederick R. Bolton's more specialized study, *The
Caroline Tradition of the Church of Ireland: With Particular Reference to
Bishop Jeremy Taylor*, does, however, supplement and modify the standard
interpretations of Taylor's "Irish period" (1658–67).

Although the content of Anglican thought varied widely among leading Churchmen even in the seventeenth century, the attitude toward religious authority which underlay these differences was shared by all. The locus of that authority was to be found, not in a single authoritarian source, whether ecclesiastical, scriptural, rational, or subjective, but in a consonance of them all.[16] In effect, these four were seen as reducible to two: (1) the dictates of Christian tradition—determined above all by an infallible Scripture, but a Scripture interpreted and supplemented (in nonessentials) by the historic Church—and (2) the claims of reason—including, in its widest sense, private spiritual insight and moral sensitivity as well as the strictly ratiocinative faculty. Individual Churchmen disagreed as to the relative significance of these authorities in the determination of religious truth; hence their many arguments over specific issues. Taylor himself wavers from time to time, but in *Holy Dying* appeals over and over again to the authority of "reason and religion" together. On the whole, his insistent pairing of the two is reminiscent of Lupset's—with one all-important qualification. For Taylor, as for Hooker, reason supports revelation and explores its meaning, rather than vice versa.[17] Furthermore—and most signifi-

16. For a more precise statement of the interrelationships among these four sources as they are set forth by leading Anglican divines from Jewell and Whitgift to Taylor, Whichcote, and Stillingfleet, see James Thayer Addison, "Early Anglican Thought 1559–1667," *Historical Magazine of the Protestant Episcopal Church* 22 (1953), chap. 1, "The Sources of Religious Authority." Cf. Henry R. McAdoo, *The Spirit of Anglicanism: A Survey of Anglican Method in the Seventeenth Century*, pp. vi, 51–52.

17. See Stranks, app. F, and cf. Richard Hooker, *The Laws of Ecclesiastical Polity*, I:4. As Brown puts it, reason suggested for Taylor the "whole personality—thought, will, feeling—illuminated by the Holy Spirit" (p. 77). Hence the Christian's duty as rational man comprehended spiritual as well as intellectual discipline and growth. King's opinion that Taylor exalted the role of reason to the verge of heterodoxy (pp. 163–64) does not seem to take sufficiently into account these nonratiocinative aspects of "right reason" as Taylor interpreted the concept. In the most fundamental sense he simply "does not think of reason apart from revelation" (Hughes, p. 28). Cf. Robert Hoopes, *Right Reason in the English Renaissance*, pp. 165–67; John F. H. New, *Anglican and Puritan: the Basis of Their Opposition, 1558–1640*, p. 25; and McAdoo, p. 56–65.

cantly—he and his learned peers felt none of the constraints on
their intellectual independence that Churchmen such as Becon had,
despite Hooker's pleas, imposed on themselves. Quite to the contrary. It was in truth Taylor's religious *duty* to make the fullest
possible use of his capacities for absorbing non-Christian culture as
well as for advancing biblical and historical scholarship.

He responded to this challenge by acquiring a wealth of learning
which was impressive even in his own astonishingly learned age.
The precocious sizar of Caius College, the promising Fellow of All
Souls, came to suffer tribulations that exiled him for years from
both scholarly libraries and sophisticated conversation. Yet besides
the indirect evidence we have in his published works, both biographical data and personal letters testify directly to his lifelong
intellectual curiosity and delight in study.[18] A "rare humanist, and
hugely versed in all the polite parts of learning," he was a master of
"all the Greek and Roman poets, historians, and philosophers," and
"not unacquainted with the refined wits of the later ages, whether
French or Italian." Indeed, according to Duyckinck, his reading in
these "later ages" extended not only to contemporary scientific and
medical studies, but even to "fashionable novels."[19] His accom-

18. In his later forties, Taylor found refuge in Ireland from the difficulties besetting royalist and Laudian Churchmen such as he. Apparently
he reveled in the "opportunities of study and devotion" at Portmore; see
his letter of gratitude to Lord Conway, March 10, 1658/9 (quoted in
Bolton, p. 29), and the supporting comments in Rust's funeral sermon
(p. cccxxiii). The clichés of well-mannered and conventional divines?
Possibly. Certainly the available resources for study fell far short of the
"opportunities": aside from adequate libraries, he must have missed the
intellectual stimulation provided by Evelyn's hospitality. In any case, a
subsequent letter to Evelyn (April 9, 1659) sounds as wistful as it does
genuinely curious:

> But, Sir, I pray say to me something concerning the state of learning;
> how is any art or science likely to improve: What good bookes are
> lately publike? what learned men abroad or at home begin anew
> to fill the mouth of fame, in the places of the . . . excellent persons of
> yesterday? [E. S. de Beer, ed., *The Diary of John Evelyn*, 6 vols.,
> 3:169–70]

19. In order, Rust, p. cccxxv; Stranks, p. 129; Rust, p. cccxxv; and
Duyckinck, pp. 176–77.

plishments in the field of religious studies stagger the modern imagination. Church history, together with related secular history, martyrology, and monastic legends; ancient liturgies; "all the major Fathers of East and West"; "masses of school theology" and polemical treatises of the Reformation; the Hebrew language and Rabbinical scholarship; "medieval legend, speculations, and chronicles"; the "best casuistical literature of all ages"; masses of devotional literature and "everything of any importance which was produced in his own day"—in all these his knowledge ranged from "wide" to "immense" to "perfect."[20] Even making all possible allowances for the assistance available to Taylor in commonplace book, glosses, and anthologies, those able to judge such matters agree that Bishop Rust did not exaggerate in attributing to his friend "stupendous parts, and learning" (p. cccxxvi).

These resources he exploited with all the enthusiasm of the earlier humanists—but with somewhat more discrimination. For Lupset, veneration of antiquity per se tends to outweigh appreciation of more recent insights. For Taylor, "although they that are dead some ages before we were born have a reverence due to them, yet more is due to truth that shall never die. I must go after truth wherever it is."[21] In short, within the limits of his Anglican perspective he is Eliot's traditional artist in his attitude toward the past. Its literature "has a simultaneous existence" for him, and "composes a simultaneous order" (p. 4).

This traditionalism of Taylor was reinforced by his wholehearted commitment to the Anglican understanding of "practical piety" as the ideal for Christian behavior. Here, too, individual variations in thought were predicated on a common assumption: that the

20. Stranks, pp. 91, 129, 213. The "Index of Authors Quoted or Referred To" in the Heber-Eden edition (vol. 1, pp. [ccclix]-cccxcv) includes over sixteen hundred names, from A. L. and Abailardus to Zoroaster, Zosimus, and Zuinglius—an impressive list no matter how many dozen we attribute to Bishop Rust or the editors alone. Coleridge's epithet for Taylor's reading is *"oceanic"* (*Notes on English Divines* [1853], 1:209; quoted in Brinkley, p. 295).

21. *"Deus Justificatus,"* in *Works,* 7:519; quoted in Addison, "Early Anglican Thought," p. 281.

Christian response to grace (whether of reason or of revelation)
should be to "worship the Lord in the beauty of holiness"—a descriptive phrase beloved of Laud, and instinct for all non-Calvinists
with connotations of "decency and order."[22] It was this essentially
nonrational conviction, of course, that undergirded many of those
specific tenets attacked with such bitter zeal by the Puritan polemi-
cists. In public worship, it implied the familiar Anglican position
on behalf of adorned churches, liturgical forms of worship, and
artistically elaborated sermons. In private devotion, it implied an
interpretation of practical piety which has remained central to
Anglicanism ever since. This interpretation is almost identical with
that of Roman Catholic *humanistes dévots* such as de Sâles and
Fénelon; but it is as distinct from more ardent types of Roman
Catholic spirituality as it is from the zealous godliness of Puritanism—not to mention the "practical" ethic of non-Christian humanism. For convenience of reference, therefore, it is often called
"Anglican piety"; and it seems appropriate to adopt this name here.
Because this piety lies at the heart of Taylor's thought and style,
some understanding of its distinctive quality is essential to an appreciation of the artistic values of *Holy Dying.*

Anglican piety, then, is "in the world but not of it" in a uniquely tempered way: too public, or "sober" (in the emotional sense),
to encompass the transfiguring heights of solitary spiritual growth;
but too private, or "godly" (in the devotional sense) to envisage the
splendid achievements of a prophetic interpenetration of society.
It is "in the world" to a degree unacceptable to ascetic tradition,
for it sees all life as sacramental, as infused with God's glory or
truth or grace; yet it is not "of it," for it accepts self-discipline as
a necessary condition for keeping heart and soul (and mind as well)
"ever ready up to Godward." It therefore resolves the conflict between faith and works by identifying the response of faith *with*
works, including not only action in the world, but also prayer and

---

22. In his *Holy Living,* Taylor distills this attitude in a pronunciamento
so abnormally abrupt for him as to be amusing: "we cannot love God too
much," he states firmly, "but we may proclaim it in undecent manners"
(*Works,* 3:159).

self-conquest. Similarly, it resolves the conflicting emphases as to the nature of man by affirming both his actual sinfulness and his divine potentialities, and then identifying the Christian life with progressive sanctification in and through the Church, as the Body of Christ. Hence it is a piety both solitary and public. It is solitary, or private, because it emphasizes God's quest for the individual soul, his outpouring of grace through an infinite number of channels, perhaps the majority of which are extra-ecclesiastical. And the Christian responds as a unique personality, growing in grace in accordance with the rules of his own nature. In another sense, though, it is ineluctably corporate. Not only must that individual response express itself at least partly in terms of active interrelationships in the world, but it must also be guided and furthered and delimited by the community of the historic Church. Anglican spirituality is therefore necessarily conservative, though not to the point where one can equate it with simple "obedience to Holy Mother Church," as in the *Crafte*. It allows some room for the independent spiritual experimentation, and for independent prophetic activity; but it tests the results by the experience of the Church, particularly as embodied in its liturgy. Its persistent temptation, logically and historically, is to come to terms with the world too easily, in a relaxed sort of compromise which becomes a major target of Anglican devotional writers from Taylor on.[23] Its glory is the "practice of the presence of God" as seen in the lives of men like Andrewes and Herbert and Ferrar—free and genuinely individual in its expression, yet disciplined and familiar to the average Churchman.

Thus the seventeenth-century Anglican's normal traditionalism was actually deepened and enriched by his pursuit of a personal

23. "Like all styles of piety," as W. H. Auden observes, "it becomes detestable when the fire of love has gone out. It is no insult to say that Anglicanism is the Christianity of a gentleman, but we know what a tiny hairsbreadth there is between a gentleman and a genteel snob." His own characterization of Anglican piety "at its best" includes not only "spiritual good manners" and "reverence without religiosity," but also "humor (in which . . . it resembles Jewish piety)" (Introduction to *The Protestant Mystics*, ed. Anne Fremantle, p. 29). Cf. Hughes, p. 160.

religious life rather than, as has often happened in Christian history, being attenuated by it. In piety, as in doctrine, the personal intuition was bounded by the impersonal tradition, the immediate experience validated by the timeless witness of the past. It is therefore of the utmost significance for Taylor's development as a literary artist that he was an unusually fine Christian of this Anglican brand, with a strong *attrait* for private devotion and—in the years just preceding the writing of *Holy Dying*—plenty of time for indulging it. Moreover, this temperamental inclination toward practical piety, in both its ethical and its devotional aspects, was nurtured and encouraged by a series of potent forces that merit our attention, however briefly.

In his concern for right behavior as against right belief, Taylor was fully representative of the spirit of his age, for all its bitterness in controversy.[24] True, he received at Cambridge the usual intensive training in controversial divinity, and contributed over the years a few tracts in defense of his embattled cause. Most competent critics agree, however, that he lacked the intellectual brilliance necessary to contend more than adequately in this field.[25] More important, the futility of this form of disputation was becoming ever more evident, and was proved decisively by the outbreak of the Civil War. On the positive side, there was much to further his

24. Concerning the marked shift in emphasis from controversial divinity to "practical divinity," or moral theology, in seventeenth-century Anglicanism—its rationale and outstanding exponents—H. H. Henson's concise survey is still useful: "Casuistry," in *Studies in English Religion in the Seventeenth Century*, St. Margaret's Lectures, pp. 171–210. See also Walter E. Houghton, Jr., *The Formation of Thomas Fuller's Holy and Profane States*, chap. 4, "Casuistry"; Henry R. McAdoo, *The Structure of Caroline Moral Theology*; Thomas Wood, *English Casuistical Divinity During the Seventeenth Century: With Special Reference to Jeremy Taylor*; and Hughes, esp. chaps. 3 and 4. Wood, in particular, insists upon the "representative" nature of Taylor's contributions to this field (p. 56 and passim).

25. See, e.g., Peterson, "Theology of Jeremy Taylor," p. 3178, and Hughes, p. 153. Cf., however, the anonymous review of the latter work in *TLS*, which asserts flatly that this evaluation has been "invalidated"— that Taylor had, "in fact, an acute and deep mind in metaphysical matters" (July 29, 1960, "Christian Cadences," p. 482).

natural bent toward moral philosophy. His friendships with More at Cambridge and, later, with Chillingworth at Oxford certainly contributed to the latitudinarianism so evident in his famous *Discourse on the Liberty of Prophesying* (1647), and probably to his moral sensitivity as well. At any rate, his study of casuistry while at Oxford under Laud's sponsorship was more than an academic discipline, a necessary evil: he plunged into it so intensively that by the age of twenty-five he enjoyed a reputation already as a casuist-confessor.

The growing demand of the age for specific moral guidance paralleled that for devotional literature. Ever since Perkins's ground-breaking efforts at the turn of the century, the handling of "cases of conscience" had become more and more central in pastoral work, and casuistical sermons and treatises increasingly popular.[26] As a High Churchman urging confession on his people, Taylor was almost as subject as his Calvinist counterpart to this insistent pressure to focus his teaching upon concrete moral problems. Such an orientation not only suited his pastoral temperament, but also gave free rein to his scholarly interests. In Anglican terms, all classical moral philosophy was as pertinent to the determination of right and wrong as was the Roman Catholic literature of casuistry itself. Both, that is, needed modification, for a truly reformed and catholic casuistical guide had yet to be written.[27] Even though Taylor left

26. "Indeed," Wood observes wryly, "the seventeenth century is the only century in our history when casuistical divinity could be truly described as a subject of popular interest" (p. 36). T. G. Steffan attributes this phenomenon not only to the increasingly obvious futility of doctrinal disputation, but also to the increasing demoralization of the laity under the pressures of civil war; see "Jeremy Taylor's Criticism of Abstract Speculation," University of Texas *Studies in English* 20 (1940):96–98, 103. Both McAdoo and Wood, on the other hand, describe the popular demand for "practical divinity" as "universal" and insistent throughout the century— i.e., it was merely the supply that increased steadily. See esp. McAdoo, *Structure*, pp. x–xi, 13; and Wood, pp. 31–41.

27. Taylor's belief that his *Ductor Dubitantium* (1660) really met this need explains his conviction, so curious to the modern reader, that this was his most important work, the masterpiece on which his fame would rest secure.

Uppingham after only three years, and probably never again min-
istered to a normal parish, his fame among his contemporaries as a
confessor is quite understandable. His "experience in the cure of
souls" (sig. [a4]ᵛ) was indeed a major source for the thought of
*Holy Dying*—and also, as we shall see, for its atmosphere and
style.

For Taylor, however, practical piety was by no means to be
equated with right behavior in the limited casuistical sense alone
—fortunately for his development as an artist. Moral instruction,
when narrowed down to rules by the merely intellectual application of principles and precedents to specific instances, inevitably
becomes sterile and legalistic. Bacon had scolded the Church in
1589 for not "breaking" the "bread of life" and applying it to individual needs;[28] the literature of casuistry witnesses eloquently
to how stale and dry the pieces become when the bread is not fresh
with devotion. Taylor was to contribute perhaps more than his
share of such desiccated instruction in his gigantic *Ductor Dubitantium* (1660). There he would, like his Roman Catholic predecessors, be addressing other spiritual directors rather than laymen. But the author of *Holy Dying* was not producing a textbook;
nor had his life yet been complicated by all the confusions and
harassments which were to fill it after he left his famed retreat at
Golden Grove in Wales. Personal holiness, as he sought to pro-
mote it in his readers, always included the practice of the presence
of God in a truly devotional spirit. And as the years following his
departure from Oxford in 1638 afforded him more and more
privacy, the list of his works reflects the increasing depth of his
concern for personal devotion as absolutely essential to the Christian life.

Thus his early years of active ministry and participation in the
Civil War are marked by polemical treatises; his settlement as
a schoolmaster into the quiet life of Wales, by the *Liberty of
Prophesying* (1647); and his idyllic years (ca. 1646–54) at the
beautiful estate of Lord Carbery, by his greatest devotional works.

28. *An Advertisement Touching the Controversies of the Church of
England,* as quoted in Houghton, p. 72.

*The Great Exemplar* (1649), a long devotional life of Christ, was
followed with astonishing speed by *Holy Living* (1650), *Holy
Dying* (1651), and *Eniautos: A Course of Sermons* (1653).[29] The
first of these at least, as well as the *Liberty of Prophesying*, had
been projected sometime around 1642. Canon Stranks concludes
that "the few years before and after 1642 [i.e. years of ministry in
Uppingham and the Army] seem to have been the germinative
period of Taylor's life, but it was not until he had settled down
into the quietness of life at Golden Grove that these early seeds
could be brought to harvest."[30] It is a curious fact that no critic
or biographer (to my knowledge) has associated either the quietness of Golden Grove, or the inspiring piety of Lady Carbery—or
even the library of devotional works which we may assume she
possessed—with an intensified practice of disciplined meditation
on the part of Taylor himself. Actually, one must infer from the
known facts of his life and character that he would make precisely this use of whatever welcome tranquility he might find.

For all the Caroline theologians, as McAdoo makes clear, meditation is as integral a part of the disciplined Christian life as ordinary verbal prayer. "It is not a luxury and it is not optional. . . . To
neglect meditation is to invite dryness and apathy and deadness."[31]
Much of his supporting material, be it noted, is drawn from
Taylor's writing of this period, *The Great Exemplar* and *Holy*

29. The thematic link between these and the *Liberty of Prophesying* is
*An Apology for Authorized and Set Forms of Liturgy* (1649), an expanded version of an anonymous booklet (issued in 1646) criticizing the
Presbyterian *Directory of Public Worship*. A controversial treatise, steeped
in biblical and ecclesiastical scholarship, it represents at the same time an
appeal to those outside his own party based on the community of Christian
devotion rather than of Christian morality; and it reflects a deep concern
for the Church's "stewardship in prayer." See *Works*, 5:229–314.

30. Taylor, Stranks adds, "seems to have found [calm] necessary to
good writing" (pp. 96, 116). Other biographers and critics make the same
point in their several ways.

31. *Structure*, pp. 164–65. As the choice of metaphors suggests, this
conviction of Caroline Anglicanism was grounded firmly in the teachings
of the devotional writers of the Counter-Reformation. See Roberts, *English
Recusant Prose*, pp. 20–21.

*Living.* Furthermore, it is also clear from numerous passages throughout Taylor's works that he found this traditional duty a congenial and rewarding one, to be practiced as intensively as possible.[32] There is no reason whatsoever *not* to assume that while at Golden Grove he practiced what he preached. Indeed, he virtually tells us as much. Discussing contentedness in the *Holy Living* (chap. 2, sec. 6), he argues *(inter alia)* that present blessings always outweigh even "the evils of a great affliction" (pt. 3). The peroration of this subsection—strikingly applicable to his own circumstances, with none of his usual broad generalizations and exotic illustrations (see below, pp. 249–52)—is almost certainly autobiographical:

> Or I am fallen into the hands of publicans and sequestrators, and they have taken all from me: what now? let me look about me. They have left me the sun and moon, fire and water, a loving wife, and many friends to pity me, and some to relieve me, and I can still discourse; and unless I list they have not taken away my merry countenance, and my cheerful spirit, and a good conscience: they still have left me the providence of God, and all the promises of the gospel, and my religion, and my hopes of heaven, and my charity to them too; and still I sleep and digest, I eat and drink, *I read and meditate,* I can walk in my neighbor's pleasant fields, and see the varieties

---

32. Years later, writing to Evelyn from Portmore, in Ireland—another tranquil retreat—he even hints strongly that he has been exploring, however tentatively and diffidently, the "unitive way" of contemplation. Despite Hughes's arguments against this interpretation of Taylor's cryptic remarks (pp. 160–67), mystical experiences would be inconsistent with neither his principles nor his temperament—just so long as we heed his double caveat that progress in the devotional life is grounded in, and must in turn nourish, holy living *in action.* Indeed, his descriptions of mystical raptures —those "joys and transportations spiritual" in the "bosom of beatitude" which may be granted, on occasion, by a gracious God—are notably eloquent. For his most concentrated discussion of the traditional stages of mental prayer, including such "affections of greater sublimity," see *The Great Exemplar,* pt. 1, sec. 5, discourse 3, "Of meditation," in *Works,* 2:129–43.

of natural beauties, and delight in all that in which God delights, that is, in virtue and wisdom, in the whole creation, and in God himself. [chap. 3, sec. 91; italics mine]

By 1651, then, Taylor was fully equipped as a traditional writer in the general area of Christian piety. His vision of timeless Christian truth confirming and transcending pagan insights, as well as those of particular Christian sects and eras, was also a vision informed and quickened by a distinctively timeless kind of private Christian devotion. Furthermore, it was a vision which had been tested on the battlefield as well as in the groves of academe, and in the disheartening defeats and destruction that had succeeded the early years of quick successes and golden expectations. When Lady Carbery, fearful not of death but of dying itself,[33] "desired to know how to dye" (sig. A4), Taylor had a subject worthy of his vision.

As it turned out, "God taught her by an experiment" before Taylor's "bundles of Cypresse" were ready to "minister to her piety" (sig. A4). His own wife, too, died at about the same time. Yet he mentions this double loss only by way of introducing his dedicatory epistle to Lord Carbery; the treatise itself is notably impersonal. What Helen C. White says of the Holy Living is scarcely less applicable to its companion work: "The whole treatment is austerely objective and controlled."[34] Nonetheless, a number of critics profess to find in the Holy Dying "more personal feeling . . . than [in] any other of [his] books."[35] Like all the other divergent estimates of this work cited at the beginning of the chapter, these opposing views are seen to be reconcilable when examined in the light of Taylor's genius as a traditional artist. He

33. For reasons firmly grounded in the ars moriendi tradition: "she feared not death, but she feared the sharp pains of death . . . believing the pangs of death were great and the use and aids of reason little" (Taylor, "A Funeral Sermon, Preached at the Obsequies of . . . Lady Frances, Countess of Carbery," in Works, 8:488).

34. English Devotional Literature, p. 264. All subsequent references to Miss White's studies are to this work.

35. Stranks, p. 112. Cf. Gosse, pp. 88–89; Addison, "Taylor," p. 162; and Nossen, "A Critical Study," pp. 36, 39.

might, and did, reject details of earlier treatises on dying well; but he accepted freely the limitations of the impersonal tradition as such. And in denying his own personality, in favor of the persona of the Traditional Pastor, he found himself fully as an individual artist.

If until recently literary historians and critics have failed to analyze *Holy Dying* in the light of its tradition, it is at least partly because of Taylor's own disclaimer of indebtedness to earlier treatises on this subject. His "endeavours," he explains in a famous passage of his dedicatory epistle to the Earl of Carbery:

> are the first intire body of directions for sick and dying people that I remember to have been published in the Church of England: In the Church of Rome there have been many, but they are dressed with such Doctrines which are sometimes uselesse, sometimes hurtfull, and their whole designe of assistance which they commonly yeeld, is at the best imperfect, and the representment is too carelesse and loose for so severe an imployment: So that in this affair I was almost forced to walk alone, onely that I drew the rules and advices from the fountains of scripture, and the purest channels of the Primitive Church, and was helped by some experience in the cure of souls. [sig. (a4)$^r$–(a4)$^v$]

Taylor's repudiation of the earlier treatises on dying is based on his independence of them in two major respects: as a theologian of Caroline Anglicanism, and as a pastor whose experience simply belies some of the traditional teaching. In the former role, he naturally emphasizes his objections to the Roman works so prevalent at the time. His equally strong objections to the Calvinist branch of the tradition he merely suggests—by the device of ignoring it altogether. *Holy Dying* is, he says, the "first intire body of directions for sick and dying people . . . published in the Church of England." Yet Becon's *Sicke Mannes Salve,* which a Puritan would assuredly think comprehensive enough, had by now been through more than twenty editions! William Perkins's *Salve for a Sicke Man* (1595), George Strode's *The Anatomie of Mortalitie*

(1618), Zachary Boyd's *The Last Battell of the Soule in Death* (1629), and Henry Montagu's *Contemplatio Mortis et Immortalitatis* (1631) are among those works which Sister Mary Catharine O'Connor considers important enough to analyze for their connections with the original *Ars moriendi;* but one could expand the list several times over with the aid of the *Short Title Catalogue*.[36] In view of Taylor's prodigious appetite for religious literature of all sorts, as well as his thorough knowledge of Roman Catholic devotional literature, it is inconceivable that he should have missed all of these works. The great majority, it is true, do not contain an "intire body of directions"—from Taylor's pastoral viewpoint—simply because they focus on the death scene itself, omitting directions for long-range preparation for that day.[37] One of the most famous of all, however, Christopher Sutton's *Disce Mori* (1600), claims in its subtitle a range fully as wide as that of *Holy Dying:*

> A religious discourse mouing euery Christian man to enter into a serious remembrance of his end. Wherein also is contained the mean and manner of disposing himselfe to God, before, and at the time of his departure. . . . In the whole . . . necessary to be thought vpon while we are aliue and when we are dying to aduise our selues, and others.[38]

This work went through at least nine editions by 1626, five of them in an enlarged form, and was reissued at least once after the Restoration. Such a strongly Puritan work, however, with its dis-

36. For a sampling of representative titles, see O'Connor, *Art of Dying Well,* p. 192.

37. The eminent Perkins's *Salve for a Sicke Man,* his major contribution to the ars moriendi tradition, is illustrative of this category—even if its Calvinistic theology were not abhorrent to Taylor.

38. Quoted from the title page of the 1607 ed. ("newly enlarged by the same author"). Similarly, the famous Lewis Bayly's sixteen chapters of "directions for sick and dying people" (including even "interrogations" clearly modeled upon those in the *Ars moriendi)* are supplemented by twenty-five chapters on "holy living." See *The Practice of Pietie: Directing a Christian how to walke that he may please God,* 21st ed., "Amplified by the Author."

approval of Renaissance learning and culture, its practical social-mindedness,[39] and its atmosphere of Reformed godliness, would not seem to Taylor a worthy representative of the Anglican position as he understood it. On his own terms, therefore, his assertion of originality was entirely truthful, although it has tended to distract critics' attention from the degree to which he has absorbed the tradition he is contemning.

In the second place, the easy independence with which Taylor handles his traditional material tends to conceal the minute critical care with which each point has been evaluated. Many a distinctive detail found in the earlier treatises he rejects explicitly—once again as both theologian and pastor—but without making an issue of it by naming names. As against the *Crafte* itself, for example, he assures the reader that dying is not necessarily painful, and that deathbed "visions" of devils, angels, and so on are "phantasme[s]" of Satan, the "abused fancies" of sick or melancholy minds (pp. 305, 30, 314, 74, 51). As against the Calvinist tradition, he charges the bystanders to draw no conclusions concerning the state of a man's soul from his manner of dying, since God orders these details "for reasons onely known to himself" (p. 305). He reproves those who occupy hours of illness with "knotty discourses of Philosophy," when "a Syllogisme makes our head ake," and we desire "onely to *know Christ Jesus and him crucified* . . . plainly, and with much heartinesse, and simplicity" (p. 106); and he warns the reader eloquently to shun disputation "above all things in the world" when ill, reciting his Creed without zealous sectarian elaboration (pp. 179–80). Finally, he opposes vehemently the extreme Puritan arguments that all mourning whatsoever is non-Christian, and that funerary ceremony should be abandoned in favor of a sermon with eulogy (chap. 5, sec. 8). Even Roman Catholic affective devotion, in this context, is not exempt from attack. Taylor does not recommend meditation even in health on Judgment, heaven, and hell, and his own treatment of these subjects is notably devoid of imaginative elaboration. Indeed, his approval of the technique itself, insofar as it aims at a specifically emotional re-

39. Cf. Wright, *Middle-Class Culture,* p. 251.

sponse, is tempered by the view, expressed elsewhere, that "tears are no duty."[40] The sick man, faced with the real duty of translating "ineffective contemplation" into exercise (p. 157), may lean on emotional supports of various kinds—but only because he is sick enough to need this type of aid, "most proper to weak persons" and those "under the dominion of fancy" (p. 161).

Three other, more fundamental propositions deserve special mention because of their far-reaching implications. All are readily predictable on the basis of his High Church Anglican theology and his Laudian convictions about Church polity. At the same time, all reflect his discriminating use of his predecessors' labors. First, he denies firmly the basic assumption of the original *Crafte* and most subsequent treatises: that holy dying is a Christian duty distinguishable in essence from holy living.[41] God, he says, "hath made no new Covenant with dying persons distinct from the Covenant of the living" (p. 242). On the other hand, he asserts just as strongly the duty of summoning clerical aid *in extremis.* The death scene, he insists, is not so unimportant as the humanist would imply, nor do fellow believers constitute an adequate priesthood, as the Calvinist maintains. Lastly, all deathbed repentance, whether Roman Catholic or Calvinist, he brands as invalid and ineffectual. Convinced that true contrition is impossible without growth in grace (chap. 4, sec. 6), he offers only a microscopic grain of traditional comfort to the "vitious" belated penitent.[42]

These major tenets alone would set *Holy Dying* apart from its predecessors, as a characteristic attempt to formulate an Anglican compromise based on Scripture, tradition, and common sense. Yet

40. *"Unum Necessarium,"* in *Works,* 7:429.

41. For further development of this point, see below, pp. 216–17. Almost every prefatory statement made in this section will be similarly elaborated upon, and documented, in the detailed analysis which follows. Textual references here have therefore been limited to sources of quotations and of minor points not discussed below.

42. See chap. 4, secs. 5 and 6 passim; and Hughes, p. 31. On the whole, Taylor's approach is severely admonitory: "A repentance upon our deathbed is like washing the coarse [corpse], it is cleanly and civil; but makes no change deeper then the skin" *(Holy Dying,* pp. 189–90).

even these are peripheral and relatively insignificant illustrations
of Taylor's method, as compared with the extraordinary density
and richness at the core of his argument: his identification of holy
dying with the very nature of the Christian life itself. The equa-
tion of "life in Christ" with "the Way of the Cross" is of course
fundamentally Pauline; but surely no devotional writer before
Taylor had developed St. Paul's theme with anything approaching
the complexity of understanding, still less the artistic intensity,
that we find here. Undergirding his structure, controlling his argument, permeating his imagery, Taylor's interpretation of the ars
moriendi epitomizes Christian traditionalism as that phrase was
understood by the Caroline Anglicans. It also provides the final
justification for his claims of independence from the tradition to
which he was so obviously indebted. Each major theme in this
study he handles in such a way as to preserve the tradition inherited
from the Middle Ages. At the same time, he modifies it in accordance with the insights of Renaissance and Reformation, and
weights it in accordance with that pastoral concern which is central to the treatise. And all the themes now blend into an intricate,
harmonious interpretation of "dying well" as the very essence of
the Christian's daily experience.

To begin with, the word *dying* does not refer exclusively to the
death scene. Taylor, as humanist, Church historian, and pastor,
rejects the notion that this closing scene differs qualitatively from
the others in the drama of a Christian life, and he strengthens his
position with the Stoic argument that all life is a progressive dying.
Unlike the *Crafte, Holy Dying* does not present man as first alive
and then dead, in an abrupt dichotomy of simple analysis. Rather,
Taylor's Moriens rushes precipitously toward his grave, dying
momently in accordance with Seneca's axiom. But the last step is
no less final for all that: the experience of death still remains an
existential challenge of ultimate significance, a reality all the more
poignantly felt because the values of the world and of human personality are now fully acknowledged. Since death is also presented
as the first of the Last Things, its terrors necessarily include the
possibility of everlasting rejection by God. Yet Taylor does not
communicate this aspect of death's fearfulness with anything like

the same force that we find in the passages on death as terminus. The reader is not allowed to forget the imminence of Judgment; but neither is he scorched imaginatively with hell's fire and suffocated with its stench. Instead, he is caught up, with almost physical immediacy, in the onrush of time. To be, for just a few fleeting instants, and then not to be—this is his life on earth. Properly understood, *dying* is indeed synonymous with *living,* just as the Stoics maintained.

Taylor's response to the threat of death is not, however, the Stoic proposition accepted by Lupset. The Christian humanist's teaching that dying well is to be equated with living well is significantly reversed by the humanistic Christian: living well is to be equated with dying well. The emphasis has been shifted back from the rational virtues to the sacrificial virtues, from ethics to devotion. As in the *Sicke Mannes Salve,* the Christian covenant is interpreted as one of faith and repentance, the Christian life as the perfecting of repentance; and both Becon and Taylor identify this route to salvation with the Way of the Cross—although Becon avoids the dangerous phrase, using "the Cross" alone. For Taylor, this majestic theme of Christian devotion has an intellectual complexity and an emotional richness which are lacking in the Reformer's bleak and meager definition.[43] The human Jesus no longer has to be considered suspect as a subject of meditation and of imitation by devout Protestants. Taylor is therefore able to invest his treatment of the theme with a warmth of feeling for *"Christ Jesus and him crucified"* unknown to Becon; and his Arminian view of the Christian drama of redemption opens up for him a far more complex understanding of the implications of this traditional metaphor of the Christian life.

In *Holy Dying,* the God of holiness and righteousness is also the God who is Love, interpenetrating his world at every point[44] and striving incessantly to win man's freely proffered allegiance —to persuade him to renounce the "bondage of sin" for the "per-

43. See above, chap. 3, note 34.
44. But most conspicuously in (emblematic) nature, in human reason, and in the Church.

fect freedom" of God's service. The treatise is liberally sprinkled with wry smiles at the irony of man's persistent rejection of this outpouring of divine grace;[45] and the irony is all the more poignant because this rebellious creature is not only contingent upon his Creator, but made in his image and endowed with an inestimable wealth of divine potentialities. In conforming himself to God's will, he would also realize himself fully, would achieve "the perfective end of humane nature," as Taylor puts it (p. 124). The dramatic action of *Holy Dying* has its locus in the struggle of man—free and responsible, but called, prodded, and strengthened by God—to pursue his own best interests by overcoming gradually the drag of self-will. To one just entering upon the life of grace this drag expresses itself most clearly in terms of worldliness and spiritual inertia. Its real potency becomes clear to him when he loses both charity and faith itself the moment troubles beset him. And its continuing power is evidenced even on his deathbed, when he meets the otherworldly temptations—to spiritual presumption or excessive fear or both—and recognizes the extent to which even the good he has done has been corrupted by his basic selfishness.

This lifelong struggle of the spirit is characterized by a dramatic intensity far different in quality from that of the struggle in the *Sicke Mannes Salve.* There, the loss of one engagement will mean the forfeit of the war, and the embattled Christian has little to help him but the memory of a divine transaction in the past. Taylor's Christian does not have to grit his teeth so tightly at any single challenge, since no one defeat is fatal, and God is with him anyway. The tension of *Holy Dying* lies in a double contrast: on the one hand, the immeasurable length of his spiritual journey

45. Taylor's quiet humor is particularly delightful when he is satirizing the average Christian's attitude toward the Church's ministry to the sick. Such Laodiceans, he remarks, "fear the Priest as they fear the Embalmer; or the Sextons spade; and love not to converse with him, unlesse [they] can converse with no man else; and think his office so much to relate to the other world, that he is not to be treated with, while we hope to live in this" (pp. 245–46).

and the painful slowness with which he creeps forward; on the
other, the very limited "measure of [his] days on earth" and the
agonizing speed with which he rushes through them and "descends
into his grave."[46]

Theologically speaking, Taylor's presentation of this drama is
fully trinitarian, although in the first two chapters he tends to
avoid explicit reference to the personae of deity. Emotionally, however, *Holy Dying* is strongly Christocentric. Its focus is the living
Christ—not the hero of an historic redemptive act, but "our blessed
Lord." In muted tones at first, then in full strength from chapter 3
on, Taylor proclaims the essence of the "covenant of repentance"
to be a *"covenant of sufferings"* (pp. 195, 100), and the essence of
the Christian life a day-by-day striving to keep the *"high way of
the Crosse"* (pp. 100–01). The phrase is no longer reserved even
primarily for undeserved sufferings of a major kind such as Becon's
Christopher lists;[47] it even has decidedly positive connotations.
Christ is the Lord, the Great Exemplar of perfect manhood: to
conform oneself perfectly to God's will would be to come "unto the
measure of the stature of the fulness of Christ" (Eph. 4:13). And
to respond to God's love at all, however slightly, is to follow "the
holy Jesus" toward the goal of the "glorious liberty of the children
of God."[48] At the same time, such a response involves one inescapably in a moral struggle to substitute disciplined obedience
—"the discipline of the crosse" (p. 53)—for self-willed inertia or
worldliness. Inevitably, the more complete his obedience, the more
loving and patient will be his acceptance of all the slings and
arrows of life, however minor.

Since Taylor assumes that no man can achieve perfect love and
obedience through a single dramatic conversion experience, the
Way of the Cross becomes a daily acknowledgment of Christ as
Lord, a daily repentance before Christ as Judge, and a daily dying
to sin and rising to new righteousness through trust in Christ as

46. In *Holy Dying,* a frequent substitute for "dies."

47. See above, chap. 3, note 34.

48. Rom. 8:21; Taylor modifies this to *"the liberty* and life *of the sons
of God"* (p. 122).

Redeemer.[49] The Christian life is the "perfecting of repentance" because as the heart grows in love and the will in obedience, the conscience simultaneously grows in sensitivity; penitence becomes contrition. To live well, therefore, is really to die well: to spend all the fugitive moments of physical dying in learning, through God's grace, how to die spiritually to self and live in Christ. And to die well at the last is once again, as in early Christian experience, only the final act of the Christian's "bounden duty and service" of self-offering to God throughout his life.

The distinctive nature of the pastoral relationship which Taylor establishes with his reader follows directly from the foregoing premises. The reader is presumed to be neither radically unregenerate nor fully sanctified; he belongs to the huge majority of baptized Christians, ranging from merely nominal believers to those well advanced in spirituality, who fall into neither extreme category. He is, in short, the Everyman of the *Crafte,* depicted in a seventeenth-century context. His many possible variations in age, wealth, social position, personality, and so forth are acknowledged, but discussed only in terms of their relevance to his spiritual situation.[50] In his relationship to God he stands alone, influenced

49. Although King argues that Taylor's Christology is so "meager" as to verge on heresy, his perceptive analysis of the (baroque) portrait of Christ in the *Great Exemplar* actually supports and illuminates my argument both here and below. The Christus Triumphans, who was and is and is to be eternally present as Model, Judge, and Redeemer; the Lord of history, and of men's hearts, who is "above" time and yet "in" the Eucharist —this is precisely the Christ whom Taylor adores, and sets forth for our adoration. For many Christians, such a Christ may well be "unsatisfactory," in every sense, or even unconvincing; but he can scarcely be dismissed as "little more than an ethical model" (p. 163; and cf. pp. 177–90).

50. See, for example, the dedicatory epistle, and chap. 3, sec. 4, pt. 1 as to difference in age; chap. 5, sec. 8 and chap. 5, sec. 3, pt. 7 as to those in wealth and social position; and chap. 3, sec. 2 and chap 5, sec. 3 passim as to those in personality. Hughes's observation concerning Taylor's restrictions in his portrait of Moriens is pertinent: "Even if it be admitted that Taylor wrote mainly for the ordinary Christian who may know little of the depths of degradation or the heights of rapture, he would still have done a great service to the majority unacquainted with the extremes" (p. 15).

by his sociological context but at the same time isolated from it. And in this isolation he discovers the ultimate insignificance of secular distinctions as compared to humanity's oneness in its alienation from God. Theoretically, he might be any professing Christian of 1651, at any level of sanctification, though always capable of further growth in grace.

In artistic fact, however, as critics inevitably point out, Taylor's Everyman is rather more limited than this. To put it succinctly, he is—just as the dedicatory preface implies—Moriens "in the Church of England"; and a rather well-bred Moriens at that. Not only must he accept Anglican theology and ecclesiastical polity, but he must also bring to his reading of Holy Dying a measure of intellectual ability and cultural training which one cannot demand of the bona fide Everyman. All the more natural, then, that Taylor's Christian should be firmly attached to this world's values at the beginning of his spiritual pilgrimage, and hence peculiarly sensitive to the threat of death as terminus. In the later stages of his growth, his increasing atachment to God's values has as its corollary a sharper recognition of his own sinfulness, and hence a new sensitivity to the threat of God's rejection of him after death. But by this time, in terms of Anglican thought, he is in a state of grace sufficiently advanced to make his salvability probable, though never, of course, certain. Hence his attitude on his deathbed is properly, not the oscillation between hope and fear of the medieval sinner, but a subtler, more complex combination of the two, in which fearful hope overbalances hopeful fear (chap. 5, sec. 5). Hell's rumblings are audible (chap. 5, secs. 3 and 7), but in Taylor's quiet description they seem little more than the rumblings of a retreating thunderstorm.

As this individual Christian moves toward death on the one hand and sanctification on the other, the Church's response to his needs must—in theory, anyway—modulate accordingly. In Holy Dying, this ecclesiastical ideal is embodied in the persona of the Anglican Pastor, who guides the pilgrim along the Way of the Cross by ministering to his growth in piety with the authority of reason and revelation combined. This persona has several interrelated functions. As a cultured, learned, and urbane gentleman, he speaks to the condition of the thinking Christian, persuading him of the intellectual acceptability of the Christian religion, the reasonableness of following Christ as "the Way, the Truth, and the Life," and the rational validity of each step which his spiritual progress entails. As a trained spokesman for a distinctive ecclesiastical position, he also sets forth the basic principles on which he is grounding his direction, whenever these are called into serious question by his Church's adversaries; but he marshals his authoritarian citations and deductive arguments in a remarkably noncontroversial spirit, seeking less to confound the opposition than to confirm his own parishioner in allegiance to the Anglican understanding of the Body of Christ. As a spiritual director, he uses the affective techniques developed during the Counter-Reformation to sting the nominal Christian into action, and to spur the Laodicean to greater effort. As a confessor, he employs both the analytical methods and the jargon of casuistry in demonstrating sternly just how far "all have sinned"—whatever their level of spiritual achievement—"and come short of the glory of God" (Rom. 3:23). On the other hand, he also offers the sinner, from the wealth of his experience in the cure of souls, many sound practical suggestions to aid him in his spiritual warfare—often with a flash of humane wit. As a priest, finally, he automatically correlates growth in grace with increasing obedience to the Church's discipline and thankful acceptance of its sacramental aids. His final instructions for the dying are therefore almost as bleakly authoritarian as those of the *Crafte.*

The variety of these roles leads him not only to adopt a wide range of tone, but also to use many contrasting types of material. Yet all the variations in tone merge into one dominant one: the gracious but impersonal, informal but strongly reserved, pastoral tone of a priest whose conviction of sacerdotal dignity restrains both his sense of humor and his prophetic wrath. And all the elements in his argument are interwoven harmoniously in accordance with the same principle. His pastoral mission is neither to command (in the blunt, rubrical sense of the *Crafte)* nor to convert (in the evangelical sense of Parsons's *First Book of . . . resolution),* but to *persuade,* in every sense of the word: "to minister to practise, to preach to the weary, to comfort the sick, to assist the penitent, to reprove the confident, to strengthen weak hands and feeble knees" (sig. [a4]ᵛ). His guidance is authoritative, but not coercive; "he that hath ears to hear, let him hear."

The general pattern of this guidance is as firmly controlled by Taylor's pastoral ideal as are its contents and its tone. As he explains in the dedicatory preface, "the consideration and exercises of death" constitute both "the great *argument* and the great *instrument* of holy living" (sig. A5; italics mine). Appropriately, therefore, the structure of *Holy Dying* is a twofold one, paralleling that of the Christian life. Its primary movement, as the work's full title suggests,[51] is a chronological one, adapted from the *Crafte*. Within this, the Church provides the reader with authoritative direction at every stage of his descent from mature health into the grave. Its second movement, interlocking with the first as tightly as woof with warp, is that of the Ignatian meditation. Within this, the Church encourages and supports his efforts to grow in spiritual strength even as he declines in physical vigor. That the two types of guidance blend into a single harmonious pattern, instead of clashing incongruously, is a tribute to the dedicated skill and insight of the Traditional Pastor as Taylor depicts him.

"My Lord, it is a great art to dye well," writes Taylor to Lord Carbery, "and to be learnt by men in health" (sig. A5). The basic structure of *Holy Dying* is as obviously derivative as this prefatory remark. Five chapters set forth the "precepts of *dying well*" (sig. A6), directing the reader from the thought of death in days of health to the moment of his "departure," or "passage"—and directing those about him for a short time afterward as well. The chronological span of these chapters extends far beyond that of the *Crafte,* because Taylor's Moriens progresses methodically from good health to illness of an indeterminate sort before taking to his bed for the last time. Nonetheless, the treatise moves inexorably toward that end. Its dramatic focal point is still the deathbed, its central purpose still the effectual guidance of the Christian through the final crisis of his earthly pilgrimage. And a major proportion of the Pastor's labor consists in providing him with remedies against

51. See bibliography.

the temptations that will beset him in illness and in the face of
death.

If we disregard for the sake of convenience the office for the
visitation of the sick incorporated into chapter 5, the text of *Holy
Dying* consists of four roughly equal parts, addressed respectively
to the healthy, the sick, the gravely ill, and the dying (via the priest
ministering to him.) Yet to note only this quasi-logical ordering of
the argument is to overlook a far more significant organizing
principle: the momentum with which the treatise escorts the reader
toward the grave. Only two short chapters assume him to be
healthy. Moreover, the first of these, corresponding to the *descriptio
mortis* of the *Crafte,* identifies him promptly as Moriens and di-
rects him to practice the art of dying while in health. In effect, it
serves to establish the death-centered orientation which the medieval writer could take for granted. The second, preparing him "by
way of exercise" for a "holy and blessed Death," is alien to the
medieval work in its introduction of motifs from the literature of
the ars vivendi; but its argument is stringently delimited to include
only those rules which are immediately relevant to deathbed conduct. "Meditate on the Last Things daily, and live in accordance
with the implications of their imminence." Such advice is in one
sense merely an elaboration of the axiom that to "cun die" is to
have a "herte and . . . soule ever redy up to godward."

The third chapter, constituting the second quarter of the treatise,
moves on to discuss "the state of sicknesse, and the temptations
incident to it with their proper remedies." Presumably this sickness may or may not be fatal; but the reader is not allowed to
forget the possibility. The two temptations treated here are the
temptations to impatience and to the fear of death, in that order.
The picture is therefore darkened even before the conclusion of
this section, and the reader prepared to spend the last half of the
treatise on his deathbed. The fourth chapter, directing the sick
man's behavior until the arrival of his "Clergy Guide," assumes
that death is now probable, even though it does admit some faint
possibility of recovery. Its advice therefore corresponds in many
ways to that given by the conduct-book to the solitary Moriens.
The final chapter, instructing priests in their ministry to the dying

and the dead, and including an office for the visitation of the sick, is technically outside the scope of the *Crafte,* except insofar as the "Minister of religion" is merely replacing the "friends" of the medieval work, or leading them in bedside worship.

Because the reader of *Holy Dying* is himself Moriens hastening deathward, he is provided with authoritative guidance for each major stage of his journey, the guidance becoming increasingly explicit and directive as he nears the end. Because he is also, ideally, studying these instructions while in health, able to "discourse and consider," his "understanding, and acts of reason . . . not abated with fear or pains" (sig. A5), he is provided at the same time with an elaborately wrought *meditation* on holy dying. The first chapter leads him to visualize the truth about the brevity, vanity, and misery of man's life; to appropriate these axioms emotionally; and to resolve to "remove from hence, at least in affections and preparation of minde" (p. 47). The next three enlist his memory, his understanding, and his will on behalf of the proper Christian response to health, to sickness in general, and to his final illness in particular. The final chapter represents the specific deathbed behavior which should issue from all this preparation, as both summary and climax. The dynamic, concrete, and particular framework of this meditation is that of the *Crafte,* expanded; and because its chronological span is so much greater than that of an actual spiritual exercise, it encompasses not only analytical, abstract, and general elements of all kinds, but other meditations on a smaller scale as well.[52]

In sum, the long-range program of the Pastor as spiritual director is to guide his exercitant-reader from the widest possible consideration of human mortality to the concrete deathbed conduct of a salvable Christian. To accomplish this, he diminishes his focus gradually, forcing the reader to center his attention and response more and more specifically on his own personal duty in the face of his own personal death. Obviously, considerations may play an important role at each stage in the process—*except the last.* If the layman is to be moved to do his duty even while death is still re-

52. See, for example, below, pp. 227–32.

mote, affective aids are likley to be needed, as well as didactic instruction and rational argument. As the final hour approaches, such aids may still be very helpful in limited, specific ways. But the concluding scene of the drama will, if the director is successful, find the Christian so well prepared in mind and heart and will that further aid of this type would be superfluous. His response is to be one of faith-ful action without more ado: he will, quite simply, receive the Holy Communion and die "well."

The "logical looseness" which Miss White attributes to seventeenth-century devotional literature in general (p. 174) does not, therefore, apply to the argument of *Holy Dying.* Even those minor organizational flaws which tend to disturb the modern reader vanish entirely when considered in relation to the dual movement traced above. Individual points are numbered consecutively, without regard to the logical outline undergirding them, because the reader is to meditate on them—or practice them—in that order. Similar arguments recur from time to time, inviting the charge of repetitiousness; but they recur precisely because time is presumed to have passed, so that a basic principle of the Christian life needs to be reexamined from a different viewpoint. And even topics that are logically parallel are developed in dissimilar ways because the Pastor is not concerned with their rhetorical effectiveness, but with their existential significance for his reader. Each point receives, therefore, just the type of support it needs, and as much as it needs—no more.

As a matter of fact, Taylor established within his devotional framework a remarkably high degree of rhetorical balance. Not only is *Holy Dying* divided into four logically distinct segments of about equal length, but its five chapters are themselves symmetrical. The first and fifth contrast with each other radically, the second and fourth moderately; and the third is pivotal. The first chapter addresses the reader as Rational Man, the last as Obedient Christian. The first concerns itself with abstract and general considerations related to mortality as idea; the last, with concrete and particular actions related to dying as experience. The second and fourth are similarly oriented, one toward life, the other toward death; but the relative weighting of consideration and action is more nearly equal. The former concentrates on the healthy man's practice of the active graces relevant to dying well, the latter on the sick man's practice of the passive graces. The third chapter, finally, is pivotal both logically and chronologically. The remedies given for the two temptations are of both kinds—"by way of consideration" and "by way of exercise"—and clearly are to be pondered in health as well as acted upon in sickness. The chapter concludes, however, with the "general rules and exercises whereby our sicknesse may become safe and sanctified."

In sum, it is scarcely valid to stigmatize *Holy Dying,* as Logan Pearsall Smith does, for its "lack of lucid arrangement" (p. xxvi). Its structure is a complex fusion of several different types of arrangement, but a fusion which is entirely valid in terms of Taylor's equally complex interpretation of the Christian life and the Church's role therein. And the more closely we examine the treatise in the light of its traditionalism, the more clearly we see that the same principles are determinative throughout. *Holy Dying* is as tightly constructed in detail as it is in broad outline; and here too the catalytic agent in the synthesis of its elements is the persona of the Anglican Pastor.

The structure of the first chapter is technically analytical, but meditative in its inner movement. Taylor's opening "Consideration" seems at first glance to be obviously bipartite, with its subheadings focused on the classic themes of the vanity and miseries of life; but this appearance is deceptive. Actually the argument is tripartite. Taylor begins with the axiomatic premise of man's mortality, underlines it with mortuary truths, and deduces rapidly the reasonable generalization that one should live in the present— with the Christian qualification "in the light of eternity" suggested, but not argued. He then explores each side of this proposition in turn. His explanation of just how to seize the day centers traditionally upon the unreasonableness of man's vain waste of the little time he has;[53] the reality of eternity remains in the background

---

53. Cf. esp. Seneca, *De brevitate vitae,* which Taylor follows closely in a number of his points.

as a muted assumption. With the introduction of the more specifically Christian theme of life's misery,[54] however, the emphasis
shifts. Now the reader is urged to make the most of the present
*as a Christian*—to live "in the world but not of it" in the Christian
rather than the Stoic sense. The rhetorical organization of the argument therefore supports its meditative purpose: to establish the
precise nature of humanistic-Christian otherworldliness and move
the reader to embrace it.

Even in this short chapter, Taylor employs—in sequence—four
quite different types of structure for his major points. All recur
throughout the treatise. To analyze them here in some detail will
therefore spare us the pain of dissecting later, less aesthetically rewarding passages. All but the last, be it noted, are comfortably
traditional.

The first is that of the five-part meditation, which he adapts for
his opening affective "directed meditation" on the brevity of life
—that superlative passage so lovingly mangled by the anthologists
of English prose.[55] The fragility of human life is visualized in
concrete metaphor in the very first sentence: *"A Man is a Bubble."*
As the composition of place proceeds, the original image is enriched by allusions to the Bible, to mushrooms, to Hades, to homely
everyday experience, to the colors of a dove's neck, to the insub-
stantiality of a rainbow, and to many other images. The three
points of the meditation are the three areas in which God provides man with emblems of this text: in the human body itself, in
nature, and in the evidence of literature and history. Taylor's modification of the structure consists in treating each of these as affectively as the text itself: concrete images pour forth in astonishing
profusion. The conclusion is that "death meets us every where,"
and that "the chains that confine us to this condition are strong
as destiny and immutable as the eternal laws of God." And a final
image generalizing Taylor's pastoral experience invests the "us"

54. But cf. Cicero, *Ep.* 5, and Seneca, *Ep.* 30.
55. C. A. Patrides notes that it was probably plagiarized as early as
1657, in Richard Steward's *Catholique Divinity.* See "A Note on Renaissance Plagiarism," in *N & Q,* n. s. 3 (1956):338–39.

with personality: "we [you, the reader, and I] also shall die" (pp. 9, 10).

The second major form of organization used here and throughout the treatise is that of the classical moral essayist: the statement of a thesis; the reasonable discussion; the dramatic illustration, chosen usually from history or biography; and the reminder of the moral. Taylor employs this frequently, though always loosely. He uses it here, in section 2, to set forth the general implication of the fact of man's frailty. It is invalid to seek immortality via wealth or fame or both; to seek longer life via elaborate hopes or projects or both—such propositions lend themselves readily to this type of development. At this stage in *Holy Dying* affective elaboration still enriches the barer points in the outline. Nevertheless, the basic structure is clear; and it is eminently well suited to the "deduction" of "reasonable" conclusions which in fact simply assume the truth of Christian dogma without in any sense arguing it. The invalid responses to the challenge of mortality, we gather, are those which posit a concept of time as a meaningless stream, while the valid response asserts the meaningfulness of time in the light of eternity; but nothing whatever has been said to justify logically such an interpretation.

The third and last of the traditional structures employed in *Holy Dying* makes its appearance in the very next section. Taylor's rebuttal of the humanistic protest that life is too short takes the form of "Rules and Spiritual arts of lengthening our dayes." Here, as in other similar passages of such generalized advice, his analytical scheme is obscured by the numbering of points as if they were parallel. In this instance, though, he does not confuse the reader still further by setting topic sentences or important transitional generalizations inside the boundaries of a specific numbered point. Hence the pattern of his thought is readily seen to be a modified version of that used by the author of the *Crafte* in laying down his directions: the statement of the rule, the citation of authority which proves the necessity for obeying it, the provision of practical aids, the offering of incentives, and the recapitulation.

Taylor's modification of this "pastoral structure," if we may call it so, derives from the fact that he is no longer able simply to pronounce a rule, as appointed spokesman for "holy moder chirche." As a humanist and a Protestant, he must first establish his definitions and premises, and convince the Christian that his suggestions derive validly from them, before he can proceed with their elaboration in accordance with this pastoral outline. Hence he defines *true life* in three paragraphs, as that limited portion of a man's existence during which not only his body is mature, but his mental and spiritual faculties fully awakened and rightly used. He uses two paragraphs to establish the principles that sin shortens true life, while virtue prolongs it "enough." The philosophical definition and moral principles constitute the major and minor premises respectively of what may be called a "casuistical syllogism." The reader is now prepared to accept as valid the principles of behavior which constitute its necessary conclusion. In very general terms at first, and then in more detail, Taylor states the rule: the Christian is to eliminate vicious and wasted hours by avoiding sin and striving to develop that life which is true life. For ecclesiastical authority he substitutes that of Scripture (Dives), of history (Parsons's monk who beheld hell in a vision—now "a Melancholy person"), and of classical exempla (Xerxes, weeping over the mortality of soldiers whose deaths he was to hasten). He contributes his own practical psychological hint (to count time in small units) and a familiar practical incentive (the assurance that virtue often prolongs life literally as well as spiritually). The argument concludes with a long quotation from Seneca which summarizes his point—and, indirectly, commends it once more to the humanistic reader as an eminently sound rule, based on reason as well as revealed religion.

The fourth and final structural pattern introduced in this chapter is one not considered before in this study, but one peculiarly suitable for Taylor's own distinctive tone of meditation, since it blends the quietly thoughtful with the warmly affective. It consists of a series of points (often numbered, again), which are treated in different ways and are not tightly parallel anyway; but they do mesh together into a coherent, though imprecisely ordered, meditation. In this case (sec. 4), Taylor marshals seven points to convince the reader of the misery of the human lot. The sequence moves from (1) the general physical miseries of the world, to (2) those of men and women, to (3) those of the sick and the well, to (4) those of the bad and the good, to (5) those of the small and the great, to (6) those mixed with pleasures proportionately, for all of whatever rank, to (7) the summary: "Man never hath one day to himself of entire peace . . . he is always restlesse and uneasy, he dwells upon the waters and leans upon thorns, and layes his head upon a sharp stone" (pp. 42–44). The effect of this cumulative technique of meditative argumentation is to channel the reader's thoughts and emotions with increasing momentum in one direction, so that he is in a sense preconditioned to accept whatever inferences meet him at the end without rational, objective cross-examination. Here he accepts not only the comforting Stoic conclusion that "the sadnesses of this life help to sweeten the bitter cup of Death," but also the Christian conclusion that he should "remove from hence, at least in affections and preparation of minde" (pp. 43, 47). Taylor has never allowed the assumption of the reality of eternity to come into question at all, still less to be argued. He has simply over-whelmed his reader with such a barrage of miseries that the latter is more than willing to rest his restless heart in the peace of God.

The first chapter of *Holy Dying* provides us, therefore, with an extraordinarily full and complete illustration of Taylor's method of adapting traditional patterns freely to his own more complex purposes. The implicit structure of his general preparation is now seen to be, like its purpose, essentially meditative. The problem: What should be the Christian's response to the fact of his mortality? The starting point: a concrete visualization of the reality of that fact, by means of an Ignatian meditation. The progress from thence to resolution: an intellectual confirmation of the general implications of mortality (by means of a static, but not drab, human-istic argument); an understanding of the personal orientation de-manded logically by those truths (by means of a casuistical adapta-tion of Aristotelian logic); and an emotional commitment to the validity of such an otherworldly orientation (by means of a loosely constructed meditation with cumulative emotional impact). That is, the choice of basic organizational scheme in each partiular in-stance is determined by Taylor's target: memory (or rational acquiescence), understanding, or will. The exercitant has been led, whether consciously or not, through a meditation on Psalm 39:4–6:

> Lord, make me to know mine end, and the measure of my days, what it is; that I may know how frail I am. Behold, thou hast made my days as an handbreadth; and mine age is as nothing before thee: verily every man at his best state is altogether vanity. Selah. Surely every man walketh in a vain show; surely they are disquieted in vain: he heapeth up riches, and knoweth not who shall gather them.

The challenge to resolution is made in the last sentence of the chapter: "let us remove from hence, at least in affections and preparation of minde." The reader who moves on to chapter 2 has taken up the challenge and added of his own accord the Psalm's seventh verse: "And now, Lord, what wait I for? My hope is in thee."

The other four chapters of *Holy Dying* need not be analyzed in such detail. The same structural elements are used, though in different combinations and with steadily decreasing affective elaboration. Chapter 1 has enlisted the reader into a life of active commitment to God, and done this with notable speed. Unlike Parsons, Taylor assumes the presence of a relatively sympathetic reader. The nominal Christian to whom the first chapter is addressed is not, as he puts it, of *"an open villany"* (sig. [A9]ᵛ), but rather that nominal Christian who lurks in every one of his readers, whether more or less devout. Thus, in terms of his pastoral purpose the most significant development in the chapter is his swift creation of an I-thou relationship with the reader.[56] Because the reader is presumed to be sympathetic, Taylor can move more rapidly than Parsons could from the opening generalized statement *("A Man is a Bubble")* to the particular application *("thou art a man")*. On the other hand, for reasons which have been explored, this personal relationship, once established, remains more reserved than Parsons's for a longer period of time. The key to the structural

56. Cf. above, chap. 4, pp. 170–77 passim, 178, 179.

modulation from chapter to chapter is to be found in Taylor's gradually increasing assertion of priestly authority over his reader as the latter moves forward toward both death and sanctification.

Chapter 2, like chapter 1, is technically static and analytical in structure; but here the inner movement is theological as well as meditative, while the tone of pastoral authority is noticeably stronger. The "exercise" by which the Christian is to prepare throughout life for a holy death consists of three precepts: to anticipate death daily, to make a daily self-examination and confession of sins, and to practice charity toward his neighbors. Taylor analyzes these as exercises in the active graces of faith, hope, and charity respectively, and shows how each comprehends both devotional response and moral activity.[57] The faithful Christian meditates on and prepares for death, and embraces "a life severe, holy, and under the discipline of the crosse" (p. 53). By anticipating Judgment daily and perfecting his repentance, he makes hope possible. In responding to God's love by exercising charity himself, he participates "of the divine nature" and looks with more confidence for his own acceptance at Doomsday (pp. 67–68).

It will be observed that Taylor has so organized his analysis that the practice of the Christian virtues in life is explicitly related to meditation on the Last Things. Moreover, whereas chapter 1 challenges the reader with the fact of mortality as such, chapter 2 focuses his attention on the more concrete challenge of his own deathbed. Taylor expounds each point not only as a means of growing in grace generally, but also as a means of forestalling a miserable deathbed in particular. Thus, he climaxes the first with a reference to the traditional deathbed agonies of the voluptuous; the second, with a description (similar to Parsons's) of the agonies of the bad man; the third, with a warning against trusting to deathbed charity to save one's soul. And the chapter concludes with an "affectionate" meditation, constructed from "dispersed" thoughts of the Fathers, which describes in all its familiar detail *"the circumstances of a dying mans sorrow and danger"* (pp. 72–76). Here

---

57. For a general discussion of Taylor's teaching in regard to the three theological virtues, see Hughes, pp. 95–106.

Taylor makes room not only for the physical pain of dying but even for the "gripes of Devils," qualifying these traditional torments only slightly. The reader who resolved at the end of chapter 1 to embrace a life of practical piety has now been instructed by a rational analysis as to what such a life means—that is, the Way of the Cross—and at the same time has been provided with additional, more forceful, meditative incentives to "begin betimes, and lose no time" (p. 71).

In the pivotal third chapter, rational analysis is subordinated for the first time to authoritative pastoral guidance. The pattern adopted for the discussion of the temptations incident to sickness is a blend of the pastoral and the meditative. It starts with an affirmation of revealed Christian truth, or a statement of principles of Christian piety derived from that truth, and issues in a series of concrete "rules and exercises" for the Christian to perform. The premise in this case (sec. 1) is that the "Way" of the Cross is also the "Truth": that although sickness, death, and dissolution are inevitable because of the sin of Adam and its multiplication through intervening generations, yet through Christ's Passion these miseries may be transmuted into "rosaries, and coronets . . . *instruments, and earnests, and securities, and passages* to the greatest perfection of humane nature, and the Divine promises." The conclusion (sec. 9) is a series of general directions to obey *"whereby our sicknesse may become safe and sanctified."* As we shall see, they issue logically from the intervening remedies against impatience (secs. 2–6) and against the fear of death (secs. 7–8). Despite the striking difference in length, these two discussions are just as parallel in organization as it is psychologically valid to make them.

In the first (pp. 81–125), prefatory remarks of a distinctly pastoral nature lead into a casuistical analysis of the *"constituent or integrall parts of patience."* Authority explains why complaints in sickness must be *"without despair," "without murmure,"* and *"without peevishnesse";* it proclaims the duties of Christian piety in opposition to each—hope, faith (in the sense of "thy will be done"), and charity; and it summarizes this statement of basic principles with a (nonaffective) description of the patient man in terms of action in faith. Taylor then moves on, like the author of the *Crafte,* to provide specific help to the Christian, first in his negative battle against the temptation, and then in his positive struggle on behalf of the corresponding virtue. For the first, he persuades the mind by a "cumulative meditation" reviewing all the traditional humanistic clichés applicable to illness. For the second, he enlists the will by reminding the reader of the relevant Christian promises, and demanding from him a response of gratitude. The former consideration induces Stoic resignation; the latter exercise seeks, not merely to confirm that response by means of Christian doctrine, as with Lupset, but to invest it with a new quality altogether. The climactic argument (sec. 5, pt. 5), introduced by a traditional meditation on "Jesus crucified," is that a positive welcome of suffering, rather than mere resignation, is the Christian's most inescapable duty. As a follower of the Cross, he is to transmute evil into good by offering it to God. Taylor now closes these remedies with a few pastoral remarks about the possibility of recovery.

Then he launches wholeheartedly into a third major section, on the *"advantages of Sicknesse,"* which corresponds to the *Crafte's* marshaling of practical incentives for Moriens. But "O, what a change is here!" Three points are embedded in a superb affective meditation on the Christian soul's steps in "dressing herself" for heaven as the body lies sick. This eloquent passage not only climaxes the discussion of impatience, but also provides the chapter as a whole with a central emotional peak.[58] Two other advantages follow,[59] each elaborated with a wealth of miscellaneous images. The orchestration is perhaps even richer, but definitely reduced in intensity. After these, Taylor can move, without destroying the effect, into a coda of pastoral admonitions against postponing the practice of these graces until sick.

The second discussion, of the temptation to fear death (pp. 125–43), seems at first glance oddly truncated. Less than half as

58. Quoted in part below, p. 266.

59. It is "the opportunity and the proper scene of exercising some vertues"; and it may become a "great instrument of pardon of sins" (pp. 110, 116).

long as the first, it exemplifies that rhetorical imbalance deplored by Taylor's critics. Yet his attack on this temptation actually follows the identical tripartite organization—except for ellipses dictated by common sense. The opening analysis of the true nature of the virtue under attack is obviously unnecessary, so introductory pastoral remarks lead directly to remedies. Again the "consideration" persuades the mind of the reader with a loosely ordered collection of Stoic arguments,[60] each presented in the traditional manner, as in the earlier series: principle, historical example, and summary—or definition and logical implication—reinforced by some imagery and a good deal of pastoral experience. Again the *"remedies . . . by way of exercise"* seek to inculcate a Christian attitude that is more positive than one of mere noble resignation. The development of Christian otherworldliness and Christian fortitude[61] will increase one's love of heaven, deepen one's acceptance of God's will—and free one from enslavement to fear. Taylor is too practical to put his case any more strongly than this. The *"dead that die in the Lord"* do not cling to life, but they do not sin in fearing death to some extent, since Jesus did (pp. 138, 141). Death is among the "sowre and laborious felicities of man," and those in a state of grace will be free of "violent and transporting fear" of it (pp. 142–43). The third section—the marshaling of incentives —if balanced symmetrically with its counterpart, would have to extol some extreme form of death wish, or yearning for heaven sooner rather than later. This Taylor does not include.

The *"general rules"* which issue from these two arguments, and conclude the chapter, lead the reader one long step closer to the actual practice of holy dying. Death is becoming less and less a reality to be thought about with humanistic objectivity, or considered devoutly as an incentive to virtue, and more and more clearly an experience to be faced. After warning the Christian to be sure his illness is authentic, Taylor summarizes the general rule

60. Cf. above, chap. 2, pp. 88–91.
61. Defined simply as the strength to do one's duty regardless of possible consequences—which may well include death for Christians more often than for pagans. For a summary of Taylor's teaching in regard to the cardinal virtues, see Hughes, pp. 117–45.

pertaining to patience as centering in repentance and prayer. His eulogy of prayer rises sweepingly to the power of prayer as death approaches ("of all the actions of religion . . . the last alive"), but retreats skillfully from turning the sickbed into a deathbed as yet: prayer "therefore best dresses our bodies for *funeral, or recovery, for the mercies of restitution, or the mercies of the grave*" (pp. 151–52). In the same way, the general rule pertaining to minimizing the fear of death brings death closer to the reader. Every illness is to be treated as *"unto death,"* the sick man sending for the help of the Church, renouncing sin, and withdrawing from the world as completely as possible. Whereas much of the chapter provides food for thought, as well as encouragement to virtuous action, in health as well as illness, its conclusion is as flatly directive in spirit as the *Crafte* itself.

"Now," says Taylor, introducing the fourth chapter, "we suppose the man entring upon his Scene of sorrows, and *passive graces.*" The tone of this sentence is deceptively reserved, remote from the reader's own "practise of the graces, proper to the state of sicknesse . . . alone." "He"—someone else—who has heard "the melancholy lectures of the Crosse," must now "passe from an ineffective contemplation to . . . exercise." But even before the end of this sentence, the true orientation of the chapter begins to reveal itself. That alien, impersonal third-person "he" must "passe . . . to such an exercise as will really try whether *we* were true disciples of the Crosse" (italics mine). And the brief introduction ends: "we are to practise by the following rules" (pp. 156–57). The remainder of the chapter consists of pastoral advice of all sorts for the Christian to follow *until the arrival of the priest.* The methods by which he is to practice each grace are aligned for convenience in a set analytical order: suggestions to help him maintain the desirable attitude toward God, rules to control his behavior in accordance with that attitude, and selected readings and prayers to aid him in his devotions. The graces as a whole, however, are organized in accordance with the liturgical order of the Office for the Visitation of the Sick. The Pastor still has many homely, practical hints to offer—but he has now donned his cassock, and is reaching for his stole.

In the meantime, the Christian is to accept his illness patiently, conforming himself to God's will and behaving properly to those around him. More specifically, he is to confirm and strengthen himself in faith, at all costs; to repent and do satisfaction for his sins; and to *"set his house in order"* in terms of his practical duties to his family and to society. The basic assumption is that Moriens is by now a loyal and obedient Churchman, doing what he can by himself in preparation for the Anglican equivalent of the rite of Extreme Unction. His duties correspond to the first two elements of the office as found in Cranmer's Prayer Books: (1) acceptance of the situation in patient and loving trust, and (2) preparation for the sacramental of Penance by means of "the examination of faith and conscience, and the setting in order of the patient's affairs, spiritual and temporal."[62] Taylor includes apropos of the duty of repentance a closely reasoned, and very dreary, polemical attack (sec. 5) on the Roman Catholic view of Extreme Unction— and also, indirectly, on the Calvinist view of deathbed repentance —arguing that the repentance of the sick must be "the prosecution and consummation of the covenant of repentance, which Christ stipulated with us in Baptisme ... which we began long before this last arrest" (p. 195). He also offers the troubled sinner a résumé of the *"means of exciting contrition,"* and a Protestant confessor's analysis of the Decalogue and *"the special precepts of the Gospel"*[63] —both of these as aids to making the repentance effectual. In short, the chapter represents a well-balanced logical analysis of the reader's specific duties when he falls ill; but it is an analysis subsumed now into liturgical structure, and modified by the demands of ecclesiastical controversy as well as of practical pastoral helpfulness.

With chapter 5, the wheel of the ars moriendi tradition comes

62. The Standing Liturgical Commission of the Protestant Episcopal Church in the U.S.A., *Prayer Book Studies, III: The Order for the Ministration to the Sick,* p. 11.

63. Secs. 6 and 8; but as Sister Mary Catharine notes, the latter "sounds like the lists given in Catholic prayer books for preparation for confession," while his later argument on behalf of auricular confession (chap. 5, sec. 3) is "almost entirely Catholic" (p. 208, n.).

full circle: once again the argument becomes almost entirely liturgical in structure. Its preface is a brief defense of the Anglican view of the ministry, necessary to convince the reader that the summoning of a priest is as much a duty for Anglicans as for Roman Catholics. The body of the chapter, however, consists of what might be called footnotes of varying lengths to each of the five portions of the Office for the Visitation of the Sick, followed by the office itself—or rather, a substitute form for use while the Book of Common Prayer is suppressed.

The type of note is determined by the needs of the time, as Taylor interprets them, as well as by his avoidance of unnecessary repetition. Thus, having already discussed the first two sections of the office, he contents himself with a summary of the "ordinary offices" which the "Ministers of religion" shall perform first (chap. 5, sec. 2, pts. 5, 6). The third, confession and absolution, demands elaborate comment. He has not only many directives and helpful suggestions for his fellow confessors, but also a wealth of arguments designed to convince the more Protestant reader of the value of sacramental penance. These are represented as arguments of which "the sick man may be reminded" (p. 250); but it seems probable, on the grounds of pastoral psychology alone, that Taylor hopes to convince his reader indirectly while the latter is still healthy. "When a person is sick," as a recent Liturgical Commission says, "it is hardly the time to argue about the value of auricular confession."[64]

So, too, the notes on the administration of Holy Communion (sec. 4) include a polemical discourse on the Anglican view of excommunication as well as particular rules to guide the clergy in communicating the sick and dying.[65] And his *"considerations"* against *"unreasonable fears"* and *"Presumption"* are to be pondered by the healthy reader as well as administered to those who are not

64. *Prayer Book Studies,* p. 17.

65. Taylor naturally makes no reference to the sacramental of Unction, the fourth unit of the Sarum Office; this was incorporated by Cranmer in the 1549 Prayer Book, but dropped in his 1552 revision. In Taylor's office (and notes thereon) the administration of Holy Communion becomes the fourth portion, and the "recommendation of the soul" the fifth.

awaiting the *commendatio* in precisely the right spirit. A final curt summary of the duties of the bystanders corresponds to the prayers for them in the postlude of the office.

The fact that Taylor's ministrations to the dying are climaxed by the celebration of the Eucharist—instead of the *interrogationes* of the *Crafte* or the persevering assurance of an Epaphroditus— epitomizes his reinterpretation of the tradition in the light of "purified catholicity" as he understood it. Christ, who has been the Way in health and the Truth in sickness, is also the Life to the faithful Christian confronted by death and Judgment.[66] The point is underlined in the *"peroration"* (sec. 8), when the pastor issues directions to the mourners, but reminds them that their duties are utterly unrelated to the destiny of the departed. Unlike his Calvinist counterpart, Taylor's Everyman has not waged a solitary deathbed battle with eternal life as the stakes; rather, it is the quality of his life as a whole which has been under judgment. *Did* he die "in the Lord," or not? He had the help of sacramental grace at the last, so the Anglican reader is emotionally predisposed to answer yes, even while admitting the technical uncertainty of the outcome. The treatise ends, significantly, not with an exhortation to go and do likewise, but with a Christian moralist's précis of the duty of the living if they would "rest in the bosome of the Lord" (p. 339).

In summary, *Holy Dying* is anything but loosely or carelessly organized. Even formal balance exists. Although relatively unimportant, it suggests pleasingly the Anglican ideal of a life of order and decency, in which a life of piety is rounded out in a reasonable

66. See the sickbed prayer addressed to Christ (quoted in part below, p. 256); the context of John 14:6; and 1 Cor. 11:23–26 (one of Taylor's favorite passages). Cf. also Karl Rahner, S.J., *On the Theology of Death,* trans. C. H. Henkey, 2d English ed., revised by W. J. O'Hara, pp. 76–77 and passim. In *Holy Dying* Taylor gives relatively little space to the sacrament, not because he is "unconcerned," as Nossen implies ("Jeremy Taylor," pp. 35), but because he simply takes for granted its central, and climactic, significance. Bolton, discussing this attitude as characteristic of the Church of Ireland during this period, points out that "the rubrics before 1662 [even] required 'a good number to receive Communion with the sick person' " (p. 172).

way by the sleep of death. Far more significant, however, is Taylor's brilliant merging of traditional schemes of organization into a pattern that encompasses not only the Anglican understanding of "piety" but even the Anglican definition of "authority." Death-oriented, it rushes with Christian through time toward the grave; yet it keeps the relationship between holy dying and holy living in such delicate suspension that the reader somehow finds himself not only well prepared for dying literally when the time comes, but freshly motivated to die figuratively in a new Christ-centered life. Church-oriented, it follows the believer's sanctification from merely nominal acceptance of the Creed to full participation, "with hearty repentance and true faith," in the central act of worship of the historic Christian community; yet it allows room for the latecomer to join him along the way. For purposes of reference, in contrast to earlier structures we may call this one "Anglican pastoral."

In the light of the foregoing analysis, the stylistic variations in *Holy Dying* are seen to be organic rather than accidental, the corollaries of design rather than the incongruities of erratic genius. Anthologists quite naturally look to the first chapter for representative illustrations of Taylor's most distinctive style, since this is the locus of his most concentrated and poetic use of what we have called the style of "directed meditation." Nonetheless, such a selection inevitably suggests that Taylor faltered as he went along, recapturing only occasionally the vision with which he began. For this reason, the wholly admirable consistency which underlies the rise and fall of his style is well worth exploring. Throughout the treatise, each particular style supports the limited pastoral role appropriate at the moment, furthers the central characterization of the persona of the Traditional Pastor, and aids in the communication of Taylor's understanding of the Christian drama of redemption.[67]

67. According to Elmen, both the seventeenth-century admirers of Taylor and the enthusiasts of the Romantic Period respected the inseparability of style and content in his work, recognizing that his style was indeed the "outward and visible sign of the spiritual unity he [had] been

The several roles adopted by this Anglican Pastor in his colloquy often blend with each other, as we have seen, but they do not become blurred. As in real life, he varies his method of approach according to the given situation, and tends to weight his diction and tone according to that approach.[68] As didactic theologian, he defends those sectors under fire by direct appeal to the authority of

---

able to achieve" (p. 390; and see pp. 395, 401). Curiously enough, however, the only other close studies that have been made of Taylor's prose style as a whole, in all its range and variety, are Sister Mary Antoine, *The Rhetoric of Jeremy Taylor's Prose: Ornament of the Sunday Sermons,* and James Roy King, "Certain Aspects of Jeremy Taylor's Prose Style," *English Studies* 37 (1954):197–210. Both studies, being grounded in different premises than mine, take different approaches and employ different analytical categories.

68. Taylor's prefatory explanation of his modus operandi in the *Great Exemplar (Works,* 2:34–37) might just as well have been repeated in his dedicatory epistle to Lord Carbery: his fourfold design is identical with that which has been shown to permeate the *Holy Dying.* (1) He has "prepared considerations . . . least severe and most affectionate," designed to appeal to readers "wholly made up of passion." (2) He has so "ordered" these, and supplemented them with "practical discourses," as "may help to answer a question, and appease a scruple, and may give rule for determination of many cases of conscience." (3) For those of greater mental capacity, capable of appreciating "those old wise spirits who preserved natural reason and religion in the midst of heathen darkness," he has provided "more severe" material, including both "art" and "learning"—even though "the excellency of its [Christianity's] secret and deep reason is not to be discerned but by experience." True lovers of the moral wisdom of the Ancients, as against the "triflings" of "later schoolmen," may thus be "invited" to consider Christianity as "the great treasure house of . . . excellent, moral and perfective discourses." (4) And, finally, he must be "diligent" in correcting false doctrines which are the "seeds of evil life" —yet "without engaging in any question in which the very life of Christianity is not concerned." Even as Taylor merely defines his four concerns, and his intention of interweaving them in a Pauline fashion ("milk for babes, and for stronger men stronger meat"), his diction, sentence structure, and above all *tone* modulate appropriately—just as in the *Holy Dying.* In short, "the very manner of presentation [suggests] the appropriate response of the believer" (King, pp. 176–77). See also Robert S. Jackson, "The Meditative Life of Christ: A Study of the Background and Structure of Jeremy Taylor's *The Great Exemplar,*" *DA* 19 (1959):3296.

Scripture, history, and common sense, and also by time-honored argumentation based on such premises as the assumed will, or even nature, of God. In either case, he employs on the whole characteristically dry and precise technical diction. Arguing against excessive fear of damnation, for example, he asserts that "God glories in the titles of mercy and forgivenesse, and will not have his appellatives so finite and limited as to expire in one act, or in a seldome pardon" (p. 292). As casuist, he not only defines, analyzes, and argues moral points relevant to the effectual guidance of the Christian's conscience, but employs the clichés of his field in doing so: "the integral and constituent parts of" (a virtue); "such projects are to be reproved which"; "what is to be faulted is"; the "determination" of "cases of conscience"; and so forth. As priest, he simply orders the Christian's practice, whether in the imperative or in the subjunctive: "be sure to"; "the sick man is to"; "let him"; "a prayer to be said"; and so on.

Even when acting as spiritual director, where he is most effective when working indirectly, he frequently calls attention to this role with familiar phraseology: he urges repeatedly the practice of "affectionate" meditation, or "consideration," to "enforce" practice.[69] Sometimes he himself will "represent this scene . . . a little more dressed up in Circumstances," or "fancy" (pp. 10, 49). Sometimes he urges the reader to do it himself: "Propound to your eyes and heart . . ."(p. 101). He suggests over and over the value of warm devotion both in itself and as an incentive to holy living, and underlines this basic principle of Counter-Reformation piety with a final reference to the damnation of the Laodiceans: "a lukewarme person is . . . despised by God. . . . *a holy life* [today], in the dayes of the Apostles and holy primitives would have been esteemed *indifferent, sometimes scandalous,* and *alwayes cold."* And "to feel nothing, is not a signe *of life,* but *of death"* (pp. 257–58, 257).

69. Understanding, he maintains, makes faith "lasting and reasonable" (see above, note 17); but it is the function of imagination to make it "scrupulous, strict, operative, and effectual" (*Great Exemplar,* in *Works,* 2:325).

But just as the practicing clergyman remains himself even as he shifts his mental gears, so Taylor's style retains its integrity in spite of these modulations. Each separate role, though clearly identifiable, is modified considerably to harmonize with that of the central figure who comprehends them all: the Anglican Pastor. The dull and cold styles are enlivened to some extent by rhetoric, and even warmed occasionally by imagery. On the other hand, the colloquial and intimate styles of the spiritual director as depicted by Parsons are endued with a new restrained formality: Taylor is more self-consciously artistic than the Jesuit in his use of different syntactical patterns and supporting imagery. The result is a persona who is less formidably authoritarian in his didactic and directive pronouncements, but decidedly more remote in his personal challenge to the reader—a pastor restricted to persuasion alone as his weapon against spiritual inertia. The running metaphor which crystallizes this characterization, and which relates it in turn to each facet of the pastoral vocation, is the comprehensive medical figure identifying that work with "the cure of souls."

The theologian, for example, is conventionally dull as he argues at length a declarative interpretation of the discipline of excommunication (chap. 5, sec. 4); but he is direct and forceful when defining the nature of the ministerial office in general (chap. 5, sec. 1). In the former, the burden of thought is carried primarily by the abstract nouns and technical adjectives and adverbs of theological analysis; in the latter, by the verbs of earnest pastoral labor or the biblical images suggesting that labor. Over thirty verbs enumerate specific "channels of Ecclesiastical ministries" by which Christians "derive blessings from the fountains of grace" (p. 243). Ministers are, in sum, *"servants of the will of God,* instruments of the Divine Grace and order, *stewards and dispensers* of the mysteries, and appointed to our souls to serve and lead, and to help in all accidents, dangers, and necessities" (p. 245). The cure of souls implied here is medical only in the broadest sense of painstaking attendance and cherishing care (as in the New Testament use of *therapeuō*). Significantly, however, the ministry of the confessor is described even in this didactic passage as including the duties "to enquire into our wounds, and to infuse oil and remedy" (p. 244).

The casuist, too, more often than not brightens his pronouncements and warnings by casting them in effectively balanced sentences and supporting them with vivid metaphor. Admonishing
the sick man to make his will clear and precise, he remarks: *"He
hath done me no charity, but dies in my debt that makes me sue
for a legacy"* (p. 232). After reminding the sinner in some detail
of the many sins "condemned *in the court of conscience,* and no
where else," he concludes: "Under the dark shadow of these unhappy, and fruitlesse Yew-trees, the enemy of mankind makes a
very many to lie hid from themselves, sewing before their naked-
nesse the fig-leaves of popular and *idol reputation,* and *impunity,
publike permission, a temporall penalty, infirmity, prejudice,* and
*direct errour in judgement,* and *ignorance"* (p. 263). It is the confessor, naturally enough, who most frequently refers to the minister
as the "physician of souls." The sick man must be exhorted to
auricular confession lest the minister's "discourses . . . not wound
where they should, nor open those humours that need a lancet or
a cautery" (p. 250). Such instances could be multiplied a hundred-
fold.[70]

Even the priest avoids barren commands whenever possible.
Rubrics, of course, read as rubrics; and direct orders are often
given bluntly. Usually, however, such orders are either rephrased
or elaborated upon immediately so that they come to seem merely
the reasonable suggestions of a sympathetic and humane pastor.
One rule for the practice of patience is addressed to those who
fuss about keeping up their "exterior actions" of devotion when
sick (chap. 4, sec. 1, pt. 6). The passage begins: *"Be patient in the
desires of religion,"* and continues with specific directives for
interior meditation and prayer. Yet its conclusion is characteristic
of the warm, nonauthoritarian temper of almost all such passages:

if you can do more, do it; but if you cannot, let it not become
a scruple to thee; we must not think . . . that he who swoons

70. Hughes observes that this fact alone would identify Taylor as closer
in spirit to the Celtic Church than to the Roman, especially after Trent:
"the latter [penitential system] was judicial, the former remedial. The
Roman was concerned with the removal of guilt, the Celtic with effecting
a cure" (p. 91).

> and faints, is obliged to his usual forms and hours of prayer; *if we cannot labour, yet let us love.* Nothing can hinder us from that, but our own uncharitablenesse. [pp. 163–64]

Moreover, the priest's "secret" prayer at the beginning of the Office of Visitation (chap. 5, sec. 7) stresses rather more than an ordinary liturgical prayer his weakness, unworthiness, and need for the aid of Christ's Spirit. And, finally, even his sacerdotal functions—usually exalted stubbornly by Taylor—take their place metaphorically among all the other "medical" duties of the pastor. In *Clerus Domini* (1651), the celebrant of the Eucharist is referred to as "priest" or "minister"; in the rubrics of the substitute "Office . . . of the Lord's Supper" (1658), as "minister" alone, but in the pertinent rubric in *Holy Dying,* as "curate." The pastoral connotation is clear because the visiting "Minister of religion" (whom Taylor still feels free to call "priest" when he chooses) is not necessarily to be the curate of the local parish (chap. 5, sec. 2, pt. 4).[71]

The pastor, on the other hand—the "I" who enters at frequent intervals with casual reminiscences of his experiences, or homely observations about the vagaries of human nature, or direct challenges to "thee," the reader—is far less colloquial in his tone of voice than Parsons, less immediate in his confrontation.[72] In the first place, both his memories and his observations are so formalized rhetorically that they become largely impersonal. And in the second, they are often invested with a peculariarly impersonal type of wit: that sense of the "cosmic incongruity" of sin which is a timeless possession of the humanists and saints of all ages.[73] He "remembers," for example, conversing

71. In a later form for the Visitation of the Sick Taylor is even more explicit: the visiting priest is referred to as "Minister and Curate of Souls." See *Collection of Offices,* in *Works,* 8:674.

72. Occasional exceptions are all the more striking for their rarity: e.g., his brusque statement that the sick man, if "backward" about making a full confession, "must be hollowed [hallooed] to"; or his ingenuous admission to the reader (at another point): "Here I intend not to dispute, but to perswade" (pp. 261, 336).

73. White, p. 265; and cf. C. S. Lewis, *A Preface to Paradise Lost,* chap. 13, on the "absurdity" of Satan.

with some men who rejoyced in the death or calamity [of] others, and accounted it as a judgement upon them, for being on the other side, and against them in the contention; but within the revolution of a few moneths the same man met with a more uneasy and unhandsom death: which when I saw, I wept, and was afraid: for I knew that it must be so with all men, for we also shall die and end our quarrels and contentions by passing to a final sentence. [p. 10]

The reminiscence is expressed in such general terms, and with such biblical overtones as regards his supposed response, that one feels its literal autobiographical truth is completely irrelevant. Similarly, his trenchant comments about human nature, although in context far more convincingly his own, are couched in such balanced form that the reader is less aware of the speaker than of the observation. Apropos of the duty of patience in illness (chap. 3, sec. 2), he remarks: "Men that are in health are severe exactors of patience at the hands of them that are sick, and they usually judge it not by terms of relation, between God and the suffering man; but between him and the friends that stand by the bed-side" (p. 81). After instructing the reader firmly to treat his sickness as if it were mortal (chap. 3, sec. 9) he argues that a bold assurance is really

the greatest timorousnesse and cowardize in the world. They are so fearfull to die, that they dare not look upon it as possible; and think that the making of a Will is a mortall signe, and sending for a spirituall man an irrecoverable disease, and they are so afraid lest they should think and beleeve *now they must die,* that they will not take care that it may not be evil *in case they should.* . . . But it will be a huge folly if he shall think that confession of his sins will kill him, or receiving the holy Sacrament will hasten his agony, or the Priest shall undo all the hopefull language and promises of his Physitian. *Assure thy self thou canst not die the sooner; But by such addresses thou mayest die much the better.* [pp. 152–53]

Both the rhythmical balance and the quiet smile of this passage

seem to remove the sting of immediacy from the direct address of
the last sentence.

The same principles apply even in his most eloquent or most
severe moods. Urging the reader to welcome suffering as the discipline of the Cross (chap. 3, sec. 5), he exhorts him fervently to
follow Christ to the reward of Sonship in Heaven; but his eloquence
remains muted, controlled within the bounds of rhetorical balance. Here are the climactic clauses: "and if this [the present
suffering] be the effect or the designe of Gods love to thee; let it
be occasion of thy love to him: and remember that the truth of love
is hardly known, but by somewhat that puts us to pain" (p. 102). In
his discussion of the Christian remedies for the fear of death
(chap. 3, sec. 8), he builds up his argument to a stern pastoral
command: "Make no excuses to make thy desires of life seem
reasonable; neither cover thy fear [with] pretences, but suppresse
it rather, with arts of severity." This direct (and uncomfortably
perceptive) warning is so abrupt that it almost jolts the reader
personally; but the individual challenge is relaxed immediately by
a smiling consideration of those who are not willing to die until
they have completed some project or other now in hand. (Taylor
gives seven delightfully apt, though generalized, examples.) "It is
well for the modesty of these men that the excuse is ready; but if
it were not, it is certain they would search one out: for an idle man
is never ready to die, and is glad of any excuse; and a busied man
hath alwayes something unfinished, and he is ready for every thing
but death." By the time Taylor has added an exemplum from
Petronius and an argument with scriptural citations, the concluding imperative seems to summarize a principle rather than
command an action: "Say no more, but when God calls, lay aside
thy papers and first dresse thy soul, and then dresse thy hearse"
(pp. 139–40).

Besides the use of formal sentence structure and impersonal
humor, a third technique for maintaining a certain reserve between
Pastor and Christian is suggested by these same illustrations. This
is the deliberate shifts in pronominal usage, by which the reader
is intermittently drawn into colloquies similar to Parsons's, but
quickly released. Taylor's presumed syntactical casualness may

indeed be attributable in part, as Canon Stranks suggests (p. 290), to his reliance upon preaching techniques, when the tone of voice serves to carry the congregation safely over grammatical hurdles. Certainly the rhythms of English speech are dominant in the majority of Taylor's sentences—perhaps most of his best ones, even the most formal. Yet it seems unnecessary to consider them in any sense accidental to his writing. We have seen how appropriate such rhythms are for effective directed meditation and Taylor had excellent artistic reasons for making use of the opportunity they afforded him for "moving in and out" in his relationship with the reader. Besides, he had the best of all possible precedents: the inconsistent pronominal usage of the Psalms and the prophets. Thus, hackneyed Senecan arguments tend to be sharpened by the rather frequent use of the second person, while the pastoral "we" or impersonal "he" softens the impact of considerations, condemnations, and commands which might otherwise be too forceful, in one way or another, for the purposes of *Holy Dying.*

Finally, we may note that the reader himself is kept at a distance by the Pastor, who addresses him directly as one soul, yet as one among thousands. The constantly shifting pronouns contribute to this effect, of course; so too does the obvious technique of generalizing one's illustrations. Two other devices, however, are of particular interest to the student of Taylor's style, since they have received so much comment—*in vacuo,* for the most part— from his admirers. These are his insistent use of the most remote allusions in illustration of a homely point, and his peculiarly effective combination of such illustrations with those drawn from everyday English life.[74] A generally deprecatory tone characterizes much of the discussion of Taylor's bookishness. Delightful as it is,

74. Although these devices were characteristic of seventeenth-century devotional works in general, it is Taylor, of course, with whom we associate the technique at its most extravagant. His nineteenth-century admirers delighted, on the whole, in his "picturesque allusiveness"—save when it shocked their moral sensibilities. (See, for example, Adams, p. 320.) Twentieth-century critics are somewhat more likely to deplore the "uncontrolled exuberance, the . . . flamboyant disorder" into which it may sometimes degenerate (Pollard, p. 16; cf. Nossen, "A Critical Study," pp. 36–37).

we are told, it indicates only too clearly the fundamental snobbery of the Anglicans of his time, their alienation from the commonalty to whom the Puritans appealed so effectively with anecdotes and observations of contemporary life.[75] This accusation, though no doubt valid in its essential historical thesis, may too easily be over-emphasized in relation to *Holy Dying.* Here, over and over again, such bookishness serves not only to temper "over-affective" passages,[76] but also to universalize the particular reader—to create Everyman out of a multitude of highly diversified Christians.

Mortuary horror, for example, is always discussed at a distance, and even the most gruesome *exempla* are thereby divested of immediate repulsiveness. Juxtapositions of homely and remote imagery invest the "cold dishonour" of death with a unique atmosphere of gently poignant sadness. A few years' "sleep" in charnel houses, he says, will render men's "strength not so stubborn as the breath of an infant, and their wisdom such which can be looked for in the land where all things are forgotten" (p. 135). References of this sort to mortuary truths warn us with a melancholy reminder; but they do not shock. Keeping the reader at this aesthetic distance from his own wormy fate—so lovingly described in all its horrific detail by contemporary balladeers—Taylor may even indulge himself in a smile at men's fussiness about funeral arrangements: "For to them [the dead] it is all one whether they be carried forth upon a chariot, or a woodden bier, whether they rot in the air, or in the earth, whether they be devoured by fishes or by worms, by birds or by sepulchral dogs, by water or by fire, or by delay" (p. 331). Even the recent death of someone very close would not be likely to spoil one's appreciation of this passage. What shock potential it does contain is salutary rather than demoralizing, since it underlines

75. See, for example, King, pp. 155–56; and cf. the hostility to Taylor's style of the Puritan Robert South (1634–1716): "All dress and ornament supposes imperfection, as designed only to supply the body with something from without, which it wanted, but had not of its own" (quoted in Pollard, p. 22). For an expert summary of the modulations in Taylor's reputation over the past three centuries, see Elmen, *passim.*

76. Cf. Brown's observation that Taylor avoided "working upon the emotions of his congregation" (p. 153).

quite forcefully the universality of dissolution as a natural phenomenon.

Canon Stranks supposes that to some extent at least, Taylor was motivated to his extreme bookishness by a pastor's diffidence: a personal illustration might be too readily identifiable by the small circles of his parish and his friends (p. 130). This notion seems a bit insulting to Taylor's powers of tact and imagination, but it is suggestive. Any sort of particularization would be out of place in a work which seeks to meet the needs of every reader with the resources of the timeless best in the Western heritage. To refer to any one contemporary father's hopes for his son and methods of training him would be to introduce, however briefly and indirectly, sociological distinctions of the sort which limit Becon's treatise so drastically. But every father can identify himself with "the man that designes his son for noble imployments, to honours, and to triumphs, to consular dignities and presidences [sic] of counsels." He, too, can "rejoyce when the bold boy strikes a lyon with his hunting spear, and shrinks not when the beast comes to affright his early courage" (p. 115). To specify the miseries of seventeenth-century Englishmen would be at best distracting; but all men, however fortunate, can accept imaginatively the presence of "gnats in our chambers, and worms in our gardens, and spiders and flies in the palaces of the greatest Kings" (p. 35).

So too with Taylor's startling and delightful conjunction of the (vague, generalized) everyday image with the strikingly unusual, even esoteric. Enchanted, one is lured away from the natural urge to localize the contemporary allusion. Any intelligent man who manages to love this world, Taylor muses, must also be reconcilable "with tortures": a "witty man" might persuade him to "dwell with Vipers and Dragons, and entertain his Guests with the shrikes of Mandrakes, Cats and Scrich Owls . . . with the filing of iron, and the harshnesse of rending silk; or to admire the harmony that is made by a herd of Evening wolves when they misse their draught of blood in their midnight Revels" (p. 46). Arguing on behalf of a daily self-examination, he affirms that it sensitizes one's conscience; "And he that is used to shrink when he is pressed with a branch of twining Osier, will not willingly stand in the ruines of a house, when the beam dashes upon the pavement" (p. 61). Most men, he continues, "have been abused with false principles," and hence "are impatient to be examined, as a leper is of a comb, and are greedy of the world, as children of raw fruit; and they hate a severe reproof, as they do thorns in their beds; and they love to lay aside religion, as a drunken person does to forget his sorrow" (pp. 65–66).

Miss White has demonstrated clearly that such combinations of the homely with the odd and remote were characteristic of seventeenth-century devotional literature.[77] As used in *Holy Dying,* together with the other stylistic devices considered above, they contribute markedly to the double characterization so vital to Taylor's purposes. On the one hand is the Ideal Pastor—just as familiar with lepers' attitudes as with local laymen's, with children's tastes as with drunks' motives. On the other hand is the undifferentiated Christian to whom he is ministering—more or less committed to a pilgrimage, and straggling along more or less in the right direction, but much in need of help if he is not to fall by the wayside.[78]

Because the sine qua non of this ministry is the persuasion of the reader to an ever deepening personal commitment to Christ, the style of greatest literary significance is also the most important in terms of the treatise itself. The prose style that is distinctively Taylor's is the Pastor's unique tool for instilling in Christian that right attitude without which right belief and right conduct are alike fruitless. To this end he seeks persistently not merely to teach, or even to preach, the drama of redemption, but to *communicate* it. And the style he adopts for this purpose is, quite simply, that of the indirect meditation as developed in Counter-Reformation works such as Parsons's *First Book of . . . resolution.* Both syntax and imagery take their rise in the disciplined practice of meditation, and both are peculiarly appropriate for leading others to meditate without their recognizing the fact consciously. The meditative theme underlying all of Taylor's most exciting passages

77. Pages 240–41 and passim.
78. For other aspects of Taylor's imagery, see below.

might be any one of many suitable Pauline affirmations, but perhaps is distilled most completely in a text from the Epistle to the Romans (5:20–21): "But where sin abounded, grace did much more abound: that as sin hath reigned unto death, even so might grace reign, through righteousness, unto eternal life, by Jesus Christ our Lord."[79]

Taylor communicates this opposition between sin unto death and grace unto life even in terms of syntax alone. The long meditative sentences in *Holy Dying* consist of loosely parallel units, built either around verbs or around nouns with strong implications for concrete action. These are strung together according to some temporal sequence or theological scheme. In either case, the order is dynamic in principle and cumulative (rather than climactic) in its rhetorical effect. Such sentences move swiftly because they express, or imply, so much action; at the same time, they move slowly because one can pause to consider each item without losing the import of the sentence as a whole.

In these sentences, over and over again, natural man moves through life toward the grave, throwing his time away in sin or inertia:

79. See, in this connection, Sarah Herndon, *The Use of the Bible in Jeremy Taylor's Works: An Abridgment.* Although Miss Herndon's statistical analysis is, as she points out, necessarily imprecise, and subject to almost limitless amplification and revision (p. 2), her results are both more conclusive and more fascinating than one would anticipate. The Pauline orientation of Taylor's thought, for example, is obvious enough to any reader; so too is his recurrent citation of the Epistle to the Romans, his insistent elucidation of chaps. 5–8. Why bother with statistics? All the same, we may well be startled—and intrigued—by their forcefulness. Of the 6,842 biblical references that she found to be clearly identifiable, over 45 percent are to the New Testament epistles, "the part of the Bible most concerned with doctrine and its relation to morality" (p. 4); and *over 8 percent* (554) are to Romans alone—over 50 of them to chaps. 6–8! (pp. 7, 9). Only Matt. and 1 Cor. approach Romans in frequency of use (with 552 and 516 references respectively); and only 13 other chapters in the entire Bible are cited more than 50 times each, including (inescapably) Matt. 5–7, 1 Cor. 11 and 15, and Eph. 4 (p. 9). It is no wonder that we find in Romans the "buried text" for Taylor's most central devotional work.

we sacrifice our youth to folly, our manhood to lust and rage,
our old age to covetousnesse and irreligion, not beginning to
live till we are to die, designing that time to Vertue which
indeed is infirm to every thing and profitable to nothing . . .
we make our lives short, and lust runs away with all the vigorous and healthful part of it; and pride and animosity steal the
manly portion, and craftinesse and interest possesse old age . . .
We complain the day is long, and the night is long, and we
want company, and seek out arts to drive the time away, and
then weep because it is gone too soon. [pp. 26–27]

Over and over again, in similar sentences, God takes the initiative
and seeks man actively, pouring out blessings upon him and special
graces through the Church: he "sent His Son . . . hath appointed . . .
offers . . . intreats . . . makes. . . . sends . . . restraints . . . chastises
. . . takes care . . . preserves" (pp. 201–02).[80] The man who responds
to this divine love continues to live and act in time, but his progress
deathward is noticeably slower. Sometimes his actions are described
according to some theological pattern rather than in chronological
order, and therefore seem more measured.[81] In other instances
they are described in nouns that still suggest the passage of time,
and yet decelerate its speed by the very process of organizing it.[82]
The effectiveness of this meditative rhetoric may be demonstrated
by quoting one such sentence in full. Chosen partly because its
content seems so unpromising, it nonetheless epitomizes Taylor's

80. The ecclesiastical ministries are identified explicitly as *God's actions:*
"God comforts us by their Sermons, and reproves us by their Discipline,
and cuts off some by their severity, and reconciles others by their gentle-
nesse, and relieves us by their prayers, and instructs us by their discourses,
and heals our sicknesses by their intercession" (p. 244).

81. E.g., the sick man is patient, that "calls upon God, that hopes for
health or heaven, that believes . . . that confesses his sins and accuses himself and justifies God; that expects . . . that is civil . . . that converses . . .
and in all things submits to God's will" (pp. 86–87).

82. "Lord I will dwell . . . in thy service, religion shall be my imploy-
ment, and alms shall be my recreation, and patience shall be my rest, and
to do thy will shall be my meat and drink, and to live shall be Christ, and
then to die shall be gain" (p. 215).

techniques of communicating the reality of time by moving through it at top speed; of relating the individual inexorably to this chronological movement; of personifying authority of all kinds so that it partakes of the concreteness of God's personal will; and of controlling the conflict between physical and spiritual by a characteristically ambiguous choice of words—in this case "near" vs. "far off." This is the peroration of his argument on behalf of auricular confession when sick:

> And when a duty is so useful in all cases, so necessary in some, and encouraged by promises Evangelical, by Scripture precedents, by the example of both Testaments; and prescribed by injunctions Apostolical and by the Canon of all Churches, and the example of all ages, and taught us even by the proportions of dutie, and the Analogie to the power Ministerial, and the very necessities of every man; he that for stubbornnesse or sinful shame-fac'dnesse, or prejudice, or any other criminal weaknesse shall decline to do it in the dayes of his danger, when the vanities of the world are worn off, and all affection[s] to sin are wearied, and the sin it self is pungent and grievous, and that we are certain we shal not escape shame for them hereafter, unlesse we be ashamed of them here, and use all the proper instruments of their pardon; this man I say is very neer death, but very far off *from the kingdom of heaven.* [pp. 253–54]

It is just this syntactical aspect of Taylor's meditative style which lends to the prayers in *Holy Dying* their distinctive quality. As we should expect, their basic structure is that of liturgical prayer; but this Taylor fills out with a wealth of leisurely elaboration quite alien to the normal collect. Like Becon, he uses the prayers to some extent as review outlines of his previous instruction. More important, he uses them as concentrated opportunities for, and invitations to, meditation: they constitute the reserved Anglican's objectified and formalized version of the Ignatian colloquy. They are far more explicitly Christocentric than the argument of the treatise, even when not addressed directly to Christ; and they sharpen up its central theme of self-offering to him by dramatizing it. The reader reminds himself in some detail of what God (or Christ) has done or is doing, elaborates his petition in such a way as to review the lessons he has received, and concludes frequently with an affirmation or resolution which has been implied or encouraged. In almost every instance the diction and imagery are limited to conventional expressions of liturgical usage; the exceptions, a few rather dramatic prayers for the dying, are validated by their antiquity if not by continual use. The technique of elaboration is that which we have just analyzed. A potentially direct, straightforward petition to Christ *"for the grace and strengths of faith"* (chap. 4, sec. 4) is expanded, for example, as follows:

> O let me for ever dwell upon the rock, leaning upon thy arm, beleeving thy word, trusting in thy promises, waiting for thy mercies, and doing thy commandments, that the Devil may not prevail upon me, and my own weaknesses may not abuse or unsettle my perswasions, nor my sins discompose my just confidence in thee and thy eternall mercies. Let me alwayes be thy servant and thy disciple, and die in the communion of thy Church, of all faithfull people . . . for Thou art the Way, the Truth, and the Life. [p. 187]

As a long, loose sentence unfolds, presenting one facet of an idea after another for the reader's consideration, turning to the implications of the whole, and examining those implications with equally patient thoroughness, a wide variety of rhetorical devices operate unobtrusively to control its tendency to fall apart as an artistic unit. Others serve from time to time to sharpen up the central paradoxical theme; for example, oxymorons regarding the "severe mercies" of God, the "sowre and laborious felicities" of life. Still others support Taylor's distinctive emotional attitude toward his text. Of these devices—all of them standard equipment for the Renaissance rhetorician—the only one of marked significance for our study is the most familiar, most ordinary of them all: alliteration. This Taylor uses in a way which contrasts so strikingly with Parsons's colloquial bluntness that it invites critical attention. In *Holy Dying* both prophetic sternness and pastoral challenge are expressed without recourse to this conventional device; on the whole, we find, its use is restricted to those portions of the treatise which are permeated with Taylor's unique tone. Alliteration helps, that is, to invest the spiritual drama of the Christian life, not with the forthright vigorous belligerence of the Jesuit's spiritual combat (still less the Puritan's moral warfare), but with a poignant, often melancholy irony.

The most famous passages in *Holy Dying,* usually expressive of the haunting loveliness of the life which passes so quickly, are filled with such alliteration: the image of the rose, for instance, "fair as the Morning, and full with the dew of Heaven," until, once open, it "began to put on darknesse, and to decline to softnesse, and the symptomes of a sickly age; it bowed the head, and broke its stalk, and at night . . . fell into the portion of weeds and outworn faces" (p. 11). So, too, are those passages in which mortuary threats are hushed to sad murmurs. Death is a "house of darknesse and dishonour" (p. 49); and even the summer does not protect us from its threat, but "gives green turfe and brambles to binde upon our graves" (p. 6). Man's sinfulness unto damnation is viewed, in passages such as these, with a wistful smile: he has a "frail and a foolish spirit," only too likely to embrace "the festival follies of a soft life" (pp. 44, 54). In regard to God's action unto salvation, Taylor uses alliteration when he is concerned primarily with its quality of strength and softness combined: "Support me with thy graces, strengthen me with thy Spirit, soften my heart with the fire of thy love, and the dew of heaven, with penitentiall showers" (p. 211). The Christian life of growth in grace is not only a very busy and active one, therefore, but one filled with poignant ironies and quiet sweetness as well. The dying Christian, combating the temptation to despair (chap. 5, sec. 5) muses: "And sometimes I have had some chearful visitations of Gods Spirit, and my cup hath been crowned with comfort, and the wine that made my heart glad danced in the chalice, and I was glad that God would have me so" (p. 298).

Like its complex structure and controlled rhetoric, the rich imagery of *Holy Dying* represents the full artistic realization of the potentialities of the ars moriendi tradition. The bookishness of

the Renaissance, the scripturalism of the Reformation, and the affective power of the Counter-Reformation—all are exploited triumphantly in this masterpiece of humanistic-Christian devotional
literature. Like Lupset, Taylor turns to classical history and literature for anecdotes, quotations, and allusions which will witness to
the universality of much of his teaching; but he draws from a far
richer store of classical materials, not to mention all intervening
Western history as well. With rare exceptions, he handles these
much as the early humanist did, as appeals to the reader's understanding and appreciation rather than to the emotional sources of
behavior. Occasionally, however, he does tell a story and then ponder it in detail, working out a tropological analysis worthy of a
biblical exegete.[83] Like Becon, he turns to the plain sense of Scripture for his most telling arguments, and to its rich imagery for his
most pervasive metaphors. His scripturalism is, however, at once
more thoroughgoing and much, much freer. His diction is so saturated with its phraseology, used without self-consciousness, that the
unwary modern reader finds himself falsely attributing biblical
expressions to Taylor himself, as he would never do in reading *The
Sicke Mannes Salve.* On the other hand, Taylor handles these resources with a freedom unthinkable for a Protestant in 1560. Not
only does he approach the Bible as one source of religious authority among several—although of course the primary one—but he
also reveals a sophisticated freedom in significant minor ways, such
as the deliberate misapplication of a story to his own purposes.[84]
Above all, he uses every technique developed by Counter-Reformation devotion to revitalize Christian clichés for the reader who is
no longer responsive to them in their scriptural form.

Sometimes this procedure amounts to little more than the re-
phrasing of a metaphor which has lost its imaginative impact, or
the mere associating of two metaphors in meaningful juxtaposition.
The allusion remains clear. "Let it be enough," says Taylor, de-
nouncing zealous sectarianism on one's deathbed, "that we secure

---

83. See, e.g., the tale of Cleomenes's fate which concludes chap. 2, sec. 2.
84. E.g., his use of Jonathan's arrows as a simile for a pastor's discourses
to a sick man who has not made his confession: they "may shoot short, or
shoot over, but not wound where they should" (p. 250).

our interest of heaven, though we do not go about to appropriate the mansions to our sect" (p. 180). Let the sinner take note of both "clamorous and whispering sins" (p. 196). On the other hand, the overfearful are reminded that "God calls upon us to forgive our brother seventy times seven times, and yet all that is but like the forgiving a hundred pence for his sake who forgives us ten thousand talents" (p. 291).

Sometimes, however, even comparatively short images reflect quite clearly their genesis in meditative discipline. The great majority of images which seem to be drawn from contemporary life are actually by-products of the concrete visualization, in terms of modern English life, of biblical metaphors. The original text which provided the inspiration for the composition of place may be present in part, or it may be implicit only. Thus, the penitent is reminded of "the *by-wayes* of sins, and *the crooked lanes* in which a man may wander and be lost as certainly as in the broad high wayes of iniquity"; and Taylor provides him, therefore, with the "streight lines of scripture, by which we may . . . discover our crooked walking" (pp. 226–27, 230). Some sinners, for example, counterfeit sickness—and find that it becomes genuine; and "he that is to be carefull of his passage into sicknesse [should beware] that he fall not into it through a trap door" (p. 146). Here the reference of "passage" is not explicitly identifiable, as is the reference above of "crooked walking" to "the way . . . that leadeth to destruction." Nonetheless, Taylor obviously considers the relative clause an authoritative ecclesiastical cliché, probably derived from a combination of several relevant texts. In the following image, finally, the scriptural inspiration is completely buried in the enthusiastic scientific geographical application: the penitent need not fear excessively, for repentance is a grace which does not "expire in little accents and minutes, but hath a great latitude of signification, and a large extension of parts, under the protection of *all which* persons are safe" (pp. 286–87). The biblical authority for these reassuring words is to be found in Psalm 103:12: "As far as East is from the West, so far hath he removed our transgressions from us." Images which seem to be drawn exclusively from seventeenth-century life (chiefly medical ones) are so rare in *Holy Dying* that one is tempted to infer that they, too, are based ultimately on some literary source, classical if not Christian.[85]

Taylor's greatest passages, from the literary viewpoint, are those in which he meditates "aloud" upon the spiritual drama of the Christian life. The Pastor supports and illustrates his interpretation of this drama from every sound source available to him; but he also moves his reader to respond to it by exploring each facet affectively with the help of familiar scriptural imagery. By visualizing these stock images with "near-sighted" attention to detail,[86] and with reference to the everyday life of his time, he works out concrete metaphors so elaborated and particularized, yet so coherent and so imbued with his own devotional spirit, that most of his admirers have attributed them solely to his genius. Actually, those which recur most frequently in *Holy Dying* are firmly rooted in biblical imagery. In many, perhaps most, specific instances a particular passage seems to undergird his own; but this fact is relatively unimportant. What is of crucial significance for an appreciation of his genius as a traditional artist, is that each such meditative image evokes in the Christian reader's mind a rich complex of associations from both Old and New Testaments, and not merely the lovely scenes or daily trivia noted by critical admirers of earlier generations.

Among the dozens upon dozens of such images, a cluster of eleven stand out as basic, almost all of them because they recur throughout the treatise with significant variations from chapter to chapter. Even the first of these—the sounds of clocks and bells— is essentially biblical in inspiration. The other ten are obviously and powerfully so: swift torrents; storms, thorns, accounts, and disease; light, refreshing waters, sailing, and dressing; and a great tree. Considered together, these form a theological pattern of im-

---

85. On the other hand, Duyckinck's exquisitely tentative hypothesis is suggestive: "If inclined to the theoretical style of biography," he murmurs, "we might allege that he had been a student in his brother-in-law's apothecary shop" (p. 176). Parish priests and military chaplains are also likely to have more than ordinary familiarity with medical jargon and practice. See below, pp. 262, 264.

86. Cf. Smith, p. xlvi.

agery in perfect accord with Taylor's understanding of the Christian life under grace.

Thus, his imaginative realization of man's involvement in time, his bondage to death, occurs in *Holy Dying* primarily as a meditative exploration and elaboration of the ninetieth Psalm, especially the fourth and fifth verses: "For a thousand years in thy sight are but as yesterday when it is past, and as a watch in the night. Thou carriest them away as with a flood." But it evokes as well the entire biblical perpective on time: as a dimension created and controlled by a personal God who in the fulness of time entered history, and in due time will end it; and as the atmosphere in which individual moral endeavor must be sustained and given meaning. The sheer fact of life's swift passage is communicated by an intensification of Seneca's way of expressing it. Instead of remarking merely that we die daily, Taylor focuses upon the hackneyed truth, analyzing its implications in detail, and forcing them home imaginatively by repeated references to clocks as well as the more conventional bells. The rhythm of such sentences has a delicate appropriateness which approaches the rightness of poetry: "and while we think a thought, we die; and the clock strikes, and reckons on our portion of Eternity; we form our words with the breath of our nostrils, we have the lesse to live upon, for every word we speak" (p. 5).

The absolute irreversibility of this movement toward the grave, with all that it implies for man as moral being, haunts the treatise. In the second of his basic metaphors, Taylor describes the time allotted to us as a "torrent and sudden shower, which will quickly cease dropping from above, and quickly cease running in our chanels here below" (p. 18). And yet God "gives it to us, not as Nature gives us Rivers, enough to drown us, but drop by drop, minute after minute, so that we never can have two minutes together, but He takes away one when He gives us another." Even hyperbolic fantasy is called upon to clarify the moral implications of these truths about time. The dying man has no time left for procrastination: his duty "must be done, but cannot any more, if not now, untill [time] return[s] again, and tels the minuts backwards, so that yesterday shall be reckoned in the portions of the future" (p. 235).

For the vanity, misery, and sinfulness of man's natural life, Taylor uses four running images: storms, thorns, accounts, and disease. Again the biblical suggestions spread out through both Testaments, and again Taylor visualizes their spiritual application in concrete detail. The undifferentiated storms of Scripture are now those of a sailing ship in rough seas. Men who live "according to the flesh" are "like Sailers loosing from a port, and tost immediatly with a perpetual tempest lasting till their cordage crack," and "Mariners, and Passengers" alike "shrike [*sic*] out because their keel dashes against a Rock, or bulges under them"; and "either they sink, or return back again to the same place: they did not make a voyage, though they were long at sea" (pp. 24, 47, 24). The scriptural thorns in the side are now in men's beds. They are "gilded," and men "doat upon" them, "wear them for armelets, and knit them in [their shirts], and prefer them before a kingdom and immortality" (pp. 66, 45, 46). And the simple, straightforward accounts of biblical stewards have now become the lengthy ledgers of intricate computations kept by "Eastern Merchants," as "buisie [*sic*] as the Tables of Signes and Tangents" (p. 56). Everyone, of course, must "appear before his Judge to receive the hire of his day"; but the reprobate spirit remains "hugely in love with sin" even in "the week of the Assizes"—until he is confronted with "great bills of uncancelled crimes" (pp. 199, 154, 74).

As for the images of disease, these are so pervasive that any sampling of them seems ludicrously inadequate. The world of fallen man is under the dominion of *"death,* that is, misery and disease," and "we are to die by suffering evils, and by the daily lessening of our strength and health." Hence it is that "our dayes are full of sorrow and anguish . . . worne away with labours, loaden with diseases," and that "an Hospital . . . is indeed a map of the whole world, [where] you shall see the effects of *Adams* sin and the ruines of humane nature" (pp. 80, 44, 37). The point is underlined with numerous references to the common ailments of seventeenth-century Englishmen. Gout, kidney stones, indigestion, consumption, rotten teeth, agues, sore eyes, sciatica, and headaches by no means exhaust the list.

Since all language about God himself is necessarily metaphorical, the long lists of his gracious activity on man's behalf constitute in one sense a series of images of his essential attitude of loving concern. It is interesting, nonetheless, to observe the nearly total absence of any superimposed metaphorical elaboration of such concrete statements. God simply is, and he acts—primarily through Christ and his Church.[87] Each of the recurrent images discussed in the preceding two paragraphs plays a major role in the traditional interpretation of Christ's redemptive work in history. He shared the storms of life—and calmed them; endured literal as well as figurative thorns; and offered "full, perfect, and sufficient . . . satisfaction" for the debts of all men. Taylor's selection, from the scores of possible metaphors available to him, throws the emphasis upon Christ, not as Lupset's Teacher, but as Exemplar, suffering Redeemer, and healer. In sum,

> the condition of Nature . . . being violated by the introduction of death, Christ then repaired when he suffered and overcame death for us: that is, he hath taken away the unhappinesse of sicknesse, and the sting of death, and the dishonours of the grave, of dissolution and weaknesse, of decay and change; and hath . . . now knit them into rosaries, and coronets . . . they are *instruments,* and *earnests,* and *securities,* and *passages* to the greatest perfection of humane nature, and the Divine promises. [pp. 80–81]

The experience of one who accepts Christ as the Way, the Truth, and the Life is communicated by means of the same images, now handled with revealing differences in emphasis, and also by four new ones which are tightly interrelated to suggest the pattern of the ideal Christian response. Although the precious minutes "strike on," they are now "counted by Angels, till the period comes which must cause the passing bell to give warning to all the neighbors that thou art dead, and they must be so" (p. 126). The individual is no longer moving toward his grave by himself, but in the company of the faithful on earth and the blessed in heaven. Although God's promises let us "roul from off our thorns," at least

87. See above, note 80.

potentially (p. 99), the storms of life continue unabated. The Christian, however, recognizes them as testers and strengtheners of faith: when "all our hopes bulge under us, and descend into the hollownesse of sad misfortunes; then can you believe, when you neither hear, nor see, nor feel any thing but objections?" (p. 112). Here, for the first time, appears the familiar emblem of the Church as the ship appointed by God to carry us to the harbor of death (p. 127). Similarly, the Christian's accounts continue to pile up; but now he sums them up "at the foot of every page," in a daily self-examination. When sick, he may "represent the summe totall to God, and his conscience" through confession, "and make provisions for their remedie and pardon"; and always he seeks to perfect his repentance, knowing that "it is better to trust the goodnesse, and justice of God with our accounts then to offer him large [bills]" (pp. 56, 197, 303–04). In brief, the committed Christian remains a sinning Moriens in a fallen world—but Christ's work as the "good physician" continues through the Church, as ministers cure sick souls and heal the "wounds" of his faithful "soldiers."[88] Taylor reveals throughout the treatise a working pastor's familiarity with hospitals, ordinary medicines, and the general physiological and psychological side effects of illness and convalescence. And all this concrete knowledge, whether gleaned from books or experience, flows into his imagery when he considers sin either as injury or—more commonly—as disease.

The four new images which are most centrally related to Taylor's presentation of the life of grace not only constitute a pattern of their own, but also relate logically to those already discussed. First, and by far the most pervasive of all the images in *Holy Dying,* is that of light, which is set over against the darkness of death: the light of sun, moon, and stars, of candles and lamps, and of reason; the God-given light of day in which all men live until the night of death. The Christian walks also in the light of revelation, confronting the spirits of darkness with the light of Christ. Taylor's handling of this classic image is no more original in the intellectual sense than is his use of the others we have examined. Instead, he

88. Cf. above, pp. 244–46.

achieves his striking effects by a minute consideration of the living
phenomena behind traditional biblical metaphors. He observes, for
example, that "a Taper when its crown of flames is newly blown
off, retains a nature so symbolical to light, that it will with greed-
inesse reënkindle and snatch a ray from the neighbour fire" (p. 59).
The emblematic significance of such a factual detail occurs readily
to one saturated with biblical metaphors and accustomed to visualizing them concretely as he ponders their meaning: "So is the soul
of Man, when it is newly fallen into sin." A similarly realistic observation, applied to deathbed charity, revitalizes dozens of relevant
images from both Testaments as well as fortifying Taylor's argument with imaginative appeal:

> we must not first kindle our lights, when we are to descend
> into our houses of darknesse, or bring a glaring torch suddenly
> to a dark room, that will amaze the eye and not delight it, or
> instruct the body; but if our Tapers have in their constant
> course descended into their grave crowned all the way with
> light, then let the death-bed charity be doubled, and the light
> burn brightest when it is to deck our hearse. [p. 70]

And he describes a quiet, easy death, with exquisite appropriateness, as that of "an expiring and a spent candle" (p. 305).

Whatever the source of light in *Holy Dying,* the light itself is
characterized above all by incessant motion. Light shimmers, dances,
gleams, flickers, sparkles, glows, and so on, with a vibrancy which
suggests real life; and this living quality is enhanced by the strong
personification of the light's sources. Darkness is simply darkness
in this context: it partakes of the dull finality of the death it sym-
bolizes. Light, as the basic emblem of God and of his relationship
to man, is infinitely variable in its manifestations; but its essential
attribute is radiant activity.

The second new image of major significance for the Christian life
(the eighth in the overall pattern) is that of the waters of grace,
which pour down upon man from the fountain of God even as the
torrent of time is pouring by him. Again the concrete analysis of
a tired metaphor endures it with new vigor. Doctors, for example,
are created by God to minister to us; but Taylor urges "that we be

not too confident of the Physitian or drain our hopes of recovery from the fountain, through so imperfect chanels; laying the wells of God dry, and digging to our selves broken cisterns" (p. 164). Here, too, the attribute most emphasized is ceaseless motion, but in this case steady, dependable—even persistent—and strong rather than beautiful in its action.

Enlightened and empowered by God's activity, the Christian responds in and through action himself. This response, which is also twofold, is communicated imaginatively through the metaphors of sailing and dressing. On the one hand, he rides out the storm of life—in the ship of the Church—trustfully: "we shall sure enough be wafted to the shore, although we be tossed with the winds of our sighs, and the unevenness of our fears, and the ebbings and flowings of our passions, if we sail in a right chanel, and steere by a perfect compasse, and look up to God, and call for his help, and do our own endeavour" (p. 285). This is the response of faith, of positive commitment.

On the other hand, the specific "endeavour" which is the Christian's central duty on the journey is to "dress his soul." This metaphor appears for the first time in the magnificent meditation which climaxes chapter 3, when the soul

> begins to dresse her self for immortality: and first she unties the strings of vanity that made her upper garment cleave to the world and sit uneasily. First she puts off the light and phantastic summer robe of lust, and wanton appetite . . . and then the spirit feels it self at ease. . . .
>
> 2. Next to this; *the soul by the help of sicknesse knocks off the fetters of pride and vainer complacencies.* Then she drawes the curtains, and . . . takes the pictures down, those phantastic images of self-love, and gay remembrances of vain opinion, and popular noises. . . .
>
> 3. Next . . . *she takes off the roughnesse of her great and little angers, and animosities,* and receives the oil of mercies, and smooth forgivenesse, fair interpretations, and gentle answers, designes of reconcilement, and Christian atonement in their places. . . . [p. 105–08]

There are few passages in *Holy Dying* which demonstrate more eloquently the artistic rewards of disciplined meditation. Furthermore, the identification of the buried text is in this case very helpful, for it establishes the central importance of the image in spite of its belated introduction and comparatively meager use in later chapters, when Taylor simply reminds the Christian of his duty. Surely the reader is expected to recall, not only St. Paul's vision of the day when "this mortal shall have put on immortality" (1 Cor. 15), but also his adjurations to the Romans *now* to "put . . . on the Lord Jesus Christ, and make not provision for the flesh" (Rom. 13:14). This one extraordinarily detailed meditation therefore distills in affective form all of Taylor's "Rules and Exercises" relating to the passive graces of the Way of the Cross. In its central position, it looks backward to meditation and holy living, and forward to action and holy dying. The connection is pointed up in the paragraph which concludes this section: "The summe is this . . . an impatient person is not ready dressed for heaven. None but suffering, humble, and patient persons can go to heaven" (p. 124).

The paradoxical conflict between sin unto death and grace unto life reaches its climax when man—"*a leaf,* the smallest, the weakest piece of a short liv'd, unsteady plant" (p. 3)—finds himself upon his deathbed. He has known for years that even though his "sinews were strong as the cordage at the foot of an Oke" (p. 43), he would die all too soon. The final element in Taylor's theological pattern of imagery is the metaphor of the tree, by which he contrasts this physical weakness to the strength of faith. Warning the Christian to avoid disputation when seriously ill, he elucidates his point by working out in some detail an image of the tree of faith, which should by this time "stand firme by the weight of its own bulk and great constitution." All the sources of religious authority constitute

> the strings and branches of the roots, by which faith stands . . . unmoveable in the spirit, and understanding of a man. But in sicknesse the understanding is shaken and the ground is removed in which the root did grapple, and support its trunk, and therefore there is no way now, but that it be left to stand upon the old confidences, and by the firmament of its own weight. [p. 179]

Once again the image evokes a plethora of associations, ranging from the psalmist's description of the godly as "a tree planted by the rivers of water" (Ps. 1:3) to St. Paul's frequent exhortations to the brethren to "stand fast in the Lord." Significantly, the dominant biblical connotation for trees is one of fruitful or creative stillness, while that for "stand" is one of dignified, expectant stillness; and the two merge into a dynamic quietude which is in complete harmony with the ceaseless activity of both God and man until now. Furthermore, the major New Testament passages of which the Christian would be reminded refer him explicitly to three of the four major images just discussed: water, light, and especially dressing. The Christian stands fast in the faith and quits himself like a man only because "God is able to make him stand": he stands in grace, "by the rivers of water" (1 Cor. 16:13, Rom. 14:4, 5:2; cf. Ps. 1:3). But in order "to stand against the wiles of the devil . . . in the evil day, and, having done all, to stand," he must put on "the whole armour of God," the "armour of light"—in sum, "the Lord Jesus Christ" (Eph. 6:11–13).

And, finally, the victory which awaits those who stand so clothed is communicated by a medley of almost all the relevant metaphors in this pattern. Heaven is, as we have seen, the shore which Christian sailors will reach. If we are "embalmed in the spices and odours of a good name, and entombed in the grave of the Holy Jesus . . . we shall be dressed for a blessed resurrection"; we shall "stand upright in judgement," supported by Christ, our sins "put . . . upon the accounts of the Crosse" (pp. 20, 317, 308). In brief, life will "go from us, to lay aside its thorns, and to return again circled with a glory and a Diadem" (p. 50).

As noted in the introduction to this analysis, some of Taylor's modern admirers have reserved their warmest encomia for his supposedly modern vision of death. Remarking that he sees it as simple terminus rather than "macabre monster . . . the majestic subduer of tyrants and kings," Canon Stranks lauds him, in a representative accolade, for a "break-away from a literary convention which had been observed by too many and lasted too long" (p. 112). Such praise, we can now see, is more perceptive than that which separates Taylor's (presumably splendid) baroque prose style from the (presumably mediocre) traditional substance of his thought. Nevertheless, it is also misguided praise—on two counts.

In the first place, it misses the crucial point that death as negation is no less a challenge to Christian piety than a grinning skeleton—and may well be more. It may be true, as Lepp assures us, that

> simple people rarely think of death as a violence imposed from without by some force inimical to life. They see it as the normal fulfillment of life and it is altogether natural for them to call it the "last" sleep. [pp. 144–45]

It is certainly true, per contra, that many a contemporary intellectual accepts the existentialist view of death as an "intolerable scandal"—"that fundamental crime" which renders not only personal existence, but the universe itself, "absurd."[89] Somewhere between these two extremes, surely, we find virtually every reader of Taylor's masterpiece: not utterly despairing, one presumes, yet well aware of his own finitude. However *understood*, that is, death must at the very least remain an appalling, a "shattering" *fact*, an "event of the most radical spoliation."[90] And for the humanistic Christian, its essential threat is clearly not diminished by his full imaginative realization of the swiftness with which its cold dishonor will negate his most precious human values.

In the second place, such eulogies do not take into account the fact that *Holy Dying* belongs to another tradition than that of the *danse macabre*—one more closely allied with the timeless affirmations of Christianity than with their popular expression in any one era. Thus, the anthropomorphic presentation of death had no real place in the ars moriendi until the Counter-Reformation; and even Parsons's vivid personification of the enemy is only incidental to his central vision of death as simple experience. Rather than being a breakaway from, *Holy Dying* is in fact the noble culmination of, its devotional tradition. As Miss White says:

89. Lepp, *Death and Its Mysteries*, p. 26; Camus, *The Myth of Sisyphus*, quoted in Lepp, p. 128.
90. Rahner, pp. 10, 31.

he is but the highest peak of the intellectual and spiritual range out of which he rises. He is the greatest of these devotional writers in degree, but he is of their kind, made rich by their tradition, and his glory is rightly theirs. [p. 270]

Enriched by the religious insights and artistic contributions of Renaissance, Reformation, and Counter-Reformation, and alchemized by literary genius, Taylor's masterpiece remains in essence the *Crafte of Dyinge,* though the *Crafte* raised to the $n^{th}$ power: the Church's proclamation to Everyman, mortal and sinful, of the good news that "God was in Christ, reconciling the world unto himself" —and that over the faithful "death shall have no dominion."

# Bibliography of Works Cited

PRIMARY SOURCES, 1450–1651

*Ars moriendi,* Editio princeps [ca. 1450]. Edited by W. H. Rylands. London: Wyman & Sons, 1881.

Bacon, Sir Francis. "On Death," in *The Essayes or Counsels Civill and Morall . . . ,* in *Selected Writings of Francis Bacon.* Edited by Hugh G. Dick. New York: Modern Library [1955].

Bayly, Lewis. *The Practice of Pietie: Directing a Christian how to walke that he may please God.* 21st ed. ("Amplified by the Author"). London, 1628.

Becon, Thomas. "The Prayse of Death, set forth in a dialogue betwene man and Reason . . ." in *Worckes,* 1563 (STC #1710), vol. 3, fols. [ccccx]–[cccccxxi].

——. *The Sicke mannes Salve, wherein the faithfull Christians may learne both how to behave themselves paciently and thankefully in the tyme of sickenes, and also vertuously to dispose their temporall goods, and finally to prepare themselves gladly and godly to dye . . .* in *Worckes,* 1563 (STC #1710), vol. 2, fols. [ccxvii<sup>v</sup>]–cclxxxiii<sup>v</sup>.

*The Boke of crafte of dyinge,* in vol 2 of *Yorkshire Writers: Richard Rolle of Hampole and his Followers.* Edited by Carl Horstmann. London: Swan Sonnenschein, 1896.

Colet, John. "A ryght fruitfull monicion concerning the order of a good christen mannes lyfe, very profitable for all maner of estates, and other, to beholde and loke vppon . . ." (Johan Byddell, 1534). Appendix D, pp. [305]–10, in Joseph H. Lupton, *A Life of John Colet.* 2d ed. London: Bell, 1909.

Erasmus, Desiderio. *A Comfortable exhortacion against the chances of death.* Translated by Sir Frances Poyngz, in *The Table of*

271

*Cebes the Philosopher.* . . . [London: Thomas Berthelet, 1530?]

——. *Preparation to deathe, A boke as devout as eloquent.* Translated anonymously. [London, Thomas Berthelet, 1543.]

Evelyn, John. *The Diary of John Evelyn.* Edited by E. S. de Beer. 6 vols. Oxford: Clarendon Press, 1955. Vol. 3.

Greene, Robert. "The Repentance of Robert Greene," in *The Life and Complete Works . . . of Robert Greene.* Edited by Alexander B. Grosart. Huth Library Series. 15 vols. [London and Aylesbury], "Printed for Private Circulation Only," 1881–86.

Hooker, Richard. *The Laws of Ecclesiastical Polity.* 2 vols. Everyman's Library. Edited by Ernest Rhys. New York: E. P. Dutton [1907].

Loarte, Gaspar. *The Exercise of a Christian Life.* Translated by Stephen Brinkley [James Sancer]. [Rheims?], 1584.

Loyola, St. Ignatius. *The Text of the Spiritual Exercises of St. Ignatius.* Translated by John Morris. 4th ed. Westminster, Md.: Newman Bookshop, 1943.

Lupset, Thomas. *A compendious and a very fruteful treatyse, teachynge the waye of Dyenge well, written to a frende* . . . in *The Life and Works of Thomas Lupset.* Edited by John A. Gee. New Haven: Yale University Press, 1928.

More, St. Thomas. *A Dyalogue of Coumfort agaynst Tribulacion,* with the *Utopia,* in Everyman's Library. Edited by Ernest Rhys. New York: E. P. Dutton [1910].

——. "A Treatyce vnfynyshed vppon these wordes of holye Scrypture, *Memorare nouissima, & ineternum non peccabis* . . ." in *The workes of Sir Thomas More Knyght. . . . wrytten by him in the Englysh tonge.* London: John Cawod, John Waly, and Richard Tottell, 1557.

P[arsons], R[obert]. *A Booke of Christian Exercise Appertaining to Resolution, that is, shewing how that wee shoulde resolve our selves to become Christians indeede.* "Perused" by Edmund Bunny. Oxford: Joseph Barnes, 1585.

——. *A Christian Directorie Gviding Men to their Salvation.* . . . [Rouen], 1585.

——. *The First Booke of the Christian Exercise, appertayning to resolution. Wherein are layed downe the causes and reasons that should move a man to resolve hym selfe to the service of God: And all the impedimentes removed, which may lett the same.* [Rouen], 1582.

Perkins, William. *A salve for a sicke man: or, a Treatise Containing the Nature, Differences, and Kindes of Death; as Also the Right Manner of Dying Well* . . . . John Legat, Printer to the University of Cambridge, 1597.

Sutton, Christopher. *Disce Mori.* . . . "Newly enlarged by the same author." London: C. Burby, 1607.

Taylor, Jeremy. *The rule and exercises of holy dying. In which are described the Means and Instruments of preparing our selves, and others respectively, for a blessed Death: and the remedies against the evils and temptations proper to the state of Sicknesse. Together with Prayers and Acts of Vertue to be used by sick and dying persons, or by others standing in their Attendance. To which are added. Rules for the visitation of the Sick, and offices proper for that Ministry.* London: R. Royston, 1651.

—————. *The Whole Works of the Right Rev. Jeremy Taylor.* . . . Edited by Reginald Heber. Revised and corrected by Charles P. Eden. 10 vols. London: Longman and Co., and others, 1847–54.

OTHER SOURCES

Ackerman, Robert W. "Middle English Literature to 1400," in *The Medieval Literature of Western Europe: A Review of Research, Mainly 1930–1960.* Edited by John H. Fisher. Published for The Modern Language Association of America. New York: New York University Press, 1966.

Adams, Robert P. *The Better Part of Valor: More, Erasmus, Colet, and Vives, on Humanism, War, and Peace, 1496–1535.* Seattle: University of Washington Press, 1962.

Adams, W. H. Davenport. *Great English Churchmen.* London: S.P.C.K., 1897.

Addison, James Thayer. "Early Anglican Thought 1559–1667." *The Historical Magazine of the Protestant Episcopal Church* 22(1953).

————. "Jeremy Taylor." *The Historical Magazine of the Protestant Episcopal Church* 21(1952):148–90.

Allison, A. F. and D. M. Rogers. *A Catalogue of Catholic Books in
English, Printed Abroad or Secretly in England, 1558–1640.*
2 parts. Bognor Regis: Arundel Press, 1956.

Antoine, Sr. Mary Salome. *The Rhetoric of Jeremy Taylor's Prose:
Ornament of the Sunday Sermons.* Washington, D.C.: Catholic
University of America Press, 1946.

Auden, W. H. Introduction to *The Protestant Mystics,* edited by
Anne Fremantle. Boston: Little, Brown [1954].

Bailey, Derrick S. *Thomas Becon and the Reformation of the
Church in England.* Edinburgh: Oliver & Boyd, [1952].

Bainton, Roland H. *Here I Stand: A Life of Martin Luther.* New
York: Abingdon-Cokesbury Press, 1950.

Baker, Herschel. *The Dignity of Man: Studies in the Persistence of
an Idea.* Cambridge, Mass.: Harvard University Press, 1947.

Baxter, Richard. *Reliquae Baxterianae: or, Mr. Richard Baxter's
Narrative of his Life and Times.* [London: Matthew Sylvester,
1696.]

Blench, John W. *Preaching in England in the Late Fifteenth and
Sixteenth Centuries.* Oxford: Blackwell, 1964.

Bolton, Frederick R. *The Caroline Tradition of the Church of
Ireland: With Particular Reference to Bishop Jeremy Taylor.*
London: S.P.C.K., 1958.

Bonney, Henry K. *The Life of the Rt. Rev. Father in God, Jeremy
Taylor.* London, 1815.

Brinkley, Roberta F., ed. *Coleridge on the Seventeenth Century.*
Durham, N.C.: Duke University Press, 1955.

Brown, W. J. *Jeremy Taylor.* English Theologian Series. London:
S.P.C.K., Macmillan, 1925.

Buber, Martin. *I and Thou.* Translated by Ronald G. Smith. Edinburgh: T. & T. Clark, 1937.

Bush, Douglas. *Classical Influences in Renaissance Literature.* Cambridge, Mass.: Harvard University Press, 1952.

————. *English Literature in the Earlier Seventeenth Century.*
Oxford: Clarendon Press, 1945.

————. *Prefaces to Renaissance Literature.* Cambridge, Mass.: Harvard University Press, 1965.

————. *The Renaissance and English Humanism.* 1939. Reprint (with corrections). Toronto: University of Toronto Press, 1958.

Calhoun, Robert L. *Lectures on the History of Christian Doctrine.* Privately printed. New Haven, 1948.

Chambers, R. W. "The Continuity of English Prose from Alfred to More and his School," in Nicholas Harpsfield, *The Life and Death of Sir Thomas More.* Edited by E. V. Hitchcock. Early English Text Society, O.S. 186. London: Humphrey Milford, Oxford University Press, 1932.

"Christian Cadences," review of H. Trevor Hughes's *The Piety of Jeremy Taylor. TLS,* July 29, 1960, p. 482.

Cicero, Marcus Tullius. *Cato maior de senectute.* Edited and translated by William A. Falconer. Loeb Classical Library. London: Wm. Heinemann, 1923.

————. *Letters to his Friends.* Edited and translated by W. Glynn Williams. Loeb Classical Library. 3 vols. London: Wm. Heinemann, 1927–29.

————. *Tusculan Disputations.* Edited and translated by J. E. King. Loeb Classical Library. London: Wm. Heinemann, 1950.

Colie, R. L. "Johan Huizinga and the Task of Cultural History." *American Historical Review* 69(1964):607–30.

Driscoll, John, S.J. "Robert Persons' *Book of Resolution:* A Bibliographical and Literary Study." Ph.D. dissertation. New Haven: Yale University, 1957.

————. *"The Seconde Parte:* Another Protestant Version of Robert Persons' *Christian Directorie." HLQ* 25(1962): 139–46.

————. "The Supposed Source of Persons' *Christian Directory," Recusant History* 5(1960):236–45.

Duyckinck, George L. *The Life of Jeremy Taylor.* New York, 1860.

Eliot, T. S. "Tradition and the Individual Talent," in *Selected Essays.* New ed. New York: Harcourt, Brace, 1950.

Elmen, Paul. "The Fame of Jeremy Taylor." *Anglican Theological Review* 44(1962):389–403.

Ferguson, Wallace K. *The Renaissance in Historical Thought: Five Centuries of Interpretation.* Boston: Houghton Mifflin, [1948].

Gee, John A. *The Life and Works of Thomas Lupset.* New Haven: Yale University Press, 1928.

Gilmore, Myron P. "The Renaissance Conception of the Lessons of History," in *Facets of the Renaissance.* Edited by William H. Werkmeister. The Arensberg Lectures [First Series]. Los Angeles: University of Southern California Press, 1959. Reprint. Harper Torchbooks, [1963], pp. 73–98.

Gosse, Edmund. *Jeremy Taylor.* English Men of Letters Series. London: Macmillan, 1904.

Harbison, E. H. *The Christian Scholar in the Age of the Reformation.* New York: Scribner's [1956].

Hay, Denys, ed. *The Medieval Centuries.* London: Methuen, 1964 (a revised edition of *From Roman Empire to Renaissance Europe.* London, 1953). Reprint. Harper Torchbooks [1965].

Heber, Reginald. "The Life of the Right Rev. Jeremy Taylor . . . with a Critical Examination of his Writings" (1822). Reprinted in Taylor, *Works,* 1:ix–ccl.

Helton, Tinsley, ed. *The Renaissance: A Reconsideration of the Theories and Interpretations of the Age.* Madison: University of Wisconsin Press, 1961.

Henson, H. H. *Studies in English Religion in the Seventeenth Century.* St. Margaret's Lectures. London: John Murray, 1903.

Herndon, Sarah. *The Use of the Bible in Jeremy Taylor's Works: An Abridgment.* Washington Square, N.Y.: New York University Press, 1949.

Hoopes, Robert. *Right Reason in the English Renaissance.* Cambridge, Mass.: Harvard University Press, 1962.

Houghton, Walter E., Jr. *The Formation of Thomas Fuller's Holy and Profane States.* Cambridge, Mass.: Harvard University Press, 1938.

Hughes, H. Trevor. *The Piety of Jeremy Taylor.* London: Macmillan, 1960.

Huizinga, Johan. *The Waning of the Middle Ages.* Translated by F. Hopman. London: Edward Arnold, 1924.

Hunt, Ernest William. *Dean Colet and His Theology*. London: S.P.C.K., 1956.

Jackson, Robert S. "The Meditative Life of Christ: A Study of the Background and Structure of Jeremy Taylor's *The Great Exemplar*." *DA* 19 (1959): 3296.

Jacob, E. F. *Essays in the Conciliar Epoch*. [Manchester]: Manchester University Press, 1943.

―――. "The Fifteenth Century: Some Recent Interpretations." *Bulletin of the John Rylands Library* 14 (1930): 386–409.

―――. "Johan Huizinga and the Autumn of the Middle Ages," in *Essays in Later Medieval History*. [Manchester]: Manchester University Press [1968], pp. 141–53.

Janelle, Pierre. "English Devotional Literature in the Sixteenth and Seventeenth Centuries," in *English Studies Today*. 2d ser. Edited by G. A. Bonnard. Bern: Francke Verlag, 1961.

Kaufman, U. Milo. *The Pilgrim's Progress and Traditions in Puritan Meditation*. Yale Studies in English, 163. New Haven: Yale University Press, 1966.

King, James Roy. "Certain Aspects of Jeremy Taylor's Prose Style." *English Studies* 37 (1954): 197–210.

―――. *Studies in Six 17th Century Writers*. Athens, Ohio: Ohio University Press [1966].

Knappen, Marshall. *Tudor Puritanism*. Chicago: University of Chicago Press [1939].

Kristeller, Paul O. *Renaissance Thought: The Classic, Scholastic, and Humanist Strains*. New York: Harper Torchbooks [1961]. (Revised and enlarged edition of *The Classics and Renaissance Thought*. Published for Oberlin College. Cambridge, Mass.: Harvard University Press, 1955.)

―――. *Renaissance Thought II: Papers on Humanism and the Arts*. New York: Harper Torchbooks [1965].

Ladd, William P. *Prayer Book Interleaves*. New York: Oxford University Press, 1942.

Lepp, Ignace. *Death and Its Mysteries*. Translated by Bernard Murchland. New York: Macmillan [1968].

Lewis, C. S. *A Preface to Paradise Lost*. London: Oxford University Press, 1942.

Lupton, Joseph H. *A Life of John Colet.* 2d ed. London: Bell, 1909.

McAdoo, Henry R. *The Spirit of Anglicanism: A Survey of Anglican Theological Method in the Seventeenth Century.* New York: Scribner's [1965].

——. *The Structure of Caroline Moral Theology.* London: Longmans, Green [1949].

McNeill, John. *A History of the Cure of Souls.* New York: Harper, 1951.

McNulty, Robert. "The Protestant Version of Robert Parsons' *The First Booke of the Christian Exercise.*" *HLQ* 22 (1959): 271–300.

——. "Robert Parsons' *The First Book of the Christian Exercise* (1582): An Edition and a Study." *DA* 16 (1956): 528–29.

Mâle, Emile. *L'art religieux de la fin du moyen âge en France.* Paris: Librairie Armand Colin, 1922.

Martz, Louis L. "John Donne in Meditation: The Anniversaries." *ELH* 14 (1947): 247–73.

——. *The Poetry of Meditation.* New Haven: Yale University Press, 1954.

Meadows, Denis. *Elizabethan Quintet.* London: Longmans, Green, [1956].

Miles, Leland. *John Colet and the Platonic Tradition.* Fishers with Platonic Nets, 1. LaSalle, Ill.: Open Court, 1961.

Moore, Virginia. *Ho for Heaven!: Man's Changing Attitude toward Dying.* New York: E. P. Dutton, 1946.

New, John F. H. *Anglican and Puritan: the Basis of Their Opposition, 1558–1640.* Stanford, Calif.: Stanford University Press, 1964.

Newell, A. G. "Thomas Becon and Literary Studies." *Evangelical Quarterly* 33 (1961): 93–101.

Nossen, Robert J. "A Critical Study of the *Holy Dying* of Jeremy Taylor," in *Summaries of Doctoral Dissertations* 19 (Evanston, Ill.: Northwestern University Press, 1951), pp. 35–39.

——. "Jeremy Taylor: Seventeenth-century Theologian." *Anglican Theological Review* 42 (1960): 28–39.

O'Connor, Sister Mary Catharine. *The Art of Dying Well: The Development of the Ars Moriendi.* New York: Columbia University Press, 1942.

Owst, Gerald R. *Literature and Pulpit in Medieval England*. Cambridge: Cambridge University Press, 1933.

———. *Preaching in Medieval England*. Cambridge: Cambridge University Press, 1926.

Parish, John E. "Robert Parsons and the English Counter-Reformation." Monograph in English History, *Rice University Studies* 52 (Winter 1966).

Patrides, C. A. "A Note on Renaissance Plagiarism." *N&Q*, n.s. 3 (1956): 438–39.

Peterson, Raymond A. "Jeremy Taylor's Theology of Worship." *Anglican Theological Review* 46 (1964): 204–16.

———. "The Theology of Jeremy Taylor: An Investigation of the Temper of Caroline Anglicanism." *DA* 21 (1961): 3178.

Pollard, Arthur. *English Sermons*. Writers and their Work Series, 158. Edited by Bonamy Dobrée. Published for the British Council. London: Longmans, Green [1963].

Pourrat, Pierre. *Christian Spirituality*. Translated by W. H. Mitchell and S. P. Jacques. 3 vols. London: Burns, Oates, and Washbourne, 1922–27.

Rahner, Karl, S.J. *On the Theology of Death*. Translated by C. H. Henkey. 2d English ed. Revised by W. J. O'Hara. London: Burns & Oates [1965].

Rice, Eugene F. *The Renaissance Idea of Wisdom*. Cambridge, Mass.: Harvard University Press, 1958.

Roberts, John R. *A Critical Anthology of English Recusant Prose, 1558–1603*. Duquesne Studies. Philological Series. Pittsburgh: Duquesne University Press, 1966.

Ross Williamson, Hugh. *Jeremy Taylor*. London: Dobson [1952].

Rust, George. "A Funeral Sermon Preached at the Obsequies of … Jeremy [Taylor] …" (1667), in Taylor, *Works*, 1: [cccxi]–cccxxvii.

Seneca, Lucius Annaeus. *Ad Lucilium epistulae morales*. Edited and translated by R. M. Gummere. Loeb Classical Library. 3 vols. London: Wm. Heinemann, 1925–34.

———. *Moral Essays*. Edited and translated by John W. Basore. Loeb Classical Library. 3 vols. London: Wm. Heinemann, 1935. Vol. 2.

Shepherd, Massey, ed. *Oxford American Prayer-book Commentary.*
New York: Oxford University Press, 1952.

Sitwell, Gerard. *Spiritual Writers of the Middle Ages.* New York:
Hawthorn Books [1961].

Smith, Logan Pearsall, ed. *The Golden Grove: Selected Passages
from the Sermons and Writings of Jeremy Taylor.* Oxford:
Clarendon Press, 1930.

Southern, A. C. *Elizabethan Recusant Prose 1559–1582.* London:
Sands [1950].

Spencer, Theodore. *Death and Elizabethan Tragedy.* Cambridge,
Mass.: Harvard University Press, 1936.

Standing Liturgical Commission of the Protestant Episcopal Church
in the U.S.A. *Prayer Book Studies, III: The Order for the
Ministration to the Sick.* New York: Church Pension Fund,
1951.

Steffan, T. G. "Jeremy Taylor's Criticism of Abstract Speculation."
University of Texas *Studies in English* 20 (1940):96–108.

Stranks, C. J. *The Life and Writings of Jeremy Taylor.* London:
S.P.C.K., 1952.

Swift, Jonathan. *"The Tatler,* No. 230," in *The Prose Works of
Jonathan Swift.* Edited by Temple Scott. London: Bell, 1902.

Thompson, Craig R. *The Bible in English: 1525–1611.* Washington, D.C.: Folger Shakespeare Library, 1958.

Tillich, Paul. *The Courage To Be.* New Haven: Yale University
Press, 1952.

Wakefield, Gordon S. *Puritan Devotion: Its Place in the Development of Christian Piety.* London: The Epworth Press [1957].

Walker, Daniel P. *The Decline of Hell: Seventeenth-Century Discussions of Eternal Torment.* Chicago: University of Chicago
Press, 1964.

Waugh, Evelyn. *Edmund Campion.* 2d ed. London: Hollis and
Carter, 1947.

White, Helen C. *English Devotional Literature [Prose], 1600–
1640.* University of Wisconsin Studies in Language and Literature, 29. Madison: University of Wisconsin Press, 1931.

———. *The Tudor Books of Private Devotion.* Madison: University of Wisconsin Press, 1951.

White, Lynn D. "The Significance of Medieval Christianity," in *The Vitality of the Christian Tradition*. Edited by George F. Thomas. New York: Harper [1945].

Willmott, Robert A. *Bp. Jeremy Taylor: His Predecessors, Contemporaries, and Successors*. London, 1847.

Wood, Thomas. *English Casuistical Divinity During the Seventeenth Century: With Special Reference to Jeremy Taylor*. London: S.P.C.K., 1952.

Woodhouse, Caleb R. "Religious Vitality in Fifteenth-Century England." *DA* 25(1964):3528–29.

Worley, George. *Jeremy Taylor: A Sketch of His Life and Times, with a Popular Exposition of His Work*. London: Longmans, Green, 1904.

Wright, Louis B. *Middle-Class Culture in Elizabethan England*. Chapel Hill, N.C.: University of North Carolina Press, 1935.

# Index

The major works cited in this index have been abbreviated as follows: *The Crafte of Dyinge*, CD; *The Waye of Dyenge Well*, WDW; *The Sicke Mannes Salve*, SMS; *The First Booke of . . . resolution*, FBR; "Bunny's Resolution," BR; *The Rule and Exercises of Holy Dying*, HD.

Papistry, hostility to. *See* Anti-Catholicism; Church, authority of; *Sicke Mannes Salve, The,* prose style

Parish, John E., 179*n*

Parsons, Robert, S.J.: biographical data, 159*n*, 168*n*, 183*n;* A *Christian Directorie,* 159*n;* as spiritual director, 162*n;* criticized by Baxter, 166*n*

Patristic writers, 1 and *n,* 3, 113, 184*n,* 203, 233

Paul, St., 10, 61, 62, 66*n,* 78*n,* 94, 98, 103, 113, 114, 124, 124*n,* 131*n,* 186; early humanists and, 76*n,* 77*n,* 100*n;* influence of, on HD, 199, 216, 242*n,* 253 and *n,* 267, 268, and passim. *See also* Christian life, the; Cross, Way of the; Faith, hope, and charity; Grace; Gratitude, ethic of; Reconciliation

Perkins, William, 118*n,* 127*n,* 207, 212, 213*n*

Perseverance of the saints, 119–20, 140, 143, 240

Persons, Robert. *See* Parsons, Robert, S.J.

Peter, St., 62, 66*n,* 130

Peterson, Raymond A., 198*n,* 200 and *n*

Plague, bubonic, 38

Plato, 3, 54*n,* 57, 85*n,* 115*n. See also* Socrates

Plotinus, 54*n*

Pole, Reginald Cardinal, 56, 57. *See also* Walker, John

Polemics, 127, 156. See also *Holy Dying,* prose style; Taylor, as polemicist

Pourrat, Pierre, 45*n*

Practical piety. *See* Anglicanism, 17th-c., mind of; Casuistry; Rule of life

Prayer, 118; vital to Christian life, 60; interpreted ethically, 103–04; scriptural, 129 and *n;* weapon vs. Satan, 141; interpersonal communion with God, 146; inseparable from soteriology, 147 and *n;* Taylor's eulogy of, 237

—adoration, 105, 210*n*

—benediction, 104–05

—commendation of the dying, 33–34, 129, 183*n,* 239*n*

—intercession, 112, 143*n;* duty of deathbed aides, 29, 120; for dead, 132–33, 153; more important than disputation, 159*n,* 160

—obsecration, 23–24, 24*n;* in HD, illustrated, 255–56

—petition, 24, 103, 120

—thanksgiving, 120

Prayers, 5, 6, 32–34, 140–41; liturgical, 33–34, 118*n,* 129; semiliturgical, 104–05, 128–29, 255–56; vehicles for doctrinal instruction, 124–25 and *n,* 127, 129–30, 255; reflect early Puritan spirituality, 146–47; of Ignatian meditation, 169, 175, 176, 255

Presbyterian *Directory of Public Worship,* 209*n*

Pride, spiritual. *See* Deathbed temptations, to spiritual pride

Priesthood of all believers. *See* Deathbed aides; Ministry, concepts of

*Proficiscere anima Christiana,* 33–34, 129, 183*n,* 239*n*

Pseudo-Bonaventure, 45*n*

Purgatory, 14, 50, 133, 152, 153. *See also* Last Things, the

Puritanism, Tudor, mind of. See *Sicke Mannes Salve, The,* mirror of its age

Putrefaction. See *Réalisme funèbre*